MAYO

ALSO AVAILABLE IN THIS SERIES:

Sligo, Michael Farry (2012)
Tyrone, Fergal McCluskey (2014)
Waterford, Pat McCarthy (2015)
Monaghan, Terence Dooley (2017)
Derry, Adrian Grant (2018)
Limerick, John O'Callaghan (2018)
Louth, Donal Hall (2019)
Kildare, Seamus Cullen (2020)
Leitrim, Patrick McGarty (2020)
Antrim, Brian Feeney (2021)
Roscommon, John Burke (2021)
Donegal, Pauric Travers (2022)

Mayo

The Irish Revolution, 1912–23

Joost Augusteijn

FOUR COURTS PRESS

Typeset in 10.5 pt on 12.5 pt Ehrhardt by
Carrigboy Typesetting Services for
FOUR COURTS PRESS LTD
7 Malpas Street, Dublin 8, Ireland
www.fourcourtspress.ie
and in North America for
FOUR COURTS PRESS
c/o IPG, 814 N. Franklin St, Chicago, IL 60610.

© Joost Augusteijn and Four Courts Press 2023

A catalogue record for this title
is available from the British Library.

ISBN 978–1–84682–585–9

All rights reserved. No part of this publication may be reproduced,
stored in or introduced into a retrieval system, or transmitted,
in any form or by any means (electronic, mechanical,
photocopying, recording or otherwise), without the
prior written permission of both the copyright
owner and the publisher of this book.

Printed in England
by CPI Antony Rowe, Chippenham, Wilts.

Contents

	LIST OF ILLUSTRATIONS	vi
	LIST OF ABBREVIATIONS	vii
	ACKNOWLEDGMENTS	viii
	The Irish Revolution, 1912–23 series	ix
1	County Mayo before the Revolution	1
2	'A state of great unrest and agitation': the home rule crisis in Mayo, 1912–14	13
3	'Sham feiners and sham physical force men': war and protest, 1914–16	26
4	'Up the Rebels': republicans take over local politics, 1916–18	43
5	'If the police with their local knowledge go, farewell to civil government': the struggle for dominance, 1919–20	62
6	'Sinn Féin agents were reported visiting the county to foment trouble': violence comes to Mayo, 1920–1	75
7	'Glad for the respite – glad to get home to see our people and to get proper rest and regular meals': the anti-Treatyites take control, 1921–2	94
8	'Revolver government'?: a hotbed of republicanism, 1922–3	113
9	Revolution?	134
	NOTES	136
	SELECT BIBLIOGRAPHY	159
	INDEX	165

Illustrations

PLATES

1 John Dillon MP, *c*.1915.
2 Joseph MacBride at Fairford, Glouchester in 1917 after his deportation.
3 Thomas Maguire, South Mayo IRA.
4 Bridget Walsh, member of Westport Cumann na mBan.
5 Cushlough Fife and Drum Band, 1910s.
6 Westport Sluagh – Fianna Éireann, Easter 1915.
7 Poster advertising concert in aid of arms fund, on Easter Monday night 1916.
8 RIC officers, Westport.
9 Auxilliaries based in Westport.
10 Castlebar Jail.
11 West Mayo Brigade Active Service Unit.
12 Bristol Fighter F4351 at Castlebar Aerodrome.
13 Broddie Malone, Rick Jones, Paddy Duffy and Butch Lambert.
14 Edward Moane, Jimmy Flaherty and Michael Kilroy with Lewis machine-gun captured at Carrowkennedy.
15 National army officers, including Joe Ring, with armoured car.
16 Funeral procession with National army soldiers for Joe Ring.
17 Home-made armoured car, named 'Queen of the West'.

Credits
1, 3: public domain; 2: Irish Capuchin Archives; 4, 8, 17: Harry Hughes; 5, 6: Westport Historical Society; 7: Westport Public Library; 9, 10: Wynne collection; 11, 14: Leonard Photography Collection; 12: Aiden Redmond, Westport; 13: Cashel House Hotel, Connemara; 15, 16: Michael Ring TD. All maps in this volume were created by Dr Mike Brennan.

MAPS

1	Places mentioned in the text	x
2	Local government divisions	3
3	Parliamentary constituencies, 1885–1921	6
4	Police and British army distribution, 1920–1	77
5	IRA battalion areas	79
6	Parliamentary constituencies, 1922	111

Abbreviations

AFIL	All for Ireland League
AOH	Ancient Order of Hibernians
ASU	Active Service Unit
BMH	Bureau of Military History
CBHC	Clew Bay Heritage Centre, Westport
CDB	Congested Districts Board
CI	County Inspector, RIC
CO	Colonial Office
CT	*Connaught Telegraph*
CTr	*Connacht Tribune*
FJ	*Freeman's Journal*
GAA	Gaelic Athletic Association
GHQ	General Head Quarters
IAA	Irish American Alliance
IG	Inspector-General, RIC
II	*Irish Independent*
IMA	Irish Military Archives
IPP	Irish Parliamentary Party
IRA	Irish Republican Army
IRB	Irish Republican Brotherhood
IT	*Irish Times*
ITGWU	Irish Transport and General Workers' Union
IWFL	Irish Women's Franchise League
LGB	Local Government Board
MN	*Mayo News*
MP	Member of Parliament
MSPC	Military Service Pensions Collection
NAI	National Archives of Ireland
NLI	National Library of Ireland
RDC	Rural District Council
RIC	Royal Irish Constabulary
SF	Sinn Féin
TD	Teachta Dála
TNA	National Archives, London
UCDA	University College Dublin, Archives
UDC	Urban District Council
UIL	United Irish League
UVF	Ulster Volunteer Force
WIT	*Weekly Irish Times*
WP	*Western People*
WS	Witness Statement to Bureau of Military History

Acknowledgments

This work has been a long time in the making. This is partly because a substantial part of the research on the period of the War of Independence took place in the late 1980s and early 1990s in the context of my PhD. For the 1917–21 period, I therefore draw upon my book *From public defiance to guerrilla warfare*, but with the addition of new sources and an added emphasis on events in north and east Mayo. In this context I wish to reiterate my thanks to all those who aided me in my research then, in particular I would like to remember the late Jarlath Duffy, Michael McEvilly and Mary Rose O'Brien.

In a more contemporary setting, I would like to thank a number of people who have helped me in locating photographs and providing permission to reprint them. These include James Kelly, Harry Hughes, Myles MacEvilly and various members of the Westport Historical Society. I furthermore must mention the publishers and the series editors – Mary Ann Lyons and Daithí Ó Corráin – for their patience as I had intended to complete this book many years ago, and for their detailed and helpful suggestions to improve the manuscript. If my prevarication has also stretched the patience of some prospective readers, I apologize but hope the final product does not disappoint.

The Irish Revolution, 1912–23 series

Since the turn of the century, a growing number of scholars have been actively researching this seminal period in modern Irish history. More recently, propelled by the increasing availability of new archival material, this endeavour has intensified. This series brings together for the first time the various strands of this exciting and fresh scholarship within a nuanced interpretative framework, making available concise, accessible, scholarly studies of the Irish Revolution experience at a local level to a wide audience.

The approach adopted is both thematic and chronological, addressing the key developments and major issues that occurred at a county level during the tumultuous 1912–23 period. Beginning with an overview of the social, economic and political milieu in the county in 1912, each volume assesses the strength of the home rule movement and unionism, as well as levels of labour and feminist activism. The genesis and organization of paramilitarism from 1913 are traced; responses to the outbreak of the First World War and its impact on politics at a county level are explored; and the significance of the 1916 Rising is assessed. The varying fortunes of constitutional and separatist nationalism are examined. The local experience of the War of Independence, reaction to the truce and Anglo-Irish Treaty and the course and consequences of the Civil War are subject to detailed examination and analysis. The result is a compelling account of life in Ireland in this formative era.

Mary Ann Lyons
Department of History
Maynooth University

Daithí Ó Corráin
School of History & Geography
Dublin City University

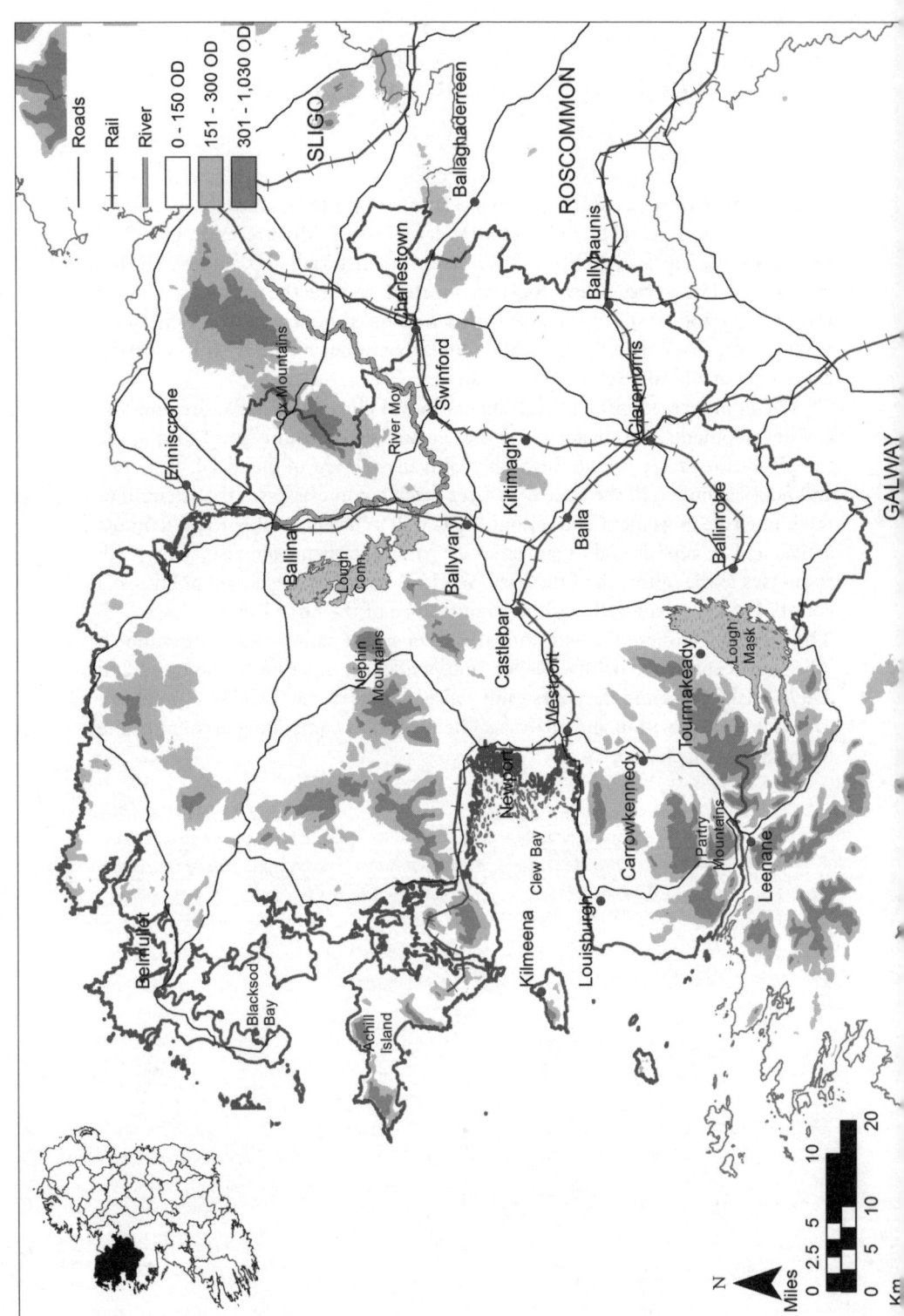

1 Places mentioned in the text

1 County Mayo before the Revolution

Although Mayo is not generally regarded as a major centre of revolutionary activity, it played a crucial role in many of the important struggles of, and within, Irish nationalism in the years before the home rule crisis of 1912. Some of the most important national movements originated here, including the Irish Land League, co-founded by Mayo native Michael Davitt, in Castlebar in 1879, and its successor organization, the United Irish League (UIL), initiated in Westport in 1898 by the town's then most prominent politician William O'Brien, who hailed from Cork. The UIL, which tried to reunite and re-energize a fragmented nationalist movement by focusing on land agitation, was supported by Davitt, then MP for South Mayo, and also by the anti-Parnellite Irish Party leader John Dillon, MP for East Mayo. Through his involvement in the Land League, Dillon became very popular, serving as MP from 1885 until 1918. The struggle over land, which was the driving force behind the founding of these two most influential movements of the late nineteenth and early twentieth centuries, was thus particularly strong in Mayo.

This long history of agitation associated with the land question and national politics in many ways foreshadowed the history of the revolutionary period. Similar to the well-organized Land League and UIL in Mayo, membership of Sinn Féin (SF) and the Irish Volunteers in the county was extremely high during the revolutionary years. Unlike its neighbouring counties and in contrast to Munster counties, in particular, this political radicalism did not occasion significant violence. The origin of these important movements in Westport and Castlebar and the power base of Dillon in Ballina also mirrored a certain division between the west and east of the county, more or less along the lines of the fertility of the soil in the east and poverty of it in the west. Radicalism was and remained very prominent in Westport, where the Irish Republican Brotherhood (IRB) and SF had their strongholds, and to a lesser extent in Castlebar, Balla and Ballinrobe, while the east remained for a long time more solidly constitutional. Although the land question was a driving force in Mayo, it did lose some of its virulence during the early revolutionary period. The fact that by 1912, fifty per cent of the tenants had become landowners, rising to seventy per cent by the start of the First World War, partly explains this. Consequently, the political issue of home rule and later the republic was foremost in people's minds, which generated almost united support locally and more so than in neighbouring Roscommon or Leitrim. It also made the Mayo SF and IRA unusually strong in the West, and the county one of the last bastions of the anti-Treaty IRA during the Civil War.

Mayo's physical features helped determine its political divisions and also the military strength of anti-treatyites. Life in the more mountainous western half of the county was in extremis represented by the history of poverty on Achill island, where people eked out a living on meagre holdings. In the eastern half, farms were generally larger although there were also many poor people. The struggle there was more about access to land which since the Famine was increasingly let to graziers. These were generally middle-class Catholics who held livestock on their farms and paid good rents to the landlords. The inequities this created were epitomized by the townland of Fallmore in the north-western tip of the county, where there were 207 people living in 43 houses on land valued at an average of £2 6s., while there was one grazing farm of 178 acres with the same value as those 43 put together. This became particularly controversial after the founding of the UIL as small farmers wanted to expand and gain control over this land. As a result, graziers became a frequent target of agrarian agitation, often taking the shape of cattle driving, the first example of which was recorded in neighbouring Roscommon in 1906.[1]

Mayo was an overwhelmingly agricultural county in 1911 with more than 86 per cent of the 192,177 strong population living in rural areas. It was the most populous county in Connacht ahead of Galway's population of 182,224. Officially, there were only three urban areas: Westport, Castlebar and Ballina, none of them matching the size of Sligo or Galway city. These substantial towns were matched with numerous smaller market towns administratively part of the rural district councils (RDCs) of Swinford, Belmullet, Claremorris, Ballinrobe and Killala (see map 2). The other RDCs in the county were linked to Westport, Castlebar and Ballina, which had their own Urban District Councils (UDCs). The largest was the port of Ballina with 914 houses and 4,662 inhabitants, followed by Westport, with its harbour, and the administrative centre of Castlebar, with almost 3,700 inhabitants each. The next largest town was Ballinrobe with just over 1,500 inhabitants. Due to the presence of the British army, Castlebar had a surplus of males, whereas Westport was female dominated. Of the working male population, 46,849 (85 per cent) were employed in agriculture; 6,792 (12 per cent) worked in the few industries such as the fish factory and the woollen mills in Foxford; the remaining 3 per cent were in the professions, domestic service and commerce. The prominence of agricultural work was less so for the 10 per cent of women who had formal employment: 40 per cent were engaged in agriculture, 26 per cent in industry, and 24 per cent in domestic service, with the remainder active in the professions, mainly as teachers and nuns.[2]

A total of 63,354 acres was used for tillage, almost six times that in Roscommon which had the second-largest acreage under tillage in Ireland. That Mayo was the poorest of the western counties was reflected in the quality of accommodation. In 1911 almost 7 per cent of families lived in one-roomed

County Mayo before the Revolution

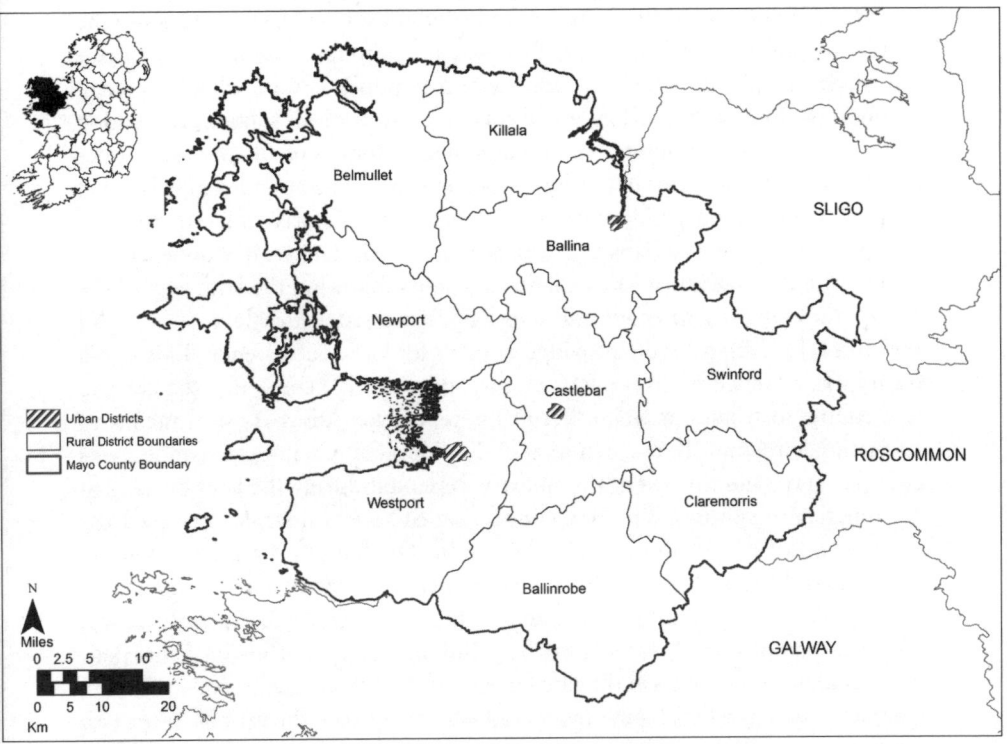

2 Local government divisions

houses and 40.8 per cent in two-roomed homes. By comparison, the proportion in this category in Sligo was 27.2 per cent, the second highest in Connacht. Out of about 36,000 inhabited houses in Mayo, 2,558 were designated as tenements. Swinford accounted for 782 with further concentrations in Westport rural district and around Belmullet, including Achill island. Despite this widespread poverty, the number receiving poor relief – 1 in every 78 – was slightly lower than in neighbouring Sligo (1 in 69) and Galway (1 in 70). Poor relief was distributed in the eight poor law unions, each with their own poor house, in Ballina, Ballinrobe, Binghamstown, Castlebar, Claremorris, Killala, Swinford and Westport.[3]

Most landowners were Protestant, but since the 1840s the steadily declining population of Mayo was almost entirely (nearly 98 per cent) Catholic. This was comparable to Galway and Roscommon, but greater than Sligo (91 per cent). The remainder of the population mainly consisted of various Protestant denominations, but there were also 2 agnostics, 1 atheist and 2 freethinkers who dared to acknowledge their life philosophy. Protestants were concentrated in north Mayo. The Church of Ireland accounted for 80 per cent and was part of the large amalgamated diocese of Tuam, Killala and Achonry. The remainder comprised mainly small Presbyterian and Methodist communities. Despite the steady decline in their numbers, Protestants maintained their own primary school system, albeit with a tiny number of fifty pupils in four schools. A small number of Protestants attended a mixed ecclesiastical school. Education attainment was higher among Protestants than Catholics of which only 0.3 per cent had received superior education, which meant having attended a school that taught a foreign language. By contrast, 0.96 per cent of Church of Ireland people, 4.01 per cent of Presbyterians and 3.25 per cent of Methodists had done so.[4]

Despite the continued sale of land to tenants following the land acts of the 1880s, 1903 and 1909, economic deprivation persisted in Mayo. The small agricultural holdings barely provided enough for basic subsistence. This harsh reality was reflected when the RIC county inspector (CI) recorded the capture of a couple of whales at Belmullet in his report for July 1912 as a means of alleviating hardship.[5] To make industrial development possible, rail connections between Mayo and the rest of the country were built during the later decades of the nineteenth century. The line connecting Sligo to Limerick traversed the eastern half of Mayo, and another opened in the 1860s that ran from Dublin through Ballyhaunis to Castlebar and from there branched out to Westport and Ballina (see map 1). A number of minor branch lines were subsequently added, the latest connected Westport with Achill in 1895. In this way the poor hinterland of the county had direct connections to Dublin, Belfast and the south, complemented by a developing main road system between the various towns (see map 1).

The improved connections enabled thousands of youths from Mayo to travel to Britain for seasonal work every spring in an effort to supplement their family incomes, returning at the approach of winter. Together with Donegal, Mayo had the highest proportion of young men engaged in this practice. The significant over-representation of young men living in the county when compared to other counties suggests that permanent emigration was not common among them. In contrast, young women left in quite large numbers. With an exodus of 15.3 out of every 100 persons between 1901 and 1911, Mayo had the highest emigration in the country. Although overall there were still slightly more women than men living in Mayo in 1911, men outnumbered women by 6,354 in the 20–35 age cohort. This meant there were three young men to every young woman, with few of them married, 3 per cent of women, and 0.6 per cent of men in this age group. Annual birth rates were, nevertheless, higher in Mayo than elsewhere at 24 per 1,000 compared to an average of 21.6.[6]

The lack of prospects in Mayo was also indicated by the fact it was the county with the fewest inhabitants born outside the county. Some 94.7 per cent of Mayo residents were born locally, whereas the comparative percentage in Galway was 93, in Sligo 90.5 and in Roscommon 88.7. As those born outside Mayo comprised equal numbers of men and women, this unusual pattern cannot be accounted for by the presence of soldiers in Castlebar or as part of the smaller garrisons in Ballinrobe, Westport and Foxford. The same applied for people born outside Ireland, who formed 0.3 per cent against an average of 0.5 per cent; most were born in England, Scotland, or the empire, with only 427 classified as foreign born. These were probably children of returned emigrants as more than half of them came from the US. All this indicated that Mayo was economically and socially less integrated in the wider world than the surrounding counties. Illiteracy rates confirmed this impression, with 21.5 per cent of those over eight years reported as being unable to read and write. Only County Galway recorded similar levels.[7]

The extent to which Irish was spoken by different age groups confirms the impression that Mayo had relatively recently developed a stronger orientation towards the outside world. Of those over sixty, 91 per cent spoke Irish, with two-thirds having no English at all. In the middle-age cohorts, monoglot Irish speakers were a small minority. The ability to speak Irish as well as English declined further with age. Only 12 per cent of those aged between 21 and 29 spoke both languages, while 2 per cent had no English. Yet overall, 46 per cent of people in Mayo still spoke Irish. Although lower than the 54 per cent in neighbouring Galway, it was substantially higher than the Connacht average of 35.5 per cent and the national figure of 14 per cent. That Irish was still spoken in many homes was reflected in the fact that 13 per cent of children under nine spoke Irish only. It seems that the efforts of the Gaelic League and the introduction of Irish in primary schools in 1893 had been fruitful, as the number of Irish speakers among those under 20 was significantly higher than in the 20–40 cohort. Monoglot Irish-speakers on the other hand learned English at school, as evidenced by the fact no one between ten and twenty had Irish alone. Despite Mayo's high number of Irish speakers, cultural organizations that tried to stimulate people's consciousness of their Irish heritage were relatively weak in the county. In 1914, according to local police reports, a mere 0.5 per cent of the population were members of the Gaelic League and 1.3 per cent were in the Gaelic Athletic Association (GAA). Although Mayo had a relatively high number of Gaelic League branches earlier in the century, they were concentrated in the towns.[8] These organizations advocating Irish-Ireland primarily represented an expression of cultural nationalist sentiment, with few signs of more radical nationalism to be found in Mayo before 1912 besides one SF branch in Westport.

The local press was an important intermediary that shaped the way Mayo's population perceived happenings at local and national levels. There were four newspapers in Mayo. The Ballina-based *Western People* served the strongly Irish Parliamentary Party (IPP)-minded north-eastern part of the county as well as north-west Sligo. Regrettably, no records from this period survive for the town's other newspaper, the *Ballina Herald*. The *Connaught Telegraph*, published in

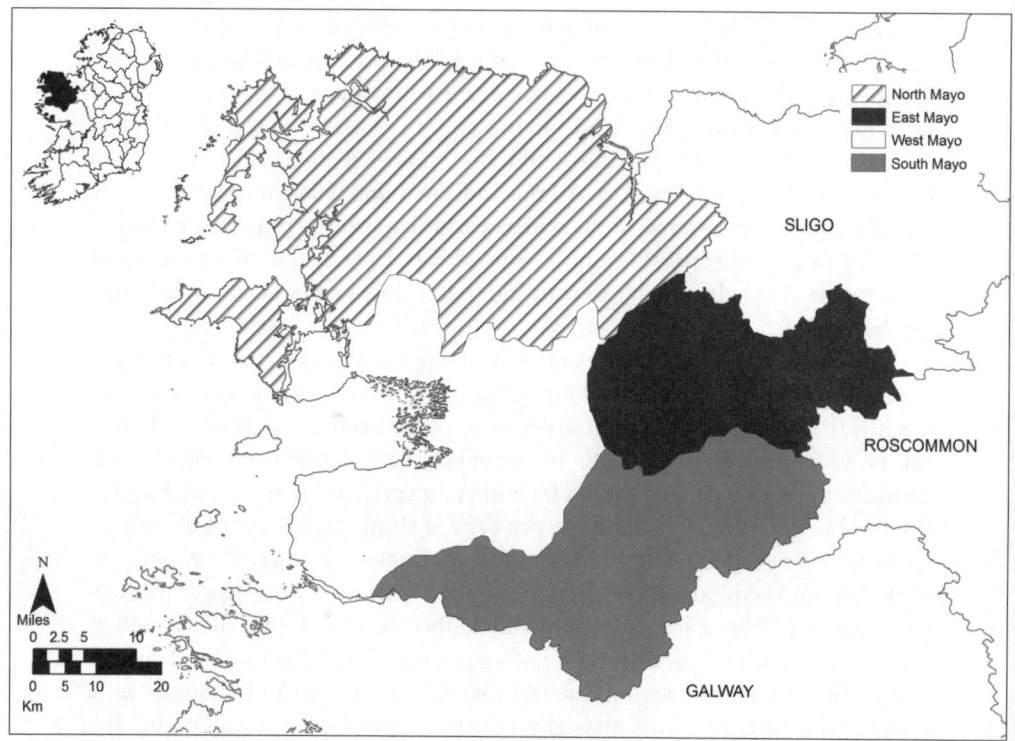

3 Parliamentary constituencies, 1885–1921

Castlebar, was more prominent in the southern and central parts of the county. Traditionally associated with the struggles of small farmers and labourers, by the early twentieth century it supported John Redmond, leader of the IPP, and strongly opposed those fomenting discord among nationalists such as William O'Brien and later SF. The Westport-based *Mayo News* was edited since 1910 by Pat Doris, an IRB man with a long involvement in the UIL and brother of William Doris MP. As the only pro-SF newspaper in the west, its editorial line was characterized by the police as disloyal. In 1919 the Castlebar reporter of the *Mayo News* started the short-lived *Mayoman*, which also identified with the SF movement. To some extent the somewhat apolitical *Connacht Tribune* from Galway was also read in parts of Mayo.[9]

The overarching political issues before the First World War were home rule and the land question: both generated disagreements. The few unionists or Protestants in Mayo were unable to make an electoral impact, meaning that 'the enemies of Home Rule' were found among nationalist rivals. Various election campaigns following the founding of the UIL in 1898 were particularly intense in Mayo and had nationwide implications. The electorate was essentially spread out over four electoral divisions for parliamentary seats (see map 3). These had roughly equal numbers of electors, around 8,000 each, but were quite different in size: North Mayo comprised 510,007 acres whereas the wealthier, more densely populated East Mayo counted only 174,008. The latter also contained a part of Roscommon around Ballaghaderreen, a district that had been transferred administratively from Mayo to Roscommon in 1898. The West and South Mayo constituencies also showed this difference in wealth, comprising 395,555 and 253,880 acres respectively. A very small portion of southern Mayo was part of the Connemara electoral division.

The first of these contested elections took place in 1900. Michael Davitt had resigned his seat in the House of Commons in protest against the imperialist connotations of the British campaign in South Africa during the Second Boer War of 1899–1902. In the ensuing elections, John O'Donnell, who was closely associated with William O'Brien and the UIL, stood against Major John MacBride, a native of Westport who had fought the British in South Africa. He was later executed following the 1916 Rising. In the 1900 elections MacBride was, nevertheless, beaten decisively by 2,401 votes to 427. The new UIL was successful in many other parts of the country as well, posing a threat to the already divided IPP. In 1903 O'Brien managed to force a coming together of the various factions of the national movement, with John Dillon becoming deputy leader under John Redmond. Fearful of O'Brien's powerful position and opposed to his support for reconciliation with unionists, Dillon and Redmond marginalized him in the newly united IPP. Frustrated and increasingly disillusioned, O'Brien subsequently left the party. In 1909 he formed the All-for-Ireland League (AFIL) in an attempt to unite nationalist with moderate unionist in favour of a separate Irish parliament. The organization's base was County Cork with some support in other counties, including Mayo where O'Brien resided.

After the unification of the IPP in 1900, the 1906 elections were uncontested. Land agitation did, however, become more intense. The transfer of land to the tenants remained slow in Mayo and neighbouring counties, with less than a third then owned by tenants. Agitation grew, especially against graziers. In 1907 and 1908 the authorities observed a large increase in cattle drivers carrying arms.[10] To ease these rising tensions, the sale of land was made more attractive for all parties through the Land Purchase Act of 1909. Although the act had a positive impact initially, it caused more conflict in the longer run as expectations rose sharply but implementation was necessarily slow. To deal with the consequent large-scale agitation, the presence of the RIC was relatively large in Mayo with sixty-eight stations of different sizes functioning in 1918. The RIC CI, George Hurst, was based in Castlebar, the administrative centre where Mayo County Council held its meetings and the local army headquarters was situated.

Despite their relative weakness in Mayo, the language movement, and to a lesser extent the GAA, were important first vehicles of political organization and radicalization of a small but influential group of men and women. Michael Kilroy, later leader of the IRA's West Mayo Brigade, mentions the influence of Irish classes in Newport during the early part of the century, which he claimed 'were a great help towards the development of a genuine national outlook.' Similarly, the centenary celebrations of 1798, which generated a plethora of leaflets and booklets about the rebellion, influenced schoolchildren who 'vied with each other as to who knew most about any one, or all of the '98 leaders'.[11] The actions of the Boers against the British in the Boer War generated another wave of enthusiasm, but only after 1910 did this lead to the founding of more radical organizations.

Around that time a concerted effort, emanating from Belfast and Dublin, was made to reorganize the IRB.[12] In Mayo a small group of generally older members took the lead and tried to introduce fresh blood. In 1905 Anthony and Joseph MacBride, brothers of John, who were then already well into their forties, had established one of the first provincial branches of SF, the most radical political movement of that period. Anthony was instrumental in organizing an IRB circle in Castlebar. His uncle, Dick Walsh, a resident of Balla, recalled how in 1911 or 1912 he was brought into the IRB by Frank Dorr, a travelling salesman for Foxford Mills. Walsh, then in his early twenties, was approached because he was GAA county treasurer and his father had been secretary of the IRB in Mayo. At this stage there was no circle in Balla so entrance requirements were minimal. Although Walsh 'could not see any prospect of success for a policy of physical force', he was inducted. Through Dorr he was eventually brought into contact with the Castlebar circle. John MacDonagh, the then 46-year-old brother of Thomas MacDonagh (later a signatory of the 1916 proclamation of the Republic), and Joseph MacBride, who both lived in Westport, initiated further organization there.[13]

These early activists took in promising young locals who often mentioned being inspired by a politically active family member or teacher and extended the organization to other areas. Joseph MacBride went as far as Kilmeena and Achill to start local circles.[14] Edward Moane, later a local IRA leader, remembered how as a young man he went for walks with John MacDonagh to discuss history and politics, and was sworn into the IRB by him in 1911. Joining this secret organization made a profound impression. Moane vividly remembered the bimonthly meetings in Westport: '[Joseph] MacBride gave us lectures on military subjects and historical items and we had discussions on various subjects.' They also paid sixpence a month towards the purchase of arms.[15] Some years afterwards, Moane swore in Tommy Heavey, a young neighbour who frequently sought his company and later became a member of the West Mayo flying column.[16] The efforts of the older IRB men thus slowly drew radical young men into the organization and established direct contacts with Dublin. This was, however, mostly confined to the towns and villages around Westport and

Castlebar. In other parts of the county development was slow, particularly in east Mayo, where John Dillon remained extremely popular.[17]

Besides this ever-widening circle of IRB men, there were others with a radical nationalist inclination, unaware of the IRB's existence, who had separately become convinced of the need to use force to obtain independence. They had joined different bodies to realize this goal. Initially, the Board of Erin faction of the Ancient Order of Hibernians (AOH) was the favoured choice. This traditionally northern organization had recently extended its activities to the south and threatened the position of the UIL. Although the Catholic Church initially tried to counter the spread of the AOH, it recognized it as a benevolent society in 1911, after which the number of Mayo divisions grew to fourteen by September 1912, as opposed to almost ninety branches of the UIL.[18] To some, like Michael Kilroy, the new members this attracted were not advanced enough. At the age of twenty-six he had left the UIL with a group of young men to join the Board of Erin, but in 1913 they moved to the more radical Irish American Alliance (IAA) faction of the AOH. A branch had formed in Westport in July, followed by others in Newport and Glenisland, and later in Kilmeena and Aughagower. The branch established in Aughagower, a village with strong personal ties to nearby Westport, was led by Owen Hughes, brother of Charles Hughes, a shopkeeper who was the local IRB 'centre' in Westport. Owen's sons and cousins were among the most energetic members of the IAA.[19]

Another avenue for activists to mobilize youngsters was the Irish boy scouts or Fianna Éireann, which was founded in Dublin in 1909. Although official Fianna records do not contain any references to them before the Rising, the RIC reported the presence in February 1912 of at least two branches in Castlebar and Westport. The latter at one point had up to fifty boys under Thomas Derrig, then a 15-year-old, bright, working-class boy with a natural flair for leadership. They were clear about their intentions. As early as February 1912, the police reported the Westport branch as being in possession of some guns.[20] According to Thomas Kettrick, this was one old revolver given to them by the MacBrides, who claimed John MacBride had used in the Boer War.[21] This led some people to question their ambitions, exclaiming: 'Does Tom Derrig and his Boy Scouts think they can beat the British Empire!'[22]

These young radicals in the IAA, the Fianna and other organizations became prime targets for IRB recruitment before the First World War. The CI, who seemed to have been well informed, observed in January 1912 that the AOH branch in Westport was very active, and that there was 'reason to believe a secret society having been formed there in connection with it'.[23] By 1912 an increasingly well-organized underground group of republicans were thus present in certain Mayo towns and villages. They were supplemented by a small but growing group of radicalized young men who often received some military training in the Fianna or other militant organizations.[24] Westport and to a lesser extent Castlebar seemed to have been hotbeds of activity on which the police kept a close watch. In most rural areas, however, little activity took place.[25]

An exceptional feature of the SF organization was its acceptance of female members. This was associated with the fight of suffragettes for the introduction of the vote for women, which came to Ireland in this period. There were also some reports of activists coming from Dublin to Mayo to promote their cause. One of the first meetings was organized in Ballina in August 1912, just after three English suffragettes had been imprisoned in Ireland for a violent attack, which had caused much indignation: 'It is pretty plain that these reckless women ... have by their organized blackguardism, killed the cause they profess to advocate.'[26] The reception of four suffragettes sporting badges and distributing pamphlets in Ballina was, nevertheless, generally friendly: 'On a few occasions some of the crowd seemed inclined to resent their intrusion, but on the whole their presence simply gave rise to a good deal of good humoured chaff.'[27]

Local newspapers attempted to avoid possible negative fallout for local suffragettes from the more extreme tactics elsewhere: 'Whilst we do not care to offer any opinion as to the practicality of their claims, we cannot endorse the use of any violence towards them'. The papers even went so far as to argue that it was 'not seemly or in accordance with the chivalrous instincts of Irishmen to treat other ladies active in the cause with contumely, because of the erring conduct of a trio of English suffragettes.'[28] Some hostility was nevertheless noticeable in Mayo County Council, where Councillor P.J. Costello objected successfully to the reading out of a letter from the Women's National Health Organization, stating that the council should not consider anything sent by the suffragettes.[29]

In Mayo, suffragette tactics were, however, never seen as a threat; instead, they were ridiculed. During a discussion in Westport UDC over safety at the New Irish Mining Company, a Mr Dever drew laughter when he stated that it was 'thought there would be an explosion and as much damage done as by the suffragettes'.[30] Jokes about suffragettes had become a genre by 1912. George Mallin's travelling company advertised with 'Comic songs, screaming sketches, mock tragedies and suffragette skits'.[31] In July 1914 Suffragette Sally was one of the horses at the races in Ballinrobe. Although she outpaced Solicitor-General, she was pipped at the post by a horse called Judith.[32]

The suffragettes' conduct contributed to them being dismissed in Mayo. During a festival, a woman delivering a speech about women's right to vote from a boat fell into the water. When she swam ashore 'Roars of laughter greeted her appearance on land, and it was then realized that "Votes for Women" had a very clever impersonator in Mr J.W. Willington, J.P.'[33] A newspaper report titled 'A Shoeless Suffragette' described how participants on an excursion to Cong in June 1914 had 'the unusual experience in this part of the country of seeing Militant Suffragette "protest" tactics in a new form.' After a group of women were shown around Lord Ardilaun's grounds, one of the party demanded an interview with the owner. When this was denied 'she sat herself down, and, to the astonishment of her friends, removed her shoes ... after great persuasion and some force she was helped to put on her shoes.'³⁴

Dublin suffragettes were nevertheless encouraged by their first visit to the county and two more visited Mayo in August 1913. On the 13th they delivered speeches which attracted large audiences on the Green in Castlebar at 2.30 and 7.00 p.m. According to the *Connaught Telegraph*, both were 'extremely fluent and pleasing speakers, and despite a good deal of heckling and badinage, made themselves heard. They claimed that the federation they represented was non-militant and non-party and they certainly put forth telling arguments in favour of the enfranchisement of women.' Although the Countess of Aberdeen was in Castlebar to visit a health and housing exhibition, the two suffragettes 'did not attempt to molest or interview' her, 'due possibly to the presence of Dublin detectives and a number of plain clothes RIC men.' The suffragettes subsequently visited other districts in Mayo and announced they would return to Castlebar on 3 September.³⁵

The campaign for votes for women largely passed Mayo by. Although the activities of Dublin suffragettes did clearly generate some response, a local organization does not seem to have been established. To some extent this applied also to another active movement of the period. Organized labour was manifesting itself with increasingly confidence in Ireland. The syndicalism of James Larkin, who came to national prominence during the Dublin lockout of 1913, also reached Mayo at this time. Although an overwhelmingly agricultural county, Westport, Castlebar and Ballina and the numerous market towns had a certain amount of labour organization. At that stage, however, the fear of 'Larkinism' was still stronger than the reality of it. When a number of RDCs contemplated the introduction of direct labour schemes for work on local roads instead of contracting the work out, opponents of the scheme in Claremorris and Castlebar argued that in a year, 'they would have Larkin down and all the labourers would be out'. Those supporting the idea claimed labour in Mayo 'can well be trusted to give a wide berth to such a nation killing system'. Based on experience of direct labour in other counties, they argued that: 'The men will have to be paid reasonably for a reasonable day's work, and when they are so paid the men can well be trusted not to kill the goose that lays the golden egg.'³⁶

Many Mayo labourers were inspired by events during the Dublin lockout. An increase in strikes was detectable afterwards, and the Irish Transport and General Workers' Union (ITGWU) managed to set up its first branches for agricultural labourers in the county.³⁷ Initially this caused discord mainly within the labour movement itself. At a meeting of the Castlebar Labourers and Tradesmen to select candidates for upcoming UDC elections on 15 January 1914, Larkinites tried to take over the organization. The *Connaught Telegraph* reported that the meeting was a 'disgrace for Castlebar'. It argued the sitting member, Joe Dwyer, had done 'his duty during the past three years and would not take dictation from strangers and idlers who wanted to introduce Larkinism'. Afterwards, Dwyer was shouted down and scuffles ensued. When order was finally restored, eight candidates were selected, but not Dwyer.[38]

The IPP was well aware of the growing presence of these new political movements. Its support for the minority Liberal government since 1910 had put the party in a difficult position. Instead of criticizing the government for its shortcomings in Ireland, the IPP was now forced to defend it, thereby creating an opportunity for radicals to attack them. John Dillon acknowledged this in September 1911 when he stated 'for two years the Liberal Ministers had been assailed by a small faction in Ireland with a torrent of scurrilous and insensate abuse unparalleled in recent politics'. Defending the IPP's actions, he cited the many achievements of the government

> which in a few years had definitively abolished coercion; dropped the Arms Act; passed the best Labourers Act ever passed for Ireland; settled the University question; done more for the National teachers and National education than any previous Government; had undertaken to put a vote for Intermediate Education on the Estimates; passed a Land Act which, with all its faults, was the best Act ever passed for the West of Ireland; had reinstated in a generous manner over two thousand evicted tenants; had given old age pensions; had passed a Town Tenants Act which was a very substantial measure of relief; and which, by the passing of the Parliament Act, had destroyed the great obstacle which has long barred the way to Irish liberty.[39]

The electorate in Mayo may have wondered whether an Irish government could deliver more. This became a realistic possibility after the elections of 1910 when the Liberal government became dependent on the support of the IPP.

2 'A state of great unrest and agitation': the home rule crisis in Mayo, 1912–14

The outcome of the two 1910 Westminster elections, the last before 1918, were crucial for the progress of home rule at a national level and greatly heightened interest in politics everywhere. A hung parliament in which the IPP could determine the shape of the next government boosted the chances of home rule being introduced. Removal of the veto power of the Conservative-dominated House of Lords – the main obstacle to home rule – loomed large in these elections. This had its origins in the political problems caused by the Lords' veto over Lloyd George's so-called People's Budget of 1909 that introduced a land tax. The Liberal minority government with the support of the IPP subsequently introduced the Parliament Act (1911), curtailing the power of the Lords, and making the introduction of home rule, on the cards since the 1880s, finally feasible.

The political situation in Mayo, which in previous years was dominated by agrarian agitation for the sale of land and the breaking up of grazier farms, was altered by the Parliament Act. The land struggle now became part of, and was eventually overtaken by, the fight for home rule. The looming introduction of self-government worried local unionists and increased pressure on the mostly Protestant owners of the remaining estates to sell to their tenants. Growing unionist resistance to home rule also brought more radical voices to the centre of politics in Mayo, particularly through their involvement in the Irish Volunteers.

In 1910 two of the Mayo constituencies were contested for the first time since 1900. The founding of William O'Brien's AFIL, which favoured a more conciliatory approach, provided a nationalist alternative. In 1906 there had been no opposing candidates in Mayo to the reunited IPP, but in January 1910 independent nationalists with a connection to the AFIL stood in the North and South Mayo constituencies. Nobody dared to challenge the all-powerful Dillon in East Mayo or Robert Ambrose in West Mayo. In North Mayo, Bernard Egan, who only later officially joined forces with O'Brien, was narrowly beaten by Daniel Boyle by a margin of forty votes, but the sitting MP in South Mayo, John O'Donnell, was successful for the AFIL. This intra-nationalist division posed a major problem for the IPP in Mayo.

Supporters of Conor O'Kelly, the defeated IPP candidate in South Mayo, complained about the role of local clergy in these elections and were not afraid to demonstrate this openly: 'They staged a concerted walk-out from Sunday Mass and overturned collection tables. A church hall and some statutes were destroyed during a riot in Claremorris.'¹ In the aftermath of the January 1910 election, the Irishtown UIL branch passed two resolutions against the interference of priests in politics. The second suggested that 'if religion is to flourish in the future as in the past, we earnestly hope His Grace [Archbishop of Tuam] will prevent the clergy from interfering with the rights of the people'.²

The IPP soon reached an agreement with the local clergy against O'Donnell. Apparently the national executive of the party stepped in and replaced O'Kelly, whose anti-clerical stance was problematic, with John Fitzgibbon, a Castlerea shopkeeper and veteran agitator, who as a rising star in the IPP in Mayo and Roscommon had just been appointed to the Congested Districts Board (CDB) and could potentially deliver the farmers' vote.³ Subsequently, O'Donnell did not stand in the December 1910 election, partly because of intimidation and partly because his newspaper, the Galway-based *Connaught Champion*, was facing ruin following the launch of the *Connacht Tribune*.⁴ The South Mayo executive of the UIL was, however, extremely annoyed by the action of the IPP national executive and passed a motion in October, criticizing them for 'foisting an outsider on them'. Adding that if this was 'the sample of Home Rule they were going to enjoy under the leadership of Mr Redmond, it was a rotten Home Rule'. The chairman subsequently announced that the Mayo executive would dissolve itself and propose an alternative candidate to the IPP.⁵

Attempts to prevent clerical interference in the political process were more successful in West Mayo, where the wishes of the majority of the clergy were disregarded. Most supporters of the sitting MP, Robert Ambrose, were physically barred from the selection convention by those in favour of William Doris, who had a long track record in the Land League and local politics, most recently as county council vice-chairman. All but two of the twenty-three priests present left the meeting with the remaining Ambrose supporters after some were prevented from speaking. Local opposition to Ambrose's candidature stemmed from his involvement in a failed attempt to develop a transatlantic port at Blacksod Bay in which many local people had lost money. Doris was duly selected as the IPP candidate.⁶

The AFIL challenge to the IPP petered out in the run-up to the December election. Although there were some reports of strong support for O'Brien, the league was not universally well-received.⁷ When an attempt was made to organize an AFIL branch in Ardagh in January 1910, the 'hostility of the crowd was ... so pronounced that the organizer was unable to get a hearing'.⁸ At the instigation of the local priest, Father Clarke, the meeting was broken up. Clarke subsequently held an impromptu meeting of the UIL, demonstrating the continued power of the local clergy as well as his affiliation and sympathy.

No alternative to Fitzgibbon subsequently came forward in South Mayo, and the announced candidacy of AFIL men in North and East Mayo never materialized. Even Bernard Egan, who had very narrowly lost in January, did not stand in North Mayo. An attempt by Conor O'Kelly to stand in North instead of South Mayo received a hostile reception.⁹ In a last-ditch effort, William O'Brien put himself forward in West Mayo, prompting the *Irish Times* to comment that 'lively times are anticipated'.¹⁰ Although this newspaper considered West Mayo to have been 'practically in possession' of the AFIL, the *Connaught Telegraph* reported that O'Brien's candidacy was 'looked upon even by some of O'Brien's best friends in the West as a rather foolhardy expedition'.¹¹

O'Brien and his supporters soon encountered opposition. When he visited Crossmolina in early September a party of police had to separate his followers from a hostile crowd. Afterwards, 'nasty scuffles' and an 'onslaught on O'Brien carriage' ensued in which a revolver was discharged.¹² At a subsequent meeting in Knockmore, which was attended by more than 1,000 people, there was a lot of cheering for national unity and the leaders of the IPP, while 'any reference to Mr Wm. O'Brien and the All-for-Ireland League was loudly groaned.'¹³ Not surprisingly perhaps, O'Brien was handsomely beaten by Doris by a margin of almost 4:1.¹⁴ Although the AFIL won eight seats nationally, this result effectively put an end to O'Brien's attempt to replace the IPP. He, nevertheless, remained a fierce critic of the party's confrontational politics.

That all successful candidates had strong links to the Land League showed the importance of the land issue in Mayo. O'Brien's policy of conciliation was clearly not popular. To his own surprise, most of O'Brien's votes were urban rather than rural. Towns like Castlebar and in particular Westport had long been hotbeds of radicalism, but now supported the moderate voice of O'Brien as they tried to challenge the ingrained power of the IPP and UIL.¹⁵ After the election, a disillusioned O'Brien, who had anticipated a sweep for the AFIL in Mayo, sold his home in Westport and moved to Cork where the party had been more successful.¹⁶ He blamed his defeat on 'the most incredible ignorance and the most shameful corruption'.¹⁷ So, following the elections all nationalist voices were again united under the IPP umbrella, although a residual AFIL presence remained in the towns of Westport, Ballina and Castlebar.¹⁸

Consequently, political candidates had much to gain from militancy on land issues and there was little room for a moderate, let alone a unionist voice. As a means of distinguishing themselves, political opponents were sought within the nationalist ranks. O'Brien's AFIL thus continued to be blamed for causing factionalism and disunity. When Dillon visited Ballyhaunis in January 1910 he was met by local representatives of the Town Tenants' League who assured him of their 'grateful, unswerving, and undivided support in its [the IPP's] present fight against faction and disruption.'¹⁹ O'Brien was also accused of siding with the landlords and encouraging them to think they could resist a divided nationalist movement striving for the sale of the land.²⁰ In a speech at Ballaghaderreen in December, Dillon denounced O'Brienites as 'traitors to the Irish cause' who sold themselves 'for Unionist votes and bribes'.²¹

After the 1910 elections the new MPs called for a speedy sale of land. The prospective introduction of home rule gave them more confidence, implying that once in power, terms might be less favourable for landlords. In July William Doris asked the chief secretary for Ireland how many landlords in Mayo had indicated a willingness to sell, and when the CDB, which was responsible for organizing the sale of estates, was intending to put the compulsory purchase clause of the 1909 act in operation. The MP was informed that 106 landlords were willing to negogiate and consequently there was no need for compulsion.[22] At monster meetings in Foxford and Ballinrobe, organized by the IPP, a letter from Dillon threatened landlords with coercion if they did not sell quickly.[23] At one of these meetings, local MP John Fitzgibbon, who was a member of the CDB, advised tenants to withhold rent to compel their landlord to sell. Subsequently, a motion calling for his removal from the CDB was put forward in the House of Lords.[24] Fitzgibbon apologized in parliament for saying more than he intended in a 'moment of excitement'. The *Irish Independent* reported how he subsequently had what it called 'other moments of excitement' in which he again advised tenants to act against the law.[25] At a meeting in Ballina, attended by 5,000 people, he congratulated the 'men of Mayo on being the means to rout landlordism', and declared 'The graziers had the fat of the land and the people the lean, but they were going to reverse the position'.[26]

Under the influence of these statements and due to a growing impatience over the effectiveness of the 1909 Land Act, agitation flared up again in Mayo and other western counties. In neighbouring Sligo the situation remained relatively quiet, but Roscommon and Galway as well as Clare were proclaimed as a result of the unrest, leading the *Irish Independent* to predict the outbreak of a new Land War.[27] In Mayo, sales were slow. The CI, who tended to view developments in a broader perspective, argued that this was mostly due to the difficulty of coming to an agreed price rather than any unwillingness by landlords to sell. In some cases, tenants refused to pay rent in line with UIL advice: this occurred on the Westport estate of Lord Sligo, the largest landlord and most powerful aristocrat in Mayo. The boycott ended in February 1912 without a reduction in rent, which in turn led to a relatively large number of evictions.[28] This was not necessarily a desireable outcome for the landlord as people often refused to take up tenancy on a farm from which others had been evicted. In February 1912 seventeen evicted farms thus lay derelict and rent was still withheld on seven other estates in Mayo, the highest number in the country. Nevertheless, intimidation and outrages of an agrarian nature remained rare in Mayo, unlike Clare and Galway.[29]

Although the RIC inspector-general stated in March that the CDB's firm stand in Mayo and Clare had prevented forced sales, the number of estates where rents were withheld only grew. A lot of graziers were also reported to have given up their land on disturbed estates, probably due to intimidation. This could be quite innocent. The family home of a young man who worked for a new grazier on the Falcon Estate near Ballina was surrounded by people blowing bottles and horns. But intimidation could also involve violence. Police serving notice on a group of tenants on the Achill Mission Estate for non-payment of rent were mobbed and pelted with turf. Other cases involved the burning of property, an assault, boycotting and a death threat. The agitation and perhaps the prospect of home rule seem to have paid off. Sales of estates increased steeply towards the end of 1912 and in December more than half of farmers owned their holding. Agitation and withholding of rents subsequently declined.[30]

At the same time, attention was diverted to bigger political issues. On 12 April 1912 the lifework of many nationalist politicians, including John Dillon, seemed to be realized when Prime Minister Asquith introduced the third home rule bill in the House of Commons. Nationalists reacted positively but did not take a formal stance until after the IPP convention the following weekend. The *Freeman's Journal* stated: 'in view of the enthusiasm with which the Bill had been received throughout the country, it is assumed that the Convention will pronounce in favour of its acceptance.' Public reaction in Mayo was, however, initially muted. Few reports of public celebrations can be found in the newspapers, possibly also due to the attention given to the sinking of the *Titanic*.[31]

The Claremorris branch of the IPP was quick to laud the party for the bill: 'the IPP, who at last have brought about our deliverance, is due the gratitude of our nation and of every Irishman the world over.'[32] The measure of self-government entailed in the bill was quite circumscribed, causing the more radical *Mayo News* to caution that it was 'by no means the broad and generous measure that a cursory glance over the speech might lead one to believe'. The paper questioned the lack of financial control accorded to the Irish parliament in particular.[33] The *Freeman's Journal* maintained that these limitations were just a formula and not real.[34] At a later stage, IPP members also voiced concerns over the possibility that a home rule government would lower subventions to county councils to make up a deficit at central level.[35]

This muted reaction changed into a more enthusiastic response in Mayo when home rule became increasingly more real with the second and especially the third reading of the bill in 1914. There were a growing number of public meetings and official bodies pledging support for home rule and IPP MPs. In March 1913 Mayo County Council unanimously passed a motion in favour of the bill. In June 1914 it congratulated the IPP on the magnificent success of passing the third reading.[36] This active support put a stop to the allegations that the party had deliberately slowed down the sale of land lest a growing proportion of farmers owning their farms would end their support for home rule. Dillon expressed his relief 'that the people of east Mayo had shown that it was not true that if the people had the land they would have no interest in Home Rule'. His fellow MP, William Doris, concurred. At a UIL branch meeting in Westport on 14 September 1913 he expressed his conviction that the bill would be enacted in the next twelve months, and they would then 'have achieved what they and their forefathers had been fighting for so long – the complete abolition of landlordism and the right to manage their own affairs'.[37] Dillon did see some remaining obstacles as there were still 'great foes to contend with'.[38]

Possibly the largest meeting in support of home rule was organized in Balla in January 1914. It was meant to represent the whole county, and special trains were commissioned to convey people from Westport, Ballina, Ballinrobe and even Athlone. Although the day was 'marred by rain which fell with pitiless incessancy' that kept thousands away, record numbers attended. Fitzgibbon and Doris, MPs for South and West Mayo, praised each other and the people of Mayo, arguing that 'The backbone of landlordism had been shattered'. A number of motions were passed in support of Redmond for his work for home rule and the emancipation of tenants. Others included a demand for compulsory purchase of the remaining land in the hands of landlords, and a call for all Irish people to help 'movements for the revival of the Irish language, the encouragements of Irish industries and national pastimes.' Fitzgibbons made another of his more radical statements, declaring they were 'ruled by a foreign power'.[39]

The IPP was confident that, as Fitzgibbon put it elsewhere that month, 'the battle was over', and even closed its home rule fund.[40] Public reactions now became more celebratory. Dillon was received with huge enthusiasm when he arrived in his constituency in June. Along the railway line 'fog signals were exploded at regular intervals' and at the two stops in Mayo he was met by crowds shouting: 'Welcome Home with Home Rule'. When he arrived at Ballaghaderreen the whole town was illuminated with bonfires and many in the huge crowds carried torches. The road from the station was lined with more than 1,000 Irish Volunteers.[41] A similar celebration in the same town when the bill reached the statute book in September drew an even larger crowd, including representatives from Mayo, Sligo and Roscommon.[42]

There were, however, still some dissenting voices, which found their main outlet in the *Mayo News*. It argued in an editorial that the bill did not give the Irish self-government but put them in a dependent position: 'The expediency of politics does not justify national dishonour.'[43] These minority voices were shouted down and accused of treachery to the Irish cause, similar to the treatment O'Brien had received in 1910. The *Mayo News* was accused of not actually having read the bill, and the people were asked to judge for themselves. A certain growth in radical support was, nevertheless, detected by the police during 1913.[44]

In these discussions, the land question was still central for many farmers. The prospect of home rule increased pressure on remaining landlords. At a meeting in Ballina in June 1912, Daniel Boyle, MP and local alderman, argued that landlords 'were making a grave mistake in not honourably meeting their tenants, and bargaining with them for the sale of their estates.' Fr Andrew Callaghan drew laughter and cheers when he suggested that a home rule government would reduce the rents of remaining tenants and then 'the landlords, may be in a little more of a hurry to sell'. Boyle added that while he 'did not wish to see these gentlemen leaving the country', he wanted 'to get rid of them as landlords'.[45]

In February 1913 the RIC inspector-general reported that boycotting and intimidation were again rife in Clare, Galway and Mayo, which had the highest number of estates, four, where tenants withheld rent, most of them in Achill. Men who worked for the local land agent were 'hooted and groaned by crowds of women when they leave home' and turf was thrown at them. Although these men received protection, they eventually felt forced to resign.[46] At a UIL meeting in Westport, Doris claimed that 'the hearts and the minds and any sympathy that the people in Westport had would go forth to the brave people of Achill in the fight that they were making', adding that apparently 'it was only by breaking the law in this country the law could be made straight.' This was taken quite far when one of the landlords, a Mrs McDonnell, was, according to a police report, 'murderously attacked' in July. She subsequently agreed to sell the estate. Other landlords followed suit. As a result, the percentage of land owned by farmer-occupiers increased to seventy by 1914.[47]

Although the county subsequently became more settled, agitation did not end. The CI reported in February 1914 that conditions had improved markedly on estates that had been sold. Farmers in possession of their land were deemed to be 'much more thrifty and contented than those who have not yet purchased', and 'do not take part in agitation'. However, on unsold land, the story was different.[48] In parliament Doris claimed that generally things were 'in a most satisfactory condition', but 'a state of great unrest and agitation prevailed in the remainder of the County owing to delays in the purchase of congested estates.' He asked the government to make funds available to enable the CDB to 'carry out their duty under the Land Acts, as otherwise they would never have peace in the County.'[49] Augustine Birrell, Irish chief secretary, defended the record of the CDB by pointing out that they had completed 247 sales totalling 822,103 acres worth £3,218,280. He added that selling land took time.[50] Nevertheless, unrest on unsold estates occasionally flared up as it did in the spring of 1914 in Crossmolina, Hollymount and Ballina with boycotts, threatening letters, and one case of firing into a house.[51] In February a farmer who had taken possession of an evicted farm was stripped naked and made to swear he would not return.[52]

Agitation against graziers also remained strong and was actively supported by the local press, which called for the breaking up of their lands.[53] Many larger farmers became fearful of taking up grazing farms. In Mayo nine such farms with an eleven-month tenancy totalling 1,952 acres remained unlet during 1913.

This was the highest number in the country with Mayo taking the lead in this form of protest from neighbouring Roscommon.[54] In a speech at Newport in September 1912, Doris had accused the CDB of giving out large tracts of lands to graziers who already owned substantial farms. The lands were, he argued, meant for the relief of congestion, and were expected to 'be distributed amongst the numerous occupiers of small uneconomic holdings in the parish'.[55]

The *Freeman's Journal* discussed some examples of townlands full of tenants with tiny holdings and on the verge of starvation with large grazier lands situated next to them. The position of farmers in remote Belmullet was described emotively: 'The gaunt spectre of famine and starvation stalks unchecked through this vast district periodically, leaving death and untold misery in its ghastly train; ... still the scores of "fodeen" landlords cling tenaciously to their estates, and wring the last copper out of a down-trodden tenantry.'[56] Any thought in Britain that the granting of home rule would settle agrarian unrest in a county like Mayo proved unfounded. In contrast to the fall in agitation for the sale of land, agitation against graziers, including much cattle driving, remained strong in 1914, particularly in Belmullet, Claremorris, Ballina and Achill.[57]

Other political and social issues also raised temperatures during this fraught period. In February 1914 a riot broke out in Westport after the staging of the play, *General John Regan*. Written by a local Protestant clergyman, J.O. Hannay, under the pseudonym of George A. Birmingham, the play was unsympathetic in its representation of nationalist conviction in Ireland and specifically in Westport where Hannay lived. According to the police, the crowd objected to the fact that the Catholic priest was played by the former Anglican rector. The stage was stormed, the actor was knocked unconscious, and the other players and the police, called in to quell the riot, were also attacked. In the ensuing mêlée, the district inspector was seriously wounded.[58]

However, the main threat to peace in the county during this period was the rise of paramilitarism. The RIC was most concerned with Ulster unionists' preparations to resist in arms a possible introduction of home rule months before the measure was introduced in parliament.[59] By July 1912 the inspector-general stated that popular feeling in that province was a 'matter of grave anxiety'. During 1913 the newly established Ulster Volunteer Force (UVF) became increasingly prominent in police reports. By July, when rumours that the UVF had been armed were confirmed, the threat caused by this organization was for the first time seen as more urgent than agrarian trouble in the inspector-general's monthly reports.[60] In August he stated that nearly all unionists of every age carried a revolver and that the organized hostility to home rule 'is a serious and growing menace to the public peace', as it had now to a large extent become 'a religious question arousing very bitter sectarian feeling'.[61]

Nationalists in Ulster initially reacted with great caution. In March 1913 the St Patrick's Day celebrations in Ulster were called off, and in August the AOH ordered its Ulster circles not to have demonstrations.⁶² This changed slowly towards the end of the year, when meetings became numerous and by November there were signs of nationalists in Ulster arming themselves.⁶³ In Mayo the events in Ulster did not generate much public interest initially.⁶⁴ In September William Doris rejected the idea that there was any serious objection to home rule: 'The people of Great Britain have satisfied themselves that the charge of bigotry against Irish Catholics is a foul slander, and this was the only serious objection now raised to Home Rule.'⁶⁵ In January 1914 John Fitzgibbon argued that 'The talk of Ulster revolt ... was only for the purpose of gulling the English people.'⁶⁶ At a large home rule meeting in Balla that month, both MPs condemned 'the ridiculous allegations of intolerance propounded by Carson [the unionist leader] and his gang of truth perverters against their Catholic fellow-countrymen.'⁶⁷ The only active response in Mayo told a slightly different story. The expulsion of Catholic and socialist workers from the Belfast shipyards in the summer of 1913 led to a boycott of Belfast goods and Belfast salesmen being intimidated by members of the AOH.⁶⁸

There was a stronger reaction from the IRB, but from 1912 this focused more on a possible war with Germany. In October several county and district circles met.⁶⁹ Richard Walsh recalled a previous meeting attended by Major John MacBride who discussed the likelihood of war between England and Germany and 'Irishmen's duty, before war broke out, of military preparedness for striking for our freedom when we found England engaged in the war'.⁷⁰ The tone of public expressions also became more radical. *Irish Freedom*, which the inspector-general argued was read by SF, the IRB and the Fianna, openly discussed the possibility of an Anglo-German war in September 1912 and the opportunity it presented for winning Irish freedom. It called on readers to collect arms for a rebellion during such a war or to join the Germans when they invaded.⁷¹

The IRB also played an important role in the foundation of the Irish Volunteers, set up at the Rotunda in Dublin on 25 November 1913, to ensure the safe introduction of the home rule bill against unionist opposition. Many of the founding members in Dublin and throughout the country were IRB men, which made the IPP initially hesitant to get involved. This was also noticed by the police, who argued that 'no persons of importance in the Nationalist organization appears to be identified with the movement, which, so far, has made no progress.' More meetings were reported in November in Galway, Cork, Limerick and other places but again no IPP officials attended. In December the inspector-general claimed the IPP opposed the founding of a Volunteer force.⁷²

This also held people back in Mayo. Early in December the formation of a branch of the Volunteers in Ballyhaunis was suggested in anticipation 'of Civil War on the passage of the Home Rule Bill a third time through the House of Commons next May'. Locals considered it doubtful that a branch would materialize '[i]n view of the mixed feelings existing in Nationalist ranks as to the advisability of establishing branches of the National Volunteer Force all over the country.'⁷³ Opposition was voiced forcefully by some:

> lest the young manhood of Ireland be misled into an orgie [sic] of misplaced militarism ... It is quite enough to have this silly gasconading going on in the North, but it is worse than mere stupidity – it is almost criminal folly – to seek to inflame the remainder of the country at this time.⁷⁴

The consequent reliance on the few IRB circles meant that the start of the Volunteers in Mayo was slow and erratic. Although Darrell Figgis, a writer and member who owned a home in Achill, claimed a company of Volunteers had been formed in Dooagh on Achill Island in 1913, the first confirmed units in Mayo were started in January 1914. The group of radicals that had emerged previously in other organizations often took the lead, starting a local Volunteer company by enlisting their own family and friends, or drawing on the IAA or Fianna.⁷⁵ Meetings were then held in Castlebar and afterwards in Newport, organized by Michael Kilroy who had also attended the meeting in Castlebar.⁷⁶ In Westport the IRB ordered its members to join the Volunteers immediately and to take control of the organization. On 21 March 1914 the *Mayo News* reported that 'on Sunday night over a hundred young man from Westport and surrounding districts were enrolled in the Irish Volunteers movement ... Instructions in drilling will commence on Monday night.' The battalion under the command of Tom Tarmey, an ex-soldier, was reviewed by Colonel Burke in May.⁷⁷ Tarmey was a former boxing and drill instructor in the British army and travelled by bicycle to instruct various companies. Later Major MacBride occasionally led the training of the company in Westport.⁷⁸

For some, the unclear political position of the Volunteers meant they did not want to join. Most of the IAA members in Newport considered the people that were in the Volunteers not radical enough. At their annual convention in July 1913, the IAA had passed two resolutions: one proclaiming that no one who served in the army of a foreign king, which included the English King, could be a member, and the other asking for the right to a separate national existence, which argued that home rule was far too circumscribed.⁷⁹ For the IPP, however, the involvement of the IRB meant they also continued to keep their distance. Dillon expressed his scepticism of mobilizing Volunteers. He felt nationalists took upon themselves a great responsibility in arming such a large body of men. Nevertheless, to ensure the continued loyalty of all, he added that the Volunteers were not a revolt against Redmond as had been alleged.⁸⁰ In newspapers the Irish Volunteers were, therefore, treated with a certain suspicion, or their importance was played down. They nevertheless frequently sported adverts for Irish National Volunteers badges 'Beautifully finished in green and gold' from 'an old design by F.J. Bigger', one of the leading men in the Gaelic League.⁸¹

Slowly the Volunteers took centre stage. The involvement of Colonel Maurice Moore, a native of Ballyglass who had been appointed inspector-general of the Volunteers, made them more acceptable to many in the following months. As the son of a former local IPP MP with a past as British army officer who had become heavily involved in the language movement, Moore was highly respected by all.[82] At a meeting in neighbouring Sligo on 7 February, he made his position, which combined loyalty with a threat of force, clear. Whilst stating that the Volunteers' aim was 'peaceful and constitutional', he argued that without an armed force, nothing would be achieved:

> It was not by hard words that Elizabeth and Cromwell and William conquered Ireland but by hard blows; it was not the eloquence of Grattan that won a Parliament for Ireland, but the fear of 40,000 Volunteers. Catholic emancipation was advocated by the greatest orators and statesmen of modern times ... but it was not till Wellington, the greatest soldier statesman of the British Empire, stated he could no longer prevent rebellion in Ireland, that emancipation was granted by the English Parliament.

The Volunteers were needed to defend Ireland in case of an invasion by foreign forces, but they were also needed to ensure Ireland would get what was lawfully hers: 'we mean not to be bullied by Sir Edward Carson, who has announced that if Parliament passes the Home Rule Bill he will resist by force, and that we Nationalists must submit to his dictation'.[83]

Volunteer companies were formed in towns throughout Mayo but membership remained still relatively small. By April 1914 it was reported that there were 520 Volunteers in Ballina, 200 in Castlebar, 300 in Achill and some more in smaller units.[84] The CI was aware of six companies all centred in towns where, according to the police, most political activists were found: 'In the country districts the people do not take the least interest in the [home rule] question.' He, nevertheless, added that the organization was actively spreading.[85] Some local IPP members, worried about the arming of the UVF following the Larne gun-running, began to support the Irish Volunteers. In Islandeady, a company was established by the commander and drill instructor of the Castlebar branch.[86] In Carracastle, Frank Fahy spoke at a public meeting where about forty men enrolled.[87] At the end of May the *Connaught Telegraph* reported that there was 'scarcely a town or village without a corps', and that the boys brigade membership had also grown considerably. The authorities were a bit more cautious but now estimated there were 2,400 Volunteers in fourteen branches.[88]

This growth was reflected nationwide, and eventually forced the IPP's hand. They realized that as the Volunteers became increasingly successful, it was important to control the force, while the Volunteers realized it would benefit the organization if the party recognized it.[89] In April Redmond initiated secret negotiations with the Volunteers executive, in which he tried to obtain a deciding voice. Initially this failed, partly due to Redmond's objections to the presence of known radicals such as Patrick Pearse and Bulmer Hobson, but also because these men resented a take-over of the Volunteers by the IPP. After an ultimatum issued by Redmond on 9 June 1914, the Volunteers executive agreed by a slim majority to allow the IPP leader to nominate twenty-five new members to it, giving him an important say in the organization.[90]

This endorsement caused a huge growth in membership. By September there were 7,406 Volunteers in 65 branches in Mayo, which made it the best-organized county in Connacht and nationwide only second in absolute numbers to Cork. The CI added that most Volunteers supported Redmond and that SF, by which they meant radicals, were only strong in Westport and to a lesser extent in Castlebar.[91] Richard Walsh recalled later how 'Companies sprang up like mushrooms all over the country. It was a common sight, if cycling along a country road on an evening, to see groups of young men forming fours at every cross-roads.' At this point, even Lord Sligo was persuaded by Maurice Moore to join up. Apparently Sligo, who did not fully appreciate the movement's association with home rule, wanted to go on an inspection tour with Moore, who asked him for tacit approval of home rule now that it was virtually on the statute book.[92]

According to the CI, this influx of new members from all shades of nationalist politics caused chaos. There was initially not really any higher form of organization above the local company, which were generally run by a self-appointed committee. Later junior officers were selected, usually through elections. Battalions or brigades did not really exist, but there was a county board comprising some of the original activists like Richard Walsh and Joseph MacBride.[93] As a result, most of the leading men at local and county level had a link to the IRB. The ordinary Volunteers came from organizations like the GAA and the AOH, which had become important recruiting grounds.[94] To maintain interest, some units became very active. In Castlebar, meetings were held six evenings a week, at which there was drill instruction, physical training and route marches led by four instructors, all ex-NCOs of the Connaught Rangers. Parades were held in a big enclosed yard and sometimes publicly on the Mall. This company also obtained some rifles and revolvers, and miniature guns used for indoor practice. Most units were somewhat less ardent, but their activities featured the same elements.[95]

An important event in the radicalization of some members was the shooting at Bachelor's Walk in Dublin, following the nationalist Howth gun-running in July 1914. One future activist from Westport remembered reading about the shootings in the paper: '"While Europe talks of war, men and women are being shot down in Dublin streets!". I was, of course, still at school and, needless to state, we were all in a furore about the landing of the guns. "Now", we said, as youngsters will, "it is the time for Ireland!"'[96] In Ballyhaunis these events forced a change in the officer corps from older respected men to a younger more activist type. Patrick Moylett sent a letter to Michael Delaney telling 'him that it was not for men like him ... to lead the Volunteers. I was elected chairman of the new Volunteer committee as from that date'.[97]

In this way politics in Mayo had shifted from focusing on land agitation linked to home rule and led by the IPP to a more unstable state. The IPP was unsure about how to make itself relevant with the prospect of home rule on the horizon, while it was confronted with a somewhat amorphous group in the Volunteers, which was prepared to bring home rule or more to Ireland, by force if necessary. This change also brought a group of radical men and some women into mainstream political organization; they became the leaders of the new form of advanced nationalism that would take control of the county during the war that followed.

3 'Sham feiners and sham physical force men': war and protest, 1914–16

The outbreak of the First World War in August 1914 heralded a new phase in the life of all sections of Irish society, but especially those engaged in various struggles – not just the men who joined the army, but also suffragettes, labour activists, radical nationalists and unionists. As a first measure, all reservists were called to join their regiments. Some new recruits also left while those who stayed behind were immediately made aware of restrictions on 'expressions likely to cause dissatisfaction' that were introduced under the Defence of the Realm Act. Anyone in breach of the act could be tried by court martial. The impact of the war on everyday life, however, remained limited in Mayo, while political allegiances only slowly became more radical prior to the Easter Rising in 1916.

The initial response in Mayo to British involvement in the war on 4 August was positive for the government. The CI reported that tensions had subsided and that local sympathies were 'entirely with England and her allies'. This was due, he claimed, to a 'general dread of German invasion'. The following month, he stated that the war was having a salutary effect on community relations with unionists and nationalists coming together to wave soldiers off. The press reported how Irish Volunteer bands escorted relatively small numbers of reservists to various railway stations. In Ballina, this was a joyous event presided over by clergymen of all denominations and for which the shops closed, two bands played and 500 Volunteers lined the streets.[1]

Yet this did not translate into immediate practical support. Some urban areas, particularly in east Mayo, provided a good number of recruits during the first weeks of the war, but in rural areas very few volunteered for service. This distinction was common throughout Ireland, but the CI, who claimed that rural districts were 'not possessed of any patriotic or martial spirit', blamed this on economic underdevelopment: 'the people in the greater portion of this County are still very backward. Living in desolation and isolation for generations on the fringe of civilization, they have experienced no influences to make them manly, sturdy or independent.'[2] The distinction also had a political dimension. Because home rule was not yet on the statute book, the IPP initially had an ambivalent attitude towards support for the war effort. The RIC inspector-general detected 'a feeling of distrust' setting in, pending the passing of the bill. He considered it 'probable the majority of Volunteers will eventually take whatever course Mr John Redmond advises'.[3]

Among nationalists, fear of conscription was widespread. In Mayo, the police reported that after the outbreak of the war a number of people rushed to America due to rumours of conscription. Although they claimed 'this cowardly action has been condemned by the clergy and by respectable people generally', the nationwide anti-recruiting campaign run by radical voices, aimed particularly at young farmers, shop assistants, clerks and teachers, was successful in Mayo. The relative radicalism in west Mayo was evident in the distribution of anti-recruiting leaflets in Castlebar and Westport, which only occurred in thirty-eight other places nationwide.[4]

Redmond's position was complicated. Without home rule on the statute book, full support for the war effort would see him lose a trump card in relation to the government and leave him in a weakened position vis-à-vis more radical elements in Ireland. He therefore publicly offered the service of the Volunteers to the government for the defence of Irish shores; however, as yet, he was unwilling to support recruitment for foreign service. In negotiations about the actual introduction of home rule and how to meet unionist opposition, Redmond accepted the controversial proposal to allow northern counties to exclude themselves temporarily from the jurisdiction of an Irish home rule parliament. In an effort to mobilize support for this stance in Mayo, leading local politicians featured prominently at the annual county demonstration of the AOH at Newport on 6 September 1914.[5] According to the *Connaught Telegraph*, this was an immense gathering of Hibernians and Volunteers, with special trains running from Achill, Ballina, Castlerea and Tubercurry. In his speech William Doris emphasized the need for a speedy introduction of home rule and warned further delays would bring back 'the old times when Ireland had no regard whatever for English promises to redress her grievances.' Acknowledging that not everyone supported the IPP stance on temporary exclusion, he promised that no amending bill that separated any portion of Ireland for all time would be passed. Doris presented temporary exclusion as an 'arrangement that will do no harm [but] will give time for reflection' before declaring to cheers that 'War or no war … Home Rule we must have without further delay'.[6]

Part of this call was heeded the following week when the House of Commons passed the home rule bill for the third time without any exclusion of northern counties, which meant it now became law despite the opposition of the Conservative-dominated House of Lords. However, at the same time a Suspensory Act was passed to delay implementation for the duration of the war. Some unionists were outraged: there were reports that some had treated the King's picture with disrespect in a picture house and that others had left divine service when the national anthem was sung, but this was also the response of some nationalists.[7]

As a result of the suspension, the news inspired little enthusiasm. The IPP, nevertheless, organized celebratory meetings. In Mayo, Doris called on all to unite behind them. He emphasized the role of the Volunteers 'in which every young fellow and every man in the country should be joined.' Although he claimed not to be a military man, he saw a fighting role for the Volunteers and declared – to cheers – that the Irish should be prepared to defend themselves and their 'interests whenever the occasion arises'. Mr Barry from Westport elaborated on this by referring to Redmond's offer that the Volunteers be used for home defence thereby freeing up the army to fight in France. Mr Moclair from Castlebar observed the dawn of a new spirit of co-operation between the English and the Irish: 'These men from Mayo were fighting England's battles, and for the first time in the history of the world Ireland's battles too, because their interests were in common.' The *Connacht Tribune* concluded that 'Where Carson divided, Redmond has united'. Even Lord Oranmore and Browne praised Redmond and the spirit of co-operation from Castle MacGarrety in Claremorris. Supportive letters by leading unionists across the country were also published in the local newspapers. In Portumna Union it was even claimed that 'some Unionists stated they were prepared to follow Mr Redmond to death's door if necessary'. Not all were so sanguine. The AOH organizer, Mr Colleary, was much more confrontational: 'if Carson raises an army to fight against Home Rule for Ireland you here in Mayo will raise a sufficient army to wipe of the face of the earth all the Unionists he can bring against you (cheers).' He was also less willing to fight for England, which he argued 'is engaged in a desperate war, she wants men and more men, to defend the vested interests of the aristocracy of England and to defend her commerce'. Only after home rule was operating would he fight with them. While some local councillors agreed, opposition to Redmond's position was still rare.[8]

It soon became clear that the IPP's conditional support for the war effort was not sustainable. Home rule was suspended and if nationalists were seen not to be co-operating fully in the fight against Germany while unionists were, the eventual implementation would be endangered. Redmond realized this quickly and changed his position on recruitment. During a speech at Woodenbridge, County Wicklow on 20 September 1914 he called on all Irishmen, especially the Volunteers, to fight for freedom not just in Ireland but anywhere the principles of 'religion and morality and right' were under attack: 'it would be a disgrace for ever to our country and a reproach to her manhood and a denial of the lessons of her history if young Ireland confined their efforts to remaining at home to defend the shores of Ireland from an unlikely invasion'.[9] Dillon claimed that fighting together with the unionists would have a positive effect. If they did not, he argued, after the war unionists would bully and use the threat of civil war to repeal the home rule act. In this way, IPP support for the war thus remained dependent on achieving home rule.

Most nationalists in Mayo and elsewhere supported the IPP position, but many doubted whether England would fulfil its promises. Some leading Volunteers and Sinn Féiners, strongly supported by radical Irish-American organizations, opposed the IPP's stance. To prevent a split, IPP MPs called on people to unite behind a renewed demand for the immediate introduction of home rule and finishing the job of smashing landlordism, 'an even greater task than achieving Home Rule'. They believed all nationalists would support these objectives, irrespective of their position on the war. In an attempt to ridicule the radicals, they declared that 'The tasks which lay before a Home Rule Parliament were too great and too serious to be interfered with by sham feiners and sham physical force men (loud laughter).' This attack made clear that O'Brien's AFIL had become irrelevant and that the IPP's new enemies were now SF and the IRB.[10]

Initially, the more radical elements among Mayo nationalists were uncertain about how to react to the outbreak of the war. However, after Redmond had called on nationalists to give the war effort their full support, they agreed on a clear anti-recruiting position and the Volunteers subsequently split in two. Opponents of Redmond still controlled the national leadership and retained the Irish Volunteers name, but the great majority followed Redmond and formed the National Volunteers, leaving both organizations in disarray. The RIC inspector-general claimed that the Volunteers were now 'little better than [a] huge mob'.[11] At a local level the confusion that followed the split meant that the Irish Volunteers often remained only nominally in existence. In Mayo, the police did not even bother to register the Irish Volunteers separately, simply stating that most Volunteers branches were following Redmond, but noting that units in Castlebar and particularly Westport were more radical.[12]

The few companies that remained with the Irish Volunteers were often directed to do so by their officers. In November 1914 Darrell Figgis, described by Dillon as 'a very objectionable and dangerous man', reviewed a unit of eighty-two men in Balla.[13] In Westport, the local branch was addressed by Major MacBride shortly after Redmond's Woodenbridge speech. Seán Gibbons recalled how MacBride laid out the choice they faced: 'Too long has England spat upon you, scorned you, reviled you! Now is your opportunity!'. A majority subsequently stayed with the Irish Volunteers.[14] It is not clear if a branch of the National Volunteers was ever established in Westport. In Castlebar, the officers also remained with the Irish Volunteers, but most men joined the rival organization. At a meeting in Newport at the beginning of October the local company decided to follow Redmond, but seventeen men led by Pat O'Donnell dissented and organized their own unit following a meeting in the town hall.[15] Soon after that some men associated with the local IAA decided to join the Irish Volunteers.[16]

The reaction of most people in Mayo to Redmond's stance was positive. There were donations to support the war effort and generally people responded to demands made from central government, especially if they were supported by Redmond or Dillon. The local press reported on the war and the fighting in a favourable light for the Allies and portrayed Germany and the Kaiser as the enemy. There were numerous reports of recruits leaving for the front and on those wounded or killed in action. In October 1914 the Mayo LGB reacted favourably to a request to prepare for the housing of a number of Belgian refugees. Although the offer was not availed of (as enough places had been offered elsewhere), money was raised in support of the Belgian Refugees Fund and an appeal was issued at Mass throughout the county in October 1914. In Castlebar, a successful fundraising dance was organized by local women and other initiatives followed.[17]

The war also affected life in Mayo more directly. The prospect of a dearth of workers strengthened the bargaining position of labourers. A few days after the declaration of war, dockers went on strike in Westport to demand higher wages, which were granted almost immediately.[18] Employers were still fearful of Larkinism or radical trade union action. This came to the fore in an apparently unrelated dispute between T.J. Kilroy and a carpenter he employed, Richard Lanigan. The latter had challenged Kilroy for deducting too much money from his wages for national insurance. In response, Kilroy struck Lanigan on the head with a poker. During the court case for assault in December 1914, the defence lawyer implied that Lanigan had intended to 'start preaching the gospel expounded by Jim Larkin' and claiming he had tried to convince Kilroy's men to go on strike as a justification for the attack.[19]

The following months witnessed increased trade union activity. The ITGWU was remarkably successful in mobilizing unskilled workers locally. In Louisburgh, Thomas J. Sweeney, secretary of the local branch, brought together all the carters whom he persuaded to join the union and demand higher wages for carting between Louisburgh and Westport. While initially it proved difficult to convince some employers, when it became clear the alternative was to employ their own horse and carts, most accepted the proposed arrangements. When one employer used a carter from Westport who was not a member of the union, the man received such a hostile reception in Louisburgh that the police were summoned to protect him. The Westport carter argued that he did not know about the carters' union and gave an undertaking not to act against their interest again.[20] Afterwards Sweeney urged the men 'to be loyal to one another, like good brothers, for upon that their success depended', and promised the union would support any strike if employers refused to accept the new wage scales.[21]

In the longer run, greater availability of workers owing to reluctance to join the army and reduced emigration undermined the bargaining power of labour. Fear of being conscripted had made men hesitant to seek work in Britain, prompting one councillor in Castlebar UDC to remark that: 'All the young fellows who used to go to England are at home this year.'[22] There was, however, less money in the hands of local authorities to provide employment. The town surveyor of Castlebar reported in February 1915 that as a result of the reduction in money spent on maintenance and scavenging, the roads were suffering. By April there were only sufficient funds for mending some small patches of road.[23]

This situation created an opportunity to reopen the discussion on direct employment of labourers by the council, which had started before the war. The chairman argued at the April meeting that they were not giving value for money, claiming that some labourers were 'sparrow-picking the roads and putting them in a worse condition, and all we receive in return is a whirlwind of dust from the motor cars enjoying the luxury of smoother roads at the expense of the ratepayers.' To allow for a reduction in the rates by 6*d*. in the pound, the council subsequently decided to reduce the budget for cleaning the roads by scavenging from £100 to £60, for road maintenance from £400 to £250, and struck out £100 for concrete footpaths altogether.[24] Labourers were not enamoured by the comments on their work ethos and the reductions which led to some redundancies. The *Connaught Telegraph* even refused to publish a letter from them criticizing Castlebar UDC because the language used was 'of a very personal and abusive nature'.[25]

Another widespread problem caused by the war was rising prices, in particular of potatoes. This hit the poor hard and put extra pressure on local politicians. A week after the decision to reduce the rates, road workers asked the Castlebar surveyor for higher wages of 3*s*. per day as they were 'unable to pay rent and support ourselves at the present wages'. At the same time the Castlebar carters sought wages of 6*s*. a day to cover the higher cost of oats for their horses.[26] Under threat of a strike, the chairman of Castlebar UDC declared that the labourers' claims were reasonable but explained that as they had not budgeted for this in the estimates, only half the increase sought could be granted.[27] At the same time, a *Connaught Telegraph* report on research showing that taking alcohol had 'no beneficial effects on curing the sick' did nothing to lift spirits locally. It seemed 'patients recovered just as well and quickly without its use'. The authorities subsequently announced that hospital patients would in future have to forego their daily dose.[28]

The creeping economic depression was brought to the attention of Lord Wimborne, the lord lieutenant, when he visited Castlebar in September 1915. The council argued that too many industries in the land were allowed to lapse into decay, and that although many improvements had been made in the town, like new cottages for the working classes and piped water, there was no more capital left for badly needed initiatives. Their pleading eventually yielded results. In May 1916 it was announced that with state support, a bacon co-operative was to be opened in Castlebar, a woollen factory in Foxford, and a knitting industry in Keel on Achill.[29]

In rural areas the war largely put a stop to agitation, as it did in neighbouring counties. The large Sligo Estate had been sold just before the outbreak of war, meaning that seventy per cent of farmers now had control of their farms, while high demand for foodstuffs raised their incomes. In the first years of the war, only a few cases of non-payment of rents occurred, which were usually quickly settled by the sale of the estate. This generally concerned smaller demesnes, with the exception of the large Achill Mission sold in June 1915 after years of agitation. Protests against graziers also died down. Incidences of cattle-driving, which had been the highest in Ireland before the war, became rare in Mayo. This was also reflected in the number of grazing farms left unlet as a result of agitation. The acreage affected in this way fell from 3,887 in 1914 to 363 acres in 1915. Although a similar reduction in agitation was recorded elsewhere, Mayo slipped down the league table of disturbed counties in which it had long featured prominently.[30]

Gradually, the position of labour improved again. Due to the demands of the war-industry, migration picked up and the numbers available for work slowly declined. The introduction by the new coalition government in August 1915 of the National Registration Act in Britain, which obliged all persons between 15 and 65 who were not already members of the armed forces to register, caused a temporary setback as many labourers returned home in fear of being conscripted. When it was made clear this did not apply to those born in Ireland, press reports of men leaving for England again appeared.[31] In March 1916 hundreds of Mayo labourers were brought to munition works in England. One reporter claimed that over 500 had gone from Achill alone and that all of them had 'been assured that they do not come under the Military Service Act'.[32]

The consequent shortage of available labour even started to be felt by the hard-hit road workers. The editor of the *Connaught Telegraph* argued in January 1916 that 'War is making labour scarcer and scarcer, the farmers are devoting more attention to their lands than they did heretofore, and as the contract prices for roads are not being increased people are commencing to shun this kind of work.'[33] The growing need for foodstuffs in Britain put further strain on the labour market. In 1917 a compulsory tillage scheme was introduced by the authorities to deal with the shortage of food that had developed as a result of the German U-boat campaign against Allied shipping. Under this, graziers were forced to convert grass land to tillage, which necessitated more workers. Early in 1916 reclamation of unused bog land to increase yields was proposed, but this was quickly shot down as a waste of time and money. The labour it would cost to drain and clear bogland could, it was argued, be used better on already reclaimed land presently used as grass land.[34]

Following the Volunteer split, the IPP again focused on the land question and the eventual introduction of home rule to retain people's attention and support. At the annual UIL convention for Mayo in March 1915 Dillon emphasized the need to force a settlement of the land question, given that 'delays had been exasperating and almost intolerable'. He suggested, to cheers, that after the institution of a home rule government, the Irish people 'would make the old land, which had for so long lain in the shadow of devastation and ruin, the home of a prosperous, a happy, and an honoured nation.' He warned of the consequences of the policies of those who had called the IPP traitors to the national cause and sought 'to pay England back for all the injury she inflicted upon Ireland' that such a stance was 'bound to end in ruin and disaster for this country'.[35] There were too many vital interests of Ireland bound up with the allies; he argued it would, therefore, be foolish to remain neutral as these people called for.

The main bone of contention between the IPP and its new nationalist adversaries remained recruitment. Having called for support for the war effort, the party now had to aid enlistment. A conscription scare was instigated by 'Sinn Féiners' in an attempt to paint the IPP as recruiting agents. During the first months of the war, the Mayo MPs did not openly advocate enlistment. In a lengthy report on a speech by Doris at Parke on 23 November, any possibility of conscription was denied and no reference was made to joining the army. Early in 1915 meetings to encourage recruitment, which were organized locally without explicit IPP support, were attended by Captain Nicholas Balfe, the recruiting officer for the Irish Brigade.[36]

In Mayo, as in neighbouring counties, the recruiting efforts had patchy results. In April the chief recruiting office in Dublin reported that Mayo had the worst record in the country. There were, however, clear differences within the county. Ballina town and district delivered 315 army recruits up to March 1915, Swinford followed with 223, Castlebar 180, Ballinrobe 130, Claremorris 87, Belmullet 72, and Newport 31 while Westport lagged well behind with a dozen recruits. Even the high numbers in Ballina did not compare to a similar town like Boyle in Roscommon where six months earlier 520 men had already enlisted, or Sligo town where it was claimed a thousand men had joined the colours. Apologetically, Doris argued this was due to all the young men working in Britain and enlisting there.[37] He also claimed that an *Irish Independent* article on the possible introduction of conscription had caused many to attempt to emigrate to America. In response, John Dillon stated that he 'was never more ashamed in my life of young Irishmen. I could understand men going away to escape conscription; but the idea of men running away to America to escape from a paragraph in the "Independent" beats all records.' A number of clergy, including the bishop of Killala and the auxiliary bishop of Tuam, condemned the young men who 'had given the name of coward to the Irish youth'.[38] Some of those seeking to leave for America were actually forced back when sailors refused to serve on boats that carried them from British ports to their destination. On their return to Ireland they were ridiculed, making them targets for the propaganda of radical activists.[39]

To counter the negative sentiments, a concerted attempt was made in early 1915 to generate enthusiasm for the army. Captain Balfe, now appointed recruiting officer for Mayo, Roscommon and parts of Galway and Sligo, instructed local politicians to organize committees. The fact that Lord Sligo had established one in Westport and appointed himself chairman was not appreciated by the local council, which was only willing to nominate a member from their own ranks if Sligo withdrew. Apart from recruiting posters, which were prominently displayed outside the RIC barracks in many towns, initiatives included the screening in Castlebar town hall of 'Defenders of the Empire'. This film was described as 'the finest image of new pictures ever seen in Castlebar, depicting striking and stirring scenes on land and sea associated with the present European War'. While the death of the son of local MP John Fitzgibbon at the Dardanelles was greeted by expressions of deep regret in Castlerea, and was an emotive issue for some, local casualties were not explicitly used to raise support for the war.[40]

Towards the end of 1915, a number of large meetings were held where the main unionist leaders of the county such as Lord Sligo and Lord Oranmore and Browne spoke. Local representatives in the Westport Union doubted whether many would follow their call as there were still evictions taking place on Lord Sligo's estate. In Ballina, the response to these efforts was good. According to one local activist, more than 800 men had joined the British army there 'to fight for small nations'. By early 1916 there were indeed 720 men from Ballina in the army, proportionally the highest number in the country together with Belfast. In other towns the response was, however, limited, and no centrally organized recruiting committee functioned in Mayo before early 1916. When the Castlebar UDC was urged to set up a committee by the Central Council for the Organization of Recruiting in May 1915, councillors treated it as a joke, putting forward known opponents of enlistment.[41]

A series of further meetings were held throughout Mayo in April 1915. The first in Crossmolina took place during a fair day and was well attended. Local members of the council paraded, accompanied by a Connaught Rangers band, and urged young men to protect their women and children from meeting the same fate as those in Belgium. The general spirit was positive. A statement that the speaker was 'loyal to King and country' was even met with applause. The main speech came from an army colonel. To demonstrate his credentials, he referred to his service with the Land Commission that had enabled the sale of land to local people. He then confronted the lack of recruits head on, emphasizing the lack of manliness: 'There were the shop assistants almost all big lusty fellows of the proper type for military duty standing behind counters measuring out yards of ribbon that was women's work and all these men should be serving their country.' He explicitly referred to the efforts of other counties and towns like Ballina, where one-fifth of the men had joined the army, including some old Fenians he claimed. He did not attempt to portray Germany as a villainous country; rather, he simply stated that if Germany won, Ireland would be treated like Belgium, taxes would go up and farmers would lose the land they had just bought. In a way, he was arguing that Germany would be a worse overlord than Britain, not that the Irish were inherently British. The proceedings ended with shows of some war pictures.[42]

Afterwards a handful of men enlisted and likewise after similar meetings in Castlebar, Achill Sound, Belmullet, Claremorris, Ballina, Swinford and Ballinrobe. Overall, the response was, however, very poor, with only nineteen recruits enlisting. Even the separation allowance that wives of those who enlisted received was not a sufficiently strong inducement. From early 1915 these ranged from 12s. for a childless wife of a private to 25s. for a sergeant's wife with three children and a further 2s. for every additional child. This 'free money' was also a cause of concern. There were complaints about women allegedly using the money for drink and neglecting their children. This was occasionally mentioned in Mayo, but it only seemed to have been a concern for those paying rates if the children had to be taken care of in the workhouse. The CI was defeatist about attracting more recruits, arguing that all towns, except Westport, had already contributed a large number of recruits and the country districts could not be induced anyway. The extra income of farmers due to wartime demand made them particularly disinclined to enlist.[43]

The response in Mayo contrasted sharply with that in other parts of the country, where the April drive brought in 5,377 new recruits, the highest monthly total since the outbreak of the war. The remainder of the year continued to witness fruitless attempts to raise enthusiasm in Mayo. In October some meetings were held but no recruits came forward at all. In November an advertisement campaign was started by the Department of Recruiting for Ireland with a large heading across a full page in the newspapers: 'Irishmen! Sign the enlistment form to-day'. This had little effect. In total the authorities recorded the enlistment of just 442 Mayomen and no women during the whole of 1915, and of these, 168 were members of the National Volunteers. In contrast, 96 men left for the US for fear of conscription in one fortnight in June 1915. In December the county controller of Mayo John Garvey DL informed a county recruitment conference that the supply of men in the towns was now exhausted but that Mayo still had 20,000 men of military age who could be spared. He initiated a new drive in March 1916 at a recruiting conference in Castlebar at which the new programme was explained to local politicians and church dignitaries of all persuasions. Part of this was the appointment of paid recruiters in each market town who visited 'recruitable men' to induce them to join up voluntarily now that compulsion was introduced in Britain. All men and women of influence were called upon to aid in the effort, and the government was asked to reward those who would serve with land through the CDB. However, fear of conscription still generated a lot of resistance, and many speakers denied even the possibility of it being introduced.[44]

Gradually, opponents of enlistment began to make themselves heard. Some anti-recruiting posters had been put up in October 1914 in Swinford. When in late 1915 the IPP brought out Lieutenant Michael O'Leary, a Cork man who had earned the Victoria Cross for bravery, at a meeting in Ballaghaderreen, he was hooted and insulted by Irish Volunteers.[45] Even O'Leary's father was apparently critical of his son, causing some consternation among the participants at a recruiting meeting in Crossmolina. A local Volunteer recalled O'Leary's father commenting on his son: 'I knew it was in me boy; how could he escape it, all the O'Learys were FENIANS and beat the hell out of the English every time and every place.'[46] The centre of opposition remained Westport. Although two recruiting meetings had been held there in May 1915, again with Lord Sligo and some prominent local businessmen speaking from the balcony of the town hall, it was the only Mayo town where nobody joined the army at this time.[47] Further meetings held there during the year were disturbed by Volunteers. Late in 1915 Patrick Dyer, the local secretary of the National Volunteers in Tubercurry, was arrested under the provisions of the Defence of the Realm Act for having anti-recruiting literature in his possession. His arrest followed a well-attended meeting at which a resolution was passed to resist conscription with their lives.[48]

Besides this anti-recruiting campaign, little activity by the Irish Volunteers was recorded after 1914. The announcement that a nationwide review of the National Volunteers would be held in Dublin at Easter 1915 prompted a flurry of activity among the Irish Volunteers. The unit in Castlebar held a raffle in January 1915 for the arms fund, following which a consignment of about 25 rifles was sent from GHQ in Dublin and kept in the Rooney hall. The Swinford company featured prominently, organizing weekly training with shooting exercises and some recruits still joining. Meetings were announced in Ballina and by a revived unit in Balcarra in February, and in March one was held to revive the Castlebar company, which had apparently again become dormant. This was successful, and also inspired the setting up of a girl scouts branch there. However, attendance at meetings varied afterwards and efforts to revitalize the organization continued throughout the year, but this remained a minor feature in newspaper reporting until the Easter Rising.[49]

The few active units attempted to rebuild the organization mainly by approaching relatives of members living in neighbouring areas. To show they were still present in Mayo, a sham battle was staged on 11 October 1914, overseen by the inspecting officer for the county, Darrell Figgis. It was intended that the Castlebar unit, supported by Volunteers from Newport, would drive the Westport men from Sheeane Hill where they had taken up positions. Although the Castlebar men were pushed back due to their lack of numbers and the failure of the Newport men to show up, Figgis commended them for their tactics.[50] Despite the limited military value, such operations had a propaganda value and created personal bonds between the various units.

To promote the movement, several national leaders visited the county during 1915. Major MacBride, who according to the police spoke with a German accent, had arrived in Westport in an expensive hired American yacht in December 1914, where he met his brother Joseph and Figgis and stayed until February.[51] Michael Kilroy recalled how Diarmuid Lynch visited Mayo in April and organized training camps and gave lectures on military topics.[52] Lynch later commented how the organization in Mayo was very weak except for Westport.[53] In August 1915 ties with Dublin were reinforced when the Castlebar branch of the Fianna, together with individual activists from other places, attended the funeral of Jeremiah O'Donovan Rossa, an old Fenian leader, in Dublin. Fianna members subsequently went around the Mayo countryside distributing leaflets detailing his life.[54] In the autumn of 1915 these reorganization attempts still had very limited effects. A formal brigade structure was created with the lead taken by Joseph MacBride and Dick Walsh, but there were only a few active units, mostly in the towns and some villages like Aughagower and Kilmeena due to strong personal ties to Westport and Newport.[55]

Significantly outnumbered, radicals felt hard-pressed. By December the authorities were aware of only four Irish Volunteer branches with 121 members in total, while the National Volunteers still officially numbered 55 units and 4,498 men, down from 66 branches the month before.[56] Even in Westport, the Irish Volunteers were locally described as 'Rainbow Chasers'. In places like Kiltimagh, Balla, and Ballina, where only six of the 83 men had remained with the Irish Volunteers, the men felt isolated and the organization had a marginal existence. In Ballyhaunis the local National Volunteers held daily drilling practice in front of the shop run by one of the five remaining Irish Volunteers, which included three brothers.[57] Together, these men nevertheless formed a sizeable group. After the Woodenbridge speech, the RIC identified 661 Mayo Volunteers who had not fallen in with Redmond's views.[58] Some of them had, however, joined organizations like the Fianna, the IAA or the Hibernian Rifles, another off-shoot of the AOH, while in Ballyvary marching practice had continued under the guise of GAA matches.[59] These alternative forms of organization may explain the small number of Irish Volunteer companies recorded by the police in Mayo compared to other counties. In spring 1916 the Irish Volunteers still only numbered 170 members, whereas the IAA grew from three branches, with 100 members, to six with 317 members.[60]

In the search for new recruits, attention shifted towards more malleable youngsters.[61] In Westport, the Fianna had even become the principal agent of radicalism after the split. At the inception of the branch in 1915, the commanding officer made clear to the fifty members that they were to become soldiers for Ireland. Accordingly, they were put through intense training, parading and a lecture scheme that included Morse code, first aid and military drill exercises. Many of the West Mayo Brigade's most active members in the

War of Independence received their first training in this Fianna branch. Some had been active in the AOH before, and many of its officers, including Tom Derrig and Tom Kettrick, both of whom became prominent in the movement later on, had been members or were taken into the IRB at this time. To heighten their profile, the Fianna and Volunteers organized a large parade following one of their recruiting meetings in Westport. Of the 150 people involved, twelve were arrested, which increased their local prestige.[62]

At this stage the Irish Volunteers had no arms that the authorities were aware of, but some individuals associated with the movement did have access to weapons. The businessman Patrick Moylett from Ballyhaunis had already purchased six rifles and military equipment for four men when the Volunteers were originally set up in 1913.[63] The rifles bought by Castlebar Volunteers early in 1915 had been taken forcibly from the Rooney hall in Castlebar by the National Volunteers while the Irish Volunteers attended a funeral of a comrade. This might have something to do with the providence of the funds used. It appears that the Irish Volunteers retook these rifles soon afterwards because there was an unsuccessful claim for compensation lodged by the National Volunteers with the Castlebar UDC for loss of rifles in April 1915.[64] In Balla a few rifles were taken from the National Volunteers, for which Dick Walsh was arrested, while in Newport two rifles were imported in a crate of glass ordered by Willie Sammon's carpentry workshop.[65] Local units began to collect money to buy weapons from GHQ, but apart from the Castlebar men, most claimed that nothing came their way before the 1916 Easter Rising.[66] By the end of 1915 the total armaments of the Mayo Volunteers amounted to a mere twenty-nine rifles, supplemented by wooden guns.[67]

Apart from these organizations, there were some other radical voices in Mayo. A small SF branch, the only party associated with opposition to the war and the IPP, had been active for a while in Westport, which was also home of the *Mayo News*, the only local newspaper that did not support Redmond or the war-effort. As in the rest of the country the clergy were generally supportive of the government and opposed radical initiatives, but some dissented early on. Fr Mulligan, parish priest of Carracastle, Fr Connolly, parish priest of Castlebar, and his curate Fr J.W. Meehan were by 1915 officially designated as disloyal.[68] The Volunteers thus did not operate in a vacuum, and radicalism was on the rise generally. Besides the Fianna, Cumann na mBan also established a presence in Mayo. Following the example of Westport, a branch was started in Newport when the wife of Michael Kilroy was visited by the sister of Edward Moane, one of the principal Volunteers in Westport.[69]

The activities initiated by these organizations inspired others. Young boys in Westport recalled the distribution by SF of song books containing patriotic songs, and a visit by Countess Markievicz to put on her play in the town hall. Afterwards, one of the players came on the stage and, before the curtains were raised, sang

'In Memory of The Dead', with a drawn sword. Some prominent activists also visited local schools to promote the Fianna. Liam Mellows 'enunciated what I would consider the clarion call of the Fianna and at this stage I can hear him – if it were he – saying, "our motto must be: strength in your arms, truth on your lips and purity in your hearts!".'[70] When Lord and Lady Wimborne visited Westport in August 1915 they were well received, but some disloyal notices, mostly aimed at Lord Sligo, had been put up before the visit, indicating the growing assertiveness of what was described as 'a disloyal element'.[71]

By 1916 there was thus a group of activists in Mayo who were supported by a small number of Irish Volunteers units and some other radical groupings. Slowly, the headquarters of the Volunteers and the IRB also extended its organizing efforts to include Mayo.[72] In August 1915 some officers, including Michael Kilroy and Peter J. McDonnell, went to a Volunteer training camp in the Galtee Mountains in Limerick.[73] Shortly afterwards, field manoeuvres and another sham battle between the Kilmeena and Westport companies were held under the supervision of John MacBride.[74] The first intimation that something serious was afoot came during a visit of Liam Mellows, Darrell Figgis and The O'Rahilly to Mayo on St Patrick's Day 1916. After they spoke at rallies in Castlebar and Westport, private meetings were held with local Volunteers officers and some IRB men: 'They said that a testing time was coming and that it was up to each person to do a man's part.'[75]

The rally in Westport attracted attention. Members of the IAA on their way to their own meeting joined in. They showed little interest in O'Rahilly's seditious speech but were attracted by the large police presence and the symbolic aspect of the Volunteer uniform that The O'Rahilly was wearing, it being the first time that many of them saw a Volunteer in uniform.[76] The Board of Erin faction subsequently challenged those present by having their band pass by playing loudly. A confrontation was prevented by The O'Rahilly, who argued that their time would come.[77]

After this visit local men began to prepare for battle by making pikes and baking biscuits. Contact with Dublin remained very limited, so nobody knew what to expect or do, or even when a rising was to start. Michael McHugh, the then 34-year-old commandant of the Castlebar unit, later claimed they did not receive any orders. It is clear that neither the countermanding order from the Irish Volunteers' chief of staff Eoin MacNeill calling off the Rising planned for Easter Sunday, nor the instructions by his opponents to proceed on Easter Monday 24 April came through.[78]

The first most Mayo activists heard about the Rising was on Easter Monday night. Without instructions and often also without arms, the local IRB leadership quickly decided that nothing could be done. The only formal action they initiated was sending a local Volunteer with a sealed letter, the content of which remains unclear, to the bishop of Killala in Ballina on Easter Tuesday.

After the bishop read the letter, he looked at the Volunteer and said: 'Go home and don't be such a foolish young man.'[79] The better-armed Volunteer units in Castlebar and Balla did mobilize, but in the absence of instructions they were also at a loss. During the week the only news that reached them were false rumours about German landings and supposed military victories. In Balla, the men eventually acted against the local National Volunteers, some of whom had responded to the CI's call to assist in quelling unrest by forming a unit of special constables. When Dick Walsh received word that the National Volunteers were going to move some rifles from Kiltimagh to Castlebar to arm these units, the Balla Volunteers held up the party transporting the arms using a brass tap as an imitation gun; they captured sixteen rifles.[80]

Only in Westport did the Volunteers engage in open defiance. The local company heard of the Rising on Easter Monday night while attending a concert. Although they were not prepared, an attack on the local RIC barracks was considered, just as the Balla men had done. Members of the Leenane company claimed that they actually marched to Westport on Tuesday night with all their arms and equipment to aid in the attack. However, on arrival they were told that the operation was cancelled and they returned home 'very down-hearted'.[81] With insufficient arms, the Westport men did not feel they could do anything significant militarily either, but nevertheless ordered a general mobilization. Unaware the rebels in Dublin had surrendered by Saturday and despite a warning from the police that any demonstration would lead to arrests, they held a parade on Sunday. At Crow Hill, 130 Volunteers and Fianna members, eighteen of them armed, assembled and marched through the town closely followed by some RIC constables.[82]

Although no fighting thus took place in Mayo during the Rising, the local authorities were extremely anxious. Immediately afterwards martial law was introduced in the county for a month, and an order was issued that all Volunteers were to surrender their arms. A large consignment of troops was brought into the county on three trains, including 400 men from the North Staffordshire Regiment, 250 officers, men and horses from the 7th Lancers, and 100 from the Staffordshire Regiment.[83] The military immediately moved to arrest eleven of the Westport men involved in the parade, while eight participants in the Balla raid were also picked up and forced to surrender the arms they had captured.[84] Known activists, such as Joe MacBride and Darell Figgis, and those from otherwise inactive areas, like Ballaghaderreen and Louisburgh, were also taken into custody as were some who had been heard to use seditious language.[85] This was given quite a wide definition. In Kiltimagh, John Corcoran (Seán) was arrested after making a joke during a visit to the bank, while Ms Gavin, a post office employee, was arrested after expressing her approval of the Rising to a commercial traveller. Due to an intervention by the local parish priest she was released, but when an IRB oath was found on Corcoran, he was detained.[86]

In total, forty-eight people were arrested between 29 April and 16 May 1916. Darrel Figgis was charged with 'attempt to cause sedition', and the Westport men were considered 'Guilty of behaviour of such a nature to be prejudicial as to the Public Safety and the Defence of the realm by marching with arms'. Colm O'Leary, a 28-year-old Gaelic League teacher from Cong, was court-martialled for drawing a gun on his arrest party. When the military came to pick up the Kilroy brothers and Pat McDonnell in Newport, the local DI prevented this, claiming these hard-working men were not in any organization. Of those arrested, five were released immediately and another five within a couple of weeks, while a total of thirty-seven people from Mayo were eventually interned in Frongoch, a detention camp in Wales. This number included eighteen men from Westport, four from nearby Aughagower, thirteen from Ballaghaderreen, as well as O'Leary and Corcoran.[87]

The authorities' decisive reaction was effective, particularly in Castlebar. Local Volunteers had been the best armed unit before 1916, but now they voluntarily gave up twenty-three rifles, while the local police retrieved two large bags from the river with bayonets and swords that had belonged to the Fianna.[88] The Castlebar UDC and the local AOH also passed resolutions against the Rising: 'we strongly condemn the actions of the pro-Germans and Sinn Féiners of Dublin in plunging portions of the country in horrors of civil war'. One of their arguments was that it was 'bad for trade'. According to the police, no one had condemned the Rising more than the farmers whose profits had been affected by the disruption of traffic. Similar resolutions were passed in other places. This led the new CI David A. Steadman, who replaced George Hurst after he retired in March following four years in office, to report that the 'People generally are pleased that the Sinn Féin rebellion ended so quietly'. He claimed that the arrests also had a sobering effect and the attitude to the government and police was generally much improved.[89]

Press reactions to the Rising as well as the internment of local people were universally negative but rather muted. In the *Mayo News* it was argued that none of the local Volunteers would have known the organization 'was, in the remotest possibility, ever to be used for any such purpose'. The execution of John MacBride, who grew up in Westport, was, according to this newspaper, 'received with deep regret by all who knew him'. Other newspapers simply gave the facts of his execution and the details of his life without any judgement.[90] Most attention in the press was devoted to the speech by John Dillon in the House of Commons in which he warned against 'the maddening effect on Ireland of Sir John Maxwell's secret trials and executions'. The introduction of martial law overseen by Maxwell was also questioned by Dillon. The speech was lauded and motions of thanks were passed by Castlebar Board of Guardians among other public bodies.[91]

There were, nevertheless, signs of sympathy for the insurgents, most clearly expressed when the arrested men were cheered on by a large crowd as they were taken away by train. More subtle acts of support were not always recognized. One young boy made a ribbon of green, white and yellow to represent the tricolour, but his friends thought it was the flag of some ally of Britain in the war. Mayo RIC noted supportive expressions in one or two places 'where the I[rish] V[olunteer] movement had of late obtained a firm footing'. Four of the now eight clergymen who were known to be sympathetic to the rebels also voiced their opinions openly. The harsh counter-measures against the Volunteers contributed to a growing feeling of sympathy for the rebels: 'Some people think there have been too many executions and deportations in connection with the Rising and sympathy in favour of clemency towards the dupes of the occasion seems on the increase.'[92] The Newport AOH passed a resolution in which they repudiated and deplored the action of the Sinn Féiners but asked 'that the Government will temper justice with mercy in dealing with those misguided men'.[93]

In this way, the scene was set for a sea-change in local politics. Where internal differences in the IPP over the approach to home rule and the land question had dominated the period before 1912, and the home rule crisis had brought a confrontation between a still-dominant IPP and a growing minority of radicals, the Easter Rising transformed SF and the Irish Volunteers into the leading voices in the county.

4 'Up the Rebels': republicans take over local politics, 1916–18

The period immediately following the Rising was crucial for future developments. In the aftermath, radical expressions were initially forced underground, but the dynamic which unfolded during the months and years that followed slowly invigorated and emboldened the movement. After an initially strong response, the authorities adopted a haphazard approach towards rebellious expressions, vacillating between repression and turning a blind eye, which in the end only strengthened the resolve of the few radically inclined local men and women and led to ever-growing support for the new republican-minded groupings such as SF and the Irish Volunteers. The IPP had difficulty maintaining its position in Mayo against this growing tide and was eventually overwhelmed and replaced by them to an exceptional degree. The First World War continued to affect the lives of people in many ways, not least by the threatened introduction of conscription, which ultimately provided a final push in this political sea-change.

Initially, it seemed as if republicans were crushed by the fall-out from the Rising. During the remainder of 1916 no open activity by advanced nationalists was reported. Activists recalled a general feeling of despair. Stephen Donnelly from Ballina felt that 'we and the rest of the country had missed a glorious opportunity to strike a blow for Ireland and that I personally would never get a chance to fire a shot'.[1] Outwardly, a sense of wartime normality set in. This was reflected in the reports of the CI which dealt mostly with the economic condition of the county and the still unsatisfactory levels of recruiting. Between five and ten men joined the army each month, all from urban areas. Even for Connacht, which had by far the lowest recruiting numbers in Ireland, this was low.[2] Underneath this calm exterior it was, however, clear that the mood had changed. The wave of sympathy that followed the executions of the rebel leaders and the arrest of many locals placed republicans everywhere in a more favourable position. Some were also inspired rather than deterred by events, like Tom Maguire from Cross, who became one of the principal IRA leaders in south Mayo: 'The Easter insurrection came to me like a bolt from the blue. I will never forget my exhilaration, it was a turning point in my life. To think that Irishmen, were fighting England on the streets of Dublin'.[3] For people like him, the Rising had not been the end, but only the beginning of a fight for independence.

As in many other counties, the main outlet for this radicalism was initially confined to a revival of local GAA and Gaelic League branches, which, as the RIC inspector-general reported, were now controlled by 'dangerous extremists'.

This was still fairly relative as illustrated by the composition of the Balla coiste ceanntair of which the local curate, Fr Andrew Moran, was the president and Dr Conor Maguire vice-president.[4] The proceedings of these organizations attracted more interest than in previous years, and the police throughout the country followed this with apprehension. The inspector-general noted that at GAA tournaments 'the Irish Republican badge is conspicuously worn, and seditious songs and cries of "Up the Rebels", "to Hell with England", etc. are indulged in'.[5]

Such expressions were not without danger. Two young men who cheered the rebels during the trial of Colm O'Leary in July were immediately court-martialled and sentenced to twenty-eight days imprisonment.[6] Although Mayo was not among the counties where sympathy for the Irish Volunteers was believed to be prevalent, the wearing of green and black mourning badges was widespread for months after the Rising. By June all republican organizations were again revived. As far as the police could ascertain, there were now five units of the Irish Volunteers with 164 members, nine branches of the Gaelic League with 350 members, eighteen of the GAA with 1,059, and one Cumann na mBan company with 40 members. In this way Mayo radicals were well organized compared to neighbouring Sligo but lagging behind Roscommon.[7]

Although open expressions of separatism, such as the annual commemoration in November of the Manchester Martyrs (three Fenians executed in 1867), were forbidden, there were other ways to make clear where one stood. These included assisting the organization of local branches of the Irish National Aid Association, which raised money to support republican families. Mayo was early in setting up a branch in June 1916 but had limited success with only £17 collected during the first month. This compared poorly to the £4,480 raised nationwide, especially considering the fact £3 had been contributed by Fr Meehan, a curate in Castlebar. A lot more money came in the next month when the Aid Association raised £400 and the more openly republican Irish Volunteers' Dependents' Fund another £50.[8] Soon after, the two bodies were amalgamated under pressure from Irish-American benefactors.

The CI noted a rise in expressions of republicanism over the summer, especially following the release of most of the Mayo internees. By August thirty-eight of the forty-eight arrested had returned home. At one meeting a large Union Jack, stolen from an improvised military camp near Balla, was burned. Such defiant events remained rare. Even the release of the last ten imprisoned men in December, including eight from Westport, was not formally celebrated apart from some public singing of seditious songs. This subdued welcome caused the CI to hope that the releases had created a better feeling. To build on this, the government called together all political parties in July 1917 in the Irish Convention. The intention was to reach an agreement for putting the suspended home rule act into operation in the hope that this would prevent further radicalization. The discussions met with little enthusiasm among all sides, being regarded as either too much, too little, or too late. SF refused to attend. The convention sat until March 1918. One of the few legal political manifestations in these months were small gatherings denouncing the convention.[9]

In the meantime membership of various radical organizations rose further. At first, this was almost entirely dependent on local initiative, but gradually it became more co-ordinated. In December 1916 Richard Walsh met with activists from all over the country in Dublin where it was agreed they would make an effort to re-establish Irish Volunteer companies in their areas. Politically, those sympathizing with the rebels were uncertain how to proceed. A number of rival organizations were established, but eventually most people joined SF in the early months of 1917. The growing number of SF cumainn also created an opportunity to revitalize or initiate Irish Volunteer companies, Fianna Éireann sluagh, and Cumann na mBan branches unnoticed by the police. The RIC did record a rise in SF membership, which was now considered to be strong in Westport, Castlebar, Ballina and Kiltimagh.[10] Nevertheless, the population and, apart from the *Mayo News*, all of the local and national press was generally not in agreement with SF or the Volunteers. 'Let nobody think that then or in later years we had all the people on our side. A large number ... thought we were mad and did not agree with our methods.' However, there was little sign that the IPP was able to mobilize its base. The UIL and AOH remained largely inactive, while an attempt to revive the ailing National Volunteers in Mayo floundered in December 1916.[11]

Walsh's first successes were in Castlebar, Balla and Ballinrobe where he had good contacts mainly through the IRB; later a company was added in Claremorris. Further expansion depended on the presence of local activists who were mostly to be found in the towns. Apart from Walsh in Balla, these again included Michael Kilroy in Newport, Seán Corcoran and Thomas Ruane in Kiltimagh, Tom Maguire in Cross, and a relatively large group in Westport. After reorganizing their own towns, these men tried to extend the movement to adjoining areas. The first such branches were observed in The Neale and Kiltimagh.[12]

The men in Westport were particularly prominent in this effort. Ned Moane remembered going mostly on foot across country during 1917, organizing companies in Derrygorman, Dromin, Belclare, Murrisk, Killevaly and Shraheen.[13] Michael Henry from Srah recalled how his company was similarly encouraged by Kilroy, although their natural connection was with Ballina. Others recounted Seán Corcoran and Tommy Ruane coming out to form companies in Lisgorman and Bohola.[14] John Timony recalled how in Crossmolina he and a fellow worker were approached by Paddy Hegarty of Lahardane and formed a company with five others at a meeting held at 2 a.m.[15] Some of these men subsequently tried to organize neighbouring villages.[16] The area covered by such a company was usually based on the parish or church catchment area. Mass was often used as a gathering point for Sunday parades and consequently for recruiting. In practice, there were many reasons for departing from this rule, ranging from working or attending Mass in another parish to personal sympathies.

As a result of the dependency on local initiative, the organization had little formal structure. By Spring 1917 Walsh found it increasingly difficult to stay in touch with all units and organized a meeting in Castlebar to set up an overarching structure. The county was divided into twelve battalions organized in four spheres of action, roughly corresponding with the four parliamentary constituencies of East, South, West and North Mayo. A brigade structure was created with the ageing Joseph MacBride as commandant, Michael McHugh from Castlebar as vice-commandant, Dick Walsh as adjutant, and Michael Kilroy as quartermaster. Anthony MacBride, well into his fifties and a doctor by profession, was appointed medical officer. According to McHugh, the battalions and its commanding officers were Castlebar, John Hoban; Westport, Joe Ring; Newport, Michael Kilroy; Claremorris, Pat Kenny; Ballina, Martin Lacken; Kiltimagh, Seán Corcoran; Ballinrobe, Seán Forde; Swinford, P. Gallagher; and Balla, J. Reilly.[17] Battalion boundaries were essentially based on the ability of officers to keep in close touch with their units, and were, therefore, often determined by natural features, like rivers and mountain ridges.[18]

This also affected the outer borders of the Mayo Brigade. Leenane parish, straddling the border of Galway and Mayo, had a local company that consisted of a fifty-fifty mix of Galway and Mayo men. Having initially had strong ties with Louisburgh, it eventually affiliated with the Connemara Brigade. Shrule, another village on the Galway–Mayo border, stayed with Mayo. Ballaghaderreen district, which historically had been part of Mayo but officially was transferred to Roscommon in 1898, also became part of the Mayo Brigade. Its leading officer, Paddy Ryan, was friends with Dick Walsh, and they had attended the Volunteers' meeting in Dublin together. Consequently, the district became a battalion of the Mayo, later East Mayo Brigade, instead of joining the Roscommon Brigade. In a similar fashion, the most western part of Sligo affiliated with Ballina.[19]

Most of this organizational work was done unbeknownst to the police and the general public. By February 1917 the RIC had only noticed one additional Volunteer company and the start of four SF clubs.[20] Although the constitutional nationalist organizations were almost dormant in Mayo during this period, there were some attempts to revive them in the autumn of 1916. In a speech to farmers in Glenisland on 3 September 1916, William Doris defended the record of the IPP against accusations of having failed to deliver on home rule and having sold out to the unionists. The local clergy and newspapers supported his attempt at reviving enthusiasm for the IPP. However, with essentially all the IPP objectives achieved and facing a political competitor that drew support by addressing new issues, even committed IPP members knew that they faced difficult times. This was exemplified in Dillon's position. Having condemned the Rising as an 'act of stupendous folly' with only dire consequences, he also commended the insurrectionists for their unselfish patriotism and splendid courage, which confused some of his supporters.[21]

This became clear in the parliamentary by-elections during 1917 in which republicans stood for the first time against the IPP. Activists who aided in election campaigns elsewhere felt empowered. A number of men from east Mayo assisted Count Plunkett, father of one of the executed 1916 leaders, who stood as an independent republican candidate in the North Roscommon by-election in February 1917. His success was celebrated openly in the hotspots of Castlebar and Westport. Although MacBride and Figgis were subsequently arrested, it inspired others to express their sympathies more openly. The Swinford Union even passed a resolution congratulating Plunkett, and withstood attempts to rescind the resolution at the next meeting, while calling on the IPP to 'absorb some of the virility of the Sinn Fein elements'. The Rising was commemorated in April when republican flags were flown in a number of the major towns, including Newport, Ballina, Swinford, Balla and Castlebar. The victory of Joseph McGuinness in the South Longford by-election in May 1917 was widely celebrated with bonfires and flag waving. Members of Swinford RDC attempted to send official congratulations to McGuinness, showing a newfound radicalism even among sitting IPP politicians.[22]

This increased willingness to display republican sympathies openly was epitomized by Patrick Moylett who painted his van green, white and yellow and used it to organize SF branches in the wider area, and aid in the by-election in Roscommon.[23] Showing the speed of change, Joe MacBride was received by a crowd of 2,000, waving what the police called SF flags, and a fyfe and drum band after his release in June. In a speech he argued that the people should not aim for a home rule parliament but should wait for the Peace Conference and obtain real independence through that. On 'Reek Sunday' in July, a tricolour was hoisted at the summit of Croagh Patrick in the presence of Darrell Figgis, while some activists went to East Clare to support the by-election campaign of Éamon de Valera. His victory led again to displays of republican flags in various Mayo towns in August. In Bohola the police were actually threatened with being shot when they attempted to remove the tricolour, while in other areas the victory was celebrated with bonfires. A further boost to morale was the participation of a deputation of Volunteers from Ballina and Westport in the funeral precession of Thomas Ashe in September 1917, the leading Dublin republican who had died as a result of forced feeding while on hunger strike. In Mayo, processions and prayer sessions were also held for the repose of his soul.[24]

The September deadline for selecting candidates for the upcoming general elections meant attention turned to organizing SF. Although there was only occasional reference to this in the local papers before the summer of 1917, even small places like Crimlin, Breaffy and Ballyheane were reported to already have started local clubs by then. After the SF convention in Dublin in October 1917 a more concerted approach was initiated and comhairle ceantair were organized in each constituency.[25] Although there was some involvement by more radical priests, they seemed only to play a minor role at this stage. Meetings were addressed by local and national leaders, including Arthur Griffith, Joseph MacBride, Darrell Figgis and even former National Volunteers inspector-general Colonel Maurice Moore, who was apparently trying to position himself as a potential local SF candidate. Persuading people to join the Volunteers was a secondary objective as members were called to 'enrol the youth so as at a suitable moment assert Ireland's right to her independent government'. The drive for SF was successful, even in remote places like Mogaugh and Kilmaclassen in the Westport district, and Loadheg in the Swinford district. Their proceedings were widely reported on, particularly in the *Mayo News*. By October, the police were aware of thirty-two SF clubs with 2,315 members. This was even higher than Roscommon and Sligo which came fourth and sixth in the country for the strength of the local SF party. At the same time, Mayo was the first county to record any significant growth in Volunteer membership with numbers more than tripling during 1917.[26]

All this made republicanism widely acceptable, especially to the younger generations, but support came from men and women of all ages. The extension of the franchise to all men over 21 and women over 30 made this particularly important and provided an opportunity for SF at the elections. The success with these groups was witnessed through the sale of SF badges and song sheets, pamphlets and radical newspapers, poems like 'Ireland over all' were widely recited while 'The Soldier's Song' was sung with the Irish republican flag flown overhead. Farmers were one of the main targets for propaganda. A leaflet entitled 'Farmers it is your turn now' was widely distributed, asking them to do their bit for Ireland in relation to the tillage scheme. In contrast to 1916, the annual Manchester commemoration was well attended in 1917, and at least in Kinaffe it was accompanied by a large parade of the Bohola Battalion, which then consisted of three companies.[27]

Open Volunteer activity was, however, still quite restricted. Route marches were a good way of getting to know the district thoroughly and make people aware of the existence of the Volunteers.[28] Military-style drilling had to be done in secret, mostly indoors or at night time in remote fields.[29] Battie Cryan recalled how they used to play football combined with drilling in a field of Lord Sligo's at Sheeane Hill, for which Joe Ring and John Walsh were summoned for trespassing, while Cryan and three others were subsequently also arrested.[30] The necessary expertise was limited, with even the brigade adjutant, Dick Walsh, admitting that his military knowledge comprised 'a rudimentary instruction I received in callisthenics'.[31] To address this the Volunteers tried, sometimes successfully, to attract ex-soldiers as instructors or in their absence obtain military instruction booklets. In Ballina, Patrick Coleman in desperation broke into his old school after he remembered how he had been drilled there by one of the teachers. Upon searching the desk of the teacher in question he found a copy of the British manual of infantry training, which he claimed was put to good use.[32]

As everywhere in Ireland, the shortage of arms was considered a major problem. Most of the few weapons the Mayo Volunteers had acquired before 1916 had been lost following the Rising and new ones were difficult to obtain during the war. Some shotguns could be acquired but rifles and revolvers were almost impossible to get, even though some might be bought from sailors on boats mooring locally or through contacts in Dublin. However, even the Dublin leadership had few rifles, with only one service rifle recorded as having come from GHQ for instruction purposes. In desperation, some units again reverted to making pikes and actively trained in the use of them, while much energy was channelled in raising money for the arms fund, through concerts and dances. On the anniversary of the Rising, a concert was also organized in Castlebar to support the children of James Connolly whose daughters were schooled in a convent in Mayo; it raised £2 5s.[33]

A more direct approach, already explored in other counties, was taking rifles from soldiers on furlough. On 13 October Thomas Kettrick and Tom Derrig, who had won a county council university scholarship and was then a student in Galway, were caught in the act. They had made a survey of soldiers on leave in Westport and raided their homes in the evening time with disguised faces and armed with a revolver. On one occasion they went to the home of the Ralph family which, as Kettrick put it, 'was composed mostly of women – one of them a soldier's wife – who screamed and brought all the neighbourhood around'. Derrig and Kettrick had to flee, but 14-year-old Annie Ralph had recognized them and the next day they were arrested. During their trial in Dublin in December, the judge drew 'the attention of the jury to the great gravity and importance of the case', adding that there have been various attempts to obtain 'instruments for taking human life' and that it was obvious that there are people in the country 'who will stop at nothing to work their wicked will by means and methods which must end in tragedy and ruin'. This was used by the defence to argue the case was prejudiced and after a number of prominent Volunteers all testified the two men had been at the SF billiards club at that time the jury failed to come to an agreed verdict so they were released on bail. The following month a rifle was successfully taken from another soldier. To prevent this recurring, in January 1918 the government forbade soldiers to take rifles home.[34] According to police returns, Mayo Volunteers then held twenty-one rifles. Although in reality this figure might have been a little higher, and there were larger numbers of shotguns and small arms available, according to their own records only about one in 6.5 of the relatively few Mayo Volunteers could be provided with a weapon at that time.[35]

As much of the organization of the Volunteers was done in secret, the RIC did not always have accurate information on them, but in general the police still kept a close eye on what transpired locally. This was shown up in October during the first Irish Volunteers general convention since the Rising. While the police were aware of 162 Volunteer branches, the organization asserted that 390 companies were affiliated at this time. The convention could be held because militia were not yet declared illegal, but expressions of republicanism were. The organization nevertheless left no doubt about its principal duty: 'To carry on the reorganization of the Irish Volunteers throughout the country, and put them in a position to complete by force of arms the work begun by the men of Easter Week.' To allay fears of renewed defeat, the Volunteers' executive guaranteed that it would not order to take to the field until they considered it possible to wage war with a reasonable hope of success. In the meantime, violence would only be resorted to if England tried to disarm them or attempted to enforce conscription in Ireland. This position concealed clear differences of opinion concerning future roles and tactics. Not all Volunteers were convinced that another military confrontation was necessary. At the Sinn Féin convention, held at the same time, a programme to attain independence principally by political means was adopted, and many members of its executive were also members of the Volunteer executive.[36]

To gain more control over local developments, the central leadership revived the IRB. Michael Collins approached Richard Walsh and asked him to reorganize the brotherhood in Mayo. Collins wanted to get rid of elderly members of the various circles and replace them with a small group of reliable young activists. To this end, Walsh approached the likes of Michael McHugh of Castlebar, Seán Corcoran of Kiltimagh, Thomas Ruane of Ballina, Pat Keville of Balla and the Westport men under Joe MacBride. The men in Ballaghaderreen organized themselves, while Michael Kilroy came into the organization later when in prison. In this way, the IRB became a moving force in these early stages in some parts of Mayo.[37]

The authorities were uncertain about how to deal with the increasingly open drill and parade exercises by Volunteers. Initially, they believed all Volunteer activity could be stopped if they singled out and discouraged the few 'bad apples'. As a result, leading Volunteers were arrested for small offences. But this policy, instituted in July 1917, only presented the republicans with occasions for inflammatory speeches and public demonstrations. In keeping with the movement's policy, those arrested generally refused to recognize the courts' right to try them, meaning all were convicted with short prison sentences. In jail these men began a hunger strike to support their demand for 'political prisoner' status. The impending death of these prisoners and the uproar this created among the population disconcerted the authorities. After Ashe's death in September 1917, they were particularly careful not to have another dead martyr on their hands, and they released the remaining hunger strikers in November. This left the police feeling powerless: 'As it is now evident to the parties concerned that they have only to hunger-strike for a couple of days in order to get them out of gaol, whether convicted or untried, it is really very little use arresting them.'[38]

The sense of power and the public admiration that released prisoners received resulted in a situation in which more and more Volunteers began to invite arrest. In November the RIC in Mayo noticed there were fewer SF meetings but greater instances of drilling. This was not universally the case. In Roscommon and Sligo, SF remained dominant at this time with the Volunteers more in the background, apparently more preoccupied with agrarian agitation. As elsewhere, however, this open defiance was met with an uncertain police response, which provided the Volunteer leadership with an opportunity to demonstrate their new-found strength, when all companies in the country were ordered to drill openly in the second week of December. Uniforms, where available, were to be worn, but no arms were to be carried. The RIC recorded 288 of these simple marching exercises nationwide and seventeen in Mayo with thirty to forty participants in most locations.

The lack of fear surprised the police: the 'men involved made no secret of their involvement'. Reflecting the continued urban nature of the organization, most of those drilling were listed as masons, carpenters, and shop assistants while only a small minority were farmers. They were generally between their late teens and early thirties, although most companies also included at least one member over fifty.[39]

The meetings were often concluded with speeches by leading activists, which in many places attracted audiences of a couple of hundred onlookers. The language used was considered to be of a 'very forcible character', and often referred to the SF policy to establish alternative government institutions. At Drummin, Ned Moane was recorded as having said: 'The men of Easter Week saved Ireland from Conscription and many a young Irishman from a grave in Flanders or France. They were not out for real revolution or blood as some said, but that their policy was for a free and Independent Ireland.' Joe Ring was more forceful: 'I'm no speechmaker. I believe in nothing but the rifle and the sword.' At a meeting in Cushlough, Moane picked up on this theme: 'Every Irishman of military age or able to march should join the Irish Volunteers, drill and equip yourselves as best you can so that when the time arrives you will be ready to strike a blow for Ireland's independence and help to make a Republic.'[40] All this understandably unnerved the police. The pro-German element in the Volunteers constituted a particular cause of concern. Although the RIC stated that they were unable to trace foreign money coming into the county, one Volunteer recalled how they could all sing the German patriotic song 'The Watch on the Rhine' from beginning to end.[41]

Only Seán Corcoran and Thomas Ruane were arrested on the first day of public drilling. During their trial in Westport, they refused to recognize the court, but this made little impact. The magistrate in Castlebar maintained: 'Unfortunately the Court recognizes you', and sentenced them to four months' imprisonment.[42] When they were subsequently taken to the railway station by armed policemen, they were escorted by a large contingent of Volunteers. In Sligo Jail they immediately went on hunger strike, during which they received support from the mayor of Sligo. Not knowing how to deal with this situation, the authorities released the men after a few days. Their homecoming was the occasion for another Volunteer mobilization of 300 men. As a result of these experiences, many Volunteers from then on felt free to defy the law and drill openly and in uniform.[43]

This heralded a period of open defiance throughout the country. In Mayo illegal drilling became the norm, with forty cases in thirty-four locations reported in March 1918 alone. Public speeches also became more and more rebellious, with national leaders visiting many units. In January 1918 de Valera was met by a parade of local Volunteers and Fianna when visiting Westport.[44] This defiant spirit also extended to other areas of activity. A favourite target were recruiting meetings for the British army, which continued to take place with little success until the end of the war. Particular attention was given to this in Ballina, where rioting broke out for a couple of weeks in a row, and twelve people were arrested. Patrick Coleman recounted how the Volunteers 'compelled them to go indoors with their meetings and even then we succeeded in creating an uproar inside, although I myself and a few others were unceremoniously chucked out several times.'[45]

The RIC inspector-general was especially concerned. Initially he stated that the military commander in Ireland considered drilling of insufficient military value to require trial by court martial. However, in January 1918 he reported to the government that the CIs opposed dispersing any massed parades of Volunteers as it might stir up more trouble than local police could handle. Consequently, the government decided to stop prosecuting men leading parades, but to keep a close eye on proceedings. Policemen were instructed to observe every parade or drilling exercise they encountered and to note the names of those involved. The increased police attention only seemed to attract more young men looking for some excitement.[46]

RIC efforts to keep track of the leading activists often led to confrontations as the Volunteers were increasingly prepared to challenge the police directly. The trials of Ned Moane early in 1918 are good examples of this. He was first charged in Westport for singing a seditious song. During the trial, the Volunteers invited the Cressenlough band to play rousing music in front of the courthouse and disabled the van waiting to bring Moane back to the police station. Subsequent attempts by the police to disperse onlookers led to serious rioting, in which the Volunteers used paving stones as ammunition. As a result, 'you could see the spikes being knocked off the padded helmets of the RIC', leading to an even stronger police response. When the RIC subsequently escorted Moane on foot, they were abused by the crowd. This led to further riots and arrests, and some injuries on both sides. Similar events took place during Moane's subsequent trial in Castlebar. The police were again attacked and the train carrying the judge home was severely damaged; further arrests followed.[47]

Every occasion was now used to mobilize people and defy the police. On St Patrick's Day 1918 all Volunteers were ordered to assemble at their battalion headquarters and put on a parade. Although the RIC tried to prevent local units from converging, according to one Volunteer in Ballina 1,200 men paraded by Humbert's monument and the post office and halted in the old Market Place.[48] There was still a playful element in the interaction. The police instructions to keep a close watch on the activities of the Volunteers inspired some units to make a sport out of having long fast route marches. As the RIC men wore heavy outfits and were often older, this could physically exhaust them. Michael Kilroy recalled how an eight-mile route march, most of it on the double, could make an RIC man 'very docile' and 'the butt of many jests'.[49]

Clashes surrounding the arrests, trials and releases became increasingly violent. In reaction to the growing use of the baton by the police, Volunteers armed themselves similarly. In this escalating conflict innocent bystanders were hurt and often turned against the authorities: 'People who were friendly to the RIC got shelfed as well as ourselves and that made them unfriendly to the RIC.'[50] The police were on occasion forced to resort to the use of firearms when in serious distress. As a culmination of this escalation, a bomb was thrown into the Westport RIC barracks in March 1918 but without causing major damage. The diminishing acceptance of the Crown forces as the legitimate authority and their indiscriminate approach increasingly justified such actions in the eyes of the majority of the population.[51]

The rise of radical politics in Mayo and Ireland generally was briefly interrupted by the death of John Redmond on 6 March 1918. Tributes to him were generous from local government boards and in most newspapers, emphasizing the loss of a great man at a time of peril. The *Mayo News*, which had clearly sided with SF, was more matter-of-fact. This paper was also very critical of John Dillon who was elected IPP leader: 'For the last ten years he has been in reality the power behind the throne, and for the disastrous mistakes made during that period he cannot disavow responsibility.' The *Connaught Telegraph* only referred to Dillon's elevation in a short notice in which his revolutionary pedigree and his role 'in saving the lives of scores of the rebels' after 1916 were recalled. In this way it sought to make him more acceptable to the new supporters of republicanism. More generous congratulations were expressed by local AOH boards.[52]

The impact of the First World War also continued to be felt locally. Although recruitment for the British army remained negligible, the compulsory tillage scheme made headway.[53] Republicans also became increasingly involved in dealing with the social effects of the war. In the winter, food shortages had developed in some parts of the county, and in January 1918 SF started to collect potatoes from farmers and distribute them among the urban poor and in the particularly deprived Achill district. The extreme poverty in parts of Mayo and the growing scarcity of workers also gave more opportunity for labour organizations to make their mark. A number of successful strikes for higher wages were recorded during 1916 and 1917, while in 1918 the ITGWU made concerted attempts to organize labourers in the west by sending out an organizer from Dublin. In January 1918 he helped set up a migratory labourers' union in Achill and Belmullet. This union notified the Scottish Potato Merchants' Association that the workers would not travel to Scotland if demands for better conditions were not met. By the end of the war, the local ITGWU thus grew to ten branches with 2,533 members in Mayo.[54] This compared very well with neighbouring counties. In Roscommon the union organizers made some headway at the end of 1918 but there was no real base to work from so growth was slow, while in Sligo, where the union had established itself early on in 1911, it had still only 810 members by July 1918.[55]

Agricultural disputes were another issue in which republicans became involved and where SF essentially took over the role of the UIL and IPP. Although more than 70 per cent of the land was now owned by farmers, on some of the unsold estates tenants continued their agitation; rents were withheld and a small number of landlords and their agents continued to receive police protection during the remainder of the war. A court case in February 1918 against the tenants of the Toromeen estate near Bohola for refusing to pay their rents, provided republicans with an opportunity to increase their popularity. The Sunday before the court session, the Volunteers deliberately took their route march past the residence of the landlord, Colonel Jordan, and when the case was heard the Bohola and Kiltimagh companies paraded in front of the courthouse.

The proceedings quickly descended into chaos and the case was adjourned. This gave SF the desired opportunity to take matters into their own hand by organizing an arbitration court. If they could force a positive settlement there, this would increase their credibility among the people, but they also realized that an unfavourable outcome would make them responsible. To deal with this, SF had arranged for Laurence Ginnell, a prominent SF lawyer and politician, to attend. After the case was deferred, Ginnell suggested to Colonel Jordan that there be arbitration between him and the tenants. Jordan agreed and was marched to the town hall by the Volunteers. Probably realizing the implicit threat, he offered favourable terms for selling, and halved the tenants' arrears. As previous attempts by the IPP to settle this case had failed, this was a great boost for SF. Subsequently, the number of rent strikes fell to one by November, possibly as a result of other SF arbitration courts.[56]

The breaking up of grazier farms for distribution among small farmers was also largely taken over from the UIL and IPP by republicans, although the UIL had made some attempts to revive local branches in early 1917, leading to occasional clashes between the two sides. The breaking up was aided by the compulsory tillage scheme that forced graziers to convert grass land to tillage, which was used as a further argument to divide these lands. A campaign to this end was started at the beginning of 1917 and was intensified during 1918. In February the local SF executive urged the taking of land for tillage by force, which was taken up vigorously in the following months, while in neighbouring Roscommon, where agrarian agitation was especially prominent, there seems to have been little emphasis on graziers during this period.[57]

In this charged atmosphere, all republican organizations grew rapidly in the opening months of 1918 as they did in neighbouring counties. Although the CI could still report in January that the movement 'has never caught on in this county up to expectation', the membership figures recorded tell a different story.[58] SF showed the biggest increase, growing from 433 members in June 1917 to 3,328 in January 1918 and 5,563 in June of that year, making it the largest organization after the largely dormant UIL. The Volunteers showed a similar but more modest rise, from 164 in September 1916 to 581 in January 1918 and 1,081 in April. The associated organizations, including Cumann na mBan, the Gaelic League and the GAA, also gained in popularity. The women's organization grew from 46 members concentrated in Westport to 326 divided over ten branches, while the Irish-language movement started eight new branches between January and April bringing its membership up from 477 to 655. These were supplemented in March with one Fianna branch and one IRB circle known to the police.[59] Despite this, not everyone in Mayo had transferred their support from the IPP to the republicans. As one Volunteer recalled: 'In March 1918 I was standing one night with a number of my school pals. They started gibing me about our drill display in the town that day. They said we were just a lot of gossoons showing off.'[60]

The accelerated pace of organization and more overt displays of Volunteer activity everywhere became intolerable to the authorities. A series of measures were taken locally and nationally in early 1918, including the suppression of the *Mayo News*, and the introduction of the Temporary Discharges or 'Cat-and-Mouse' Act to counter the undermining effects of hunger striking by prisoners. Under this legislation weakened men were released and then rearrested when in better health, thus compelling all convicted Volunteers to eventually complete their sentences or avoid re-arrest. As a result of these measures the police again felt able to act. In Mayo alone, thirty-three men from twenty-two different localities were charged with at least one case of illegal drilling in March. Anyone flying the republican flag, singing seditious songs, giving orders, wearing a uniform, or even carrying a wooden gun was now liable for prosecution. Despite ingenious ploys to avoid arrest, for instance by having each of the men take charge of a drilling party in turn, many were prosecuted. Agrarian agitation, in particular, subsided after the introduction of these measures and many active Volunteers became more cautious.[61]

This cycle of open resistance and hesitant repression was permanently broken on 21 March 1918 with the start of the Spring Offensive of the Germans in France. Although the local newspapers in Mayo were not particularly worried by it, quickly and accurately concluding that now 'the German onrush is held it will be tantamount to a German defeat', the huge allied losses and threatened breach of their lines gave the government the idea new recruits were instantly necessary. This happened to coincide with the presentation of the final report of the Irish Convention carried by a majority of delegates that called for the immediate introduction of home rule with special safeguards for unionists. The government responded by linking the introduction of conscription in Ireland to home rule. On 16 April 1918 the Military Service (Ireland) bill was passed; it was met with universal resistance by nationalist Ireland, and in effect spelled the end of home rule as it lost any popular support by this connection. According to the CI, people had lived in dread of conscription ever since its introduction in Britain in 1916, and all nationalist-minded parties, including the IPP, SF and Labour, formed a united front in opposition under the guidance of the Catholic Church, with priests presiding and speaking at a number of large public meetings. After Bishop Naughton of Killala spoke out strongly against conscription a public pledge was taken by large numbers of people after Mass 'to resist conscription by the most effective means at our disposal'. The labour movement ordered a one-day general strike for 23 April, and a fund was set up to raise money to indemnify against loss or injury all who suffered in the struggle against conscription. In Mayo the response to this was particularly strong.[62]

One of the largest protest meetings in the country was held at Ballina, with 15,000 people and more than twenty-five clergymen attending. In Ballaghaderreen another monster meeting was addressed by the national leaders of SF and the IPP, Éamon de Valera and John Dillon respectively. Most of those attending came on foot or by bicycle, including a number of Mayo Volunteer companies, which paraded through the town. The Kilkelly company brought a banner stating: 'England, we won't have your blood-tax', which was displayed prominently in front of the platform.[63] Other large manifestations in Mayo included a pilgrimage to Croagh Patrick involving hundreds of local Volunteers and Cumann na mBan members. They camped on the top from 12 o'clock to 6 a.m. with local priests in attendance. On their return the only fatality of the conscription protests was recorded when John Rowland from the Newport company fell off his bicycle on his way home. In other places meetings were held, with local leaders, including Patrick Doris, the editor of the suppressed *Mayo News*, speaking.[64]

Being seen as the strongest opponents, republicans received most of the credit for the anti-conscription campaign, and many new members flocked to their organizations. All Volunteer companies reported a flood of new recruits and better attendance at company parades in April, while new companies were started in areas which up to then had none. This was particularly evident in rural areas, where the Volunteers had been relatively weak but conscription was very unpopular. The influx of new members was further increased by the fact many migrant workers returned home from Britain to avoid conscription there. This was to some extent offset by men emigrating to the Americas to get away altogether.[65] Not all new members were considered suitable: 'Some of those were very good lads, but some of them would run from a cross gander; nevertheless, it might have been bad tactics to turn them away'. To test their resolve, new recruits were subjected to heavy marches, after which many left. The lack of officers with military knowledge was an embarrassment to the older members, which could only be remedied by recruiting ex-soldiers as drill instructors.[66]

Behind the scenes, the Volunteers prepared for armed resistance. Nationally, all imprisoned Volunteers were ordered to stop their hunger strikes, take bail and return home. Officers not released were replaced. Dick Walsh instructed local activists to sleep away from home and prepare to take to the hills, collect all arms and shotguns in the county, and hoard foodstuffs.[67] 'We made caves in the mountains and there we hid food during Conscription. The food was potatoes [and] particularly, oat-bread made and prepared by the Cumann na mBan.'[68] Although preparing could be done in secret, military training was impossible to hide completely. As one Volunteer put it, 'after nightfall every night could be heard the sounds of men drilling'.[69] The police did notice: 'Illegal drilling not so prevalent due to clerical advise and partly to the fact that drilling is now carried out by night or in out of the way places with a view to escape police observation and the prosecution of leaders.'[70]

The most confrontational aspect of Volunteers' preparations were no doubt the attempts to arm themselves: 'All shotguns, ammunition and explosives in all the local shops and private houses were taken over by the Volunteers, also some slash hooks, hay forks or anything that could be used as a weapon for hand-to-hand fighting.'[71] The houses of the gentry were a particular target for arms raids, but the military were the most promising source of coveted rifles. Some were bought, while a few soldiers, desiring to desert, were facilitated by the

Volunteers by providing them with civilian attire in exchange for their arms and equipment.⁷²

More remarkable were attempts to obtain arms by buying them from the Germans. During the war there were a number of reports of German submarines contacting locals in the West of Ireland looking for food, petrol and other supplies. On one occasion a local fisherman from Ballyderrig traded for about twenty rifles and sold them to the Volunteers through Fintan Murphy who had been sent by GHQ. In another episode, a local man, who had joined the German navy, brought some rifles ashore, but in the handover the arms were lost, either dumped in the sea or confiscated by the RIC. Local fishermen from the Blacksod area also informed Volunteers that arms were on offer. Richard Walsh asked Michael Kilroy to investigate. He paid the fishermen some money in advance and had a dugout built. However, Ned Moane missed the handover when he fell off his bike, and nothing was heard afterwards. Dominick Molloy, who had apparently handed over £100 of his own money on this occasion, recounted how in 1920 six boxes were left outside his house with twenty rifles and eight or so revolvers.⁷³ Although the CI still defined what happened as passive resistance, he was fearful of what might be coming if, as he put it, 'the extremists break away from church control'. He added that 'large numbers of younger RIC [were] expected to resign if required to enforce the conscription bill'.⁷⁴

Although the actual threat to introduce conscription dissipated quickly in the face of such opposition, the authorities took a much harder line when the crisis was over. A large number of leading Volunteers throughout the country were arrested on charges of co-operation with Germany, including prominent Westport men like Joe MacBride and Ned Moane.⁷⁵ In July SF, Cumann na mBan and the Gaelic League were proclaimed dangerous associations. Subsequently, the CI observed a marked improvement in conditions due to the firm handling of 'Sinn Feinism and sedition', which he claimed found 'general acceptance and appreciation.' He hoped the government's firm hand would not be relaxed, as this would 'enable Sinn Fein extremists to gull the countryside into an exaggerated appreciation of the power and importance of this organization which has succeeded in defying Military and Government orders'.⁷⁶

With the movement effectively forced underground, the remainder of 1918 was largely quiet. A small but steady number of illegal drilling exercises and anti-recruiting meetings, threatening notices against the police, and raids for arms were nevertheless observed.⁷⁷ There were only a few occasions of open defiance, such as a memorial parade to commemorate the death of Thomas Ashe organized by the Fianna Éireann sluagh in Ballina in September 1918. When marching up King Street with a big black banner sporting Ashe's photograph the Fianna were stopped by the police and ordered to disperse. When they refused, some street battles took place in which police batons were countered with flag poles. Four men were arrested and sentenced to five months in prison. Two recruiting meetings for the British army also led to serious rioting and twelve more arrests. The lack of open activity and the repression following the conscription crisis nevertheless caused many of those who had joined during the crisis to fall away. A subsequent effort instigated by the Dublin leadership was relatively successful in keeping numbers up. Public meetings, concerts, céilís and football matches were organized to maintain interest and raise funds. In November Volunteer membership stood at 1,592, still up by fifty per cent compared to before the conscription crisis.[78]

Remarkably, the conduct of the war in Europe had become a minor issue in the local Mayo press after the Rising. Apart from concerns about conscription, only very short notices describing major military developments appeared. Otherwise, everyday life filled the pages. Even the surrender of Turkey and Austria as well as the armistice negotiations with Germany did not get more than a simple factual reference. The end of the war itself did lead to some rejoicing in the garrison towns of Ballina and Ballinrobe, but in both cases this was inspired by soldiers based there in which some locals joined in. There were no reports of other celebrations, the CI even described Armistice night as an 'occasion for serious rioting'. The *Western People* was most enthusiastic in seeing the benefits of the victory of freedom and the defeat of the principle of a 'lust of conquest' represented by the Central Powers, which it argued would not have benefited Ireland. Its main concern, however, was the statement of the government that it would not allow the Irish claim to be 'considered at the Peace Conference', and that the chief secretary, 'a self-professed home ruler', had determined 'to cheat Ireland out of her rights and by inference expose the hypocrisy of their going into this war on behalf of the freedom of small nationalities'. In this way the paper that was strongly aligned with Dillon also took on SF thinking.[79]

During the latter half of 1918 the emphasis among republicans lay on attempts to obtain independence through political means. Volunteers turned their attention to securing the return of SF candidates in the general election called for December. The local SF clubs had set up local executives for selecting candidates for the four Mayo constituencies. This caused some tension with the Dublin leadership, which favoured political figures over military men. In East Mayo they felt a strong national figure was needed to stand successfully against IPP leader John Dillon. Eventually, de Valera was selected as the candidate best equipped to beat him. In South Mayo, another outsider, William Sears, editor of the *Enniscorthy News*, was put forward, apparently in a bid to satisfy both SF and Labour supporters. Maybe not surprisingly, the attempt to parachute another 'outsider' into North Mayo ran into trouble. SF headquarters wanted Darrell Figgis, a Dublin man who had moved to Achill in 1914 and had national standing in the movement, but the local organization favoured John Crowley, a doctor in Ballycastle who hailed from Cork. A long discussion ensued, which was apparently ended when the local branch informed headquarters that 'the people of North Mayo, had made what we thought the best selection in the interests of Sinn Féin generally, but if they, HQ, thought they could win the election by putting up Darrell Figgis, we would offer no opposition, but that we would not give one ounce of help.'[80] Things were easier in West Mayo where in Joseph MacBride the Volunteers had a strong local leader with a national standing and IRB connections.[81]

Apart from selecting candidates, raising funds was an important element of preparations. In Ballyvarry, the local SF branch even formed a dramatic cub to this end. Despite active opposition from the local parish priest and the police, which threatened to arrest the main organizer, they eventually managed to put on a performance by hiring a marquee from Dublin, making over £87.[82] In Ballina a house-to-house collection brought in £75, much to the surprise of the treasurer of the election committee.[83] Some of this was used to buy food for the needy in an effort to encourage them to vote SF. Even dependants of British soldiers were thus approached. The election campaign itself was marked by minor expressions of anti-British sentiment, ranging from singing rebellious songs to burning the Union Jack but no serious conflict arose.[84]

The campaign in East Mayo was the most interesting with a potential nationwide and international impact. Dillon received strong local support from the Protestant landowning class, most of the clergy and the police. The Volunteers had always found it hard to organize in Dillon's heartland with many areas, including a large town like Swinford, not even fielding a company.[85] De Valera supporters encountered much active opposition, particularly in rural areas. At one point the IPP supporters in Carracastle actually challenged SF to hold a meeting in the village. In response, SF mobilized every man they could and marched into town where they immediately clashed heavily with Dillon supporters. Although the RIC stepped in to separate the two parties, they did not intend to protect SF who were eventually forced out of the village without holding a meeting.[86] After a couple of similar situations in Straide and Glantaver, outside Kilkelly, the national leadership stepped in and a contingent of about fifty Volunteers were called in from Clare. Up to twenty of them were actually put out of action by the Spanish flu, but they did make a difference. When arriving at Swinford station they were observed by Dillon himself who supposedly called them 'a bunch of Clare rowdies'. Although the flu killed more than 20,000 people nationwide, Mayo like other western counties was least affected, particularly in the worst year of the flu, 1918.[87]

In other parts of Mayo republicans faced far less opposition. Sears was unopposed in South Mayo as John Fitzgibbon did not stand due to old age, dying the following year aged seventy. The poor northern part of Mayo was also a fairly safe seat for SF. Activists in the West Mayo constituency, which had always been more radical than the rest of the county, also encountered little opposition. To the surprise of SF the police did not prevent them from putting up posters and even most of the clergy now supported them.[88] The police concluded that the only real contest was in East Mayo, remarking that SF was generally much better prepared than their opponents. During election day Volunteers guarded polling booths, escorted the ballot boxes to counting centres, and brought voters to the polling stations: 'old people who had not been out of their homes for a considerable period were brought out to vote. In the townland of Tranabontna an old lady was carried from her bed and brought on a side-car to vote.'[89]

Some went a step further. In November, the CI had already reported that intimidation by SF agents was rife: 'sons are frightening their fathers as to what will happen if the fathers don't vote Sinn Féin.'[90] One Volunteer swapped the election leaflets a priest was to distribute in favour of the IPP candidate for those of SF.[91] In the polling station in Drummin 'people were to have come in, but only a few of them came, so we voted for them. There was a peeler who said to me there are dead men voting here today.'[92] Although this election rigging was observed by the police, most constables were too frightened to interfere. One local Volunteer admitted that the victory for SF in Ballaghaderreen 'was only accomplished by a great volume of personation and by falsifying the register of voters and so forth. Dead and absent voters "recorded" their votes.'[93]

All these efforts paid off. Notwithstanding the irregularities, the large support SF had gained during the previous year was still demonstrated by the results. Nationwide the party took 73 out of 105 seats. In Mayo, SF swept the board. In North Mayo, John Crowley defeated Daniel Boyle, the sitting member by 7,429 votes to 1,761. Joseph MacBride did even better in West Mayo where he outpolled William Doris by 10,195 votes to 1,568. As expected, the tightest fight was in East Mayo, but even there de Valera beat Dillon handsomely by 8,975 votes to 4,519, showing how far the unassailable position the IPP had in 1910 was eroded. Subsequently Dillon effectively retired from politics and died in 1927 at the age of seventy-six. The result in East Mayo, in particular, was seen as a great victory and was largely attributed to the efforts of local activists.[94] The CI suggested 'Sinn Fein is developing and laying its plans to promote and cause the maximum amount of trouble and unrest with the minimum amount of risk.'[95] Now the war was over and the concomitant threat of conscription had disappeared without any sign of self-government appearing, SF and the Volunteers essentially took over control of local politics. The next question was what form the struggle for dominance with the established authorities would take.

5 'If the police with their local knowledge go, farewell to civil government': the struggle for dominance, 1919–20

The end of the war, the 1918 general election and the concomitant establishment of a separate Irish parliament, Dáil Éireann, which initiated a counter-state with its own rival institutions and appealed to the peace conference in Paris for international recognition of an independent Ireland, heralded the start of a new phase of the revolution. Whereas more active Volunteers took the lead and initiated acts of violence in some parts of Ireland, the Mayo men kept their focus on organization and civil actions in line with what Charles Townshend has termed the first phase of the War of Independence. Unlike other counties, in Mayo there was little distinction between the military and civil expressions of republicanism. In an attempt to obtain popular support particular emphasis was placed on the establishment of an alternative court system, which arbitrated in civilian cases. Concomitant with this was the functioning of the Irish Volunteers as a local police force that enforced socially acceptable behaviour, such as closing down poteen-making. Politically, this period focused on the takeover of the existing local government institutions and the changing of their allegiance to Dáil Éireann. The wholesale change of loyalty of the people in most parts of Mayo made the use of force less necessary than elsewhere, while agrarian agitation also became less prominent.

A direct consequence of the founding of the Dáil was a change in the position and name of the Irish Volunteers. As the official army of the republican government, they now became the Irish Republican Army (IRA). As part of the name change, all Volunteers were asked to swear allegiance to the Dáil during the second part of 1919. Richard Walsh recalled how each brigade was asked to hold a convention and take a vote on the question of Dáil Éireann's control of the army. More than 100 battalion and company officers from Mayo attended a meeting with GHQ officer Michael Staines present. There was some opposition to the oath from older IRB men under Joe MacBride, but the convention accepted the change, an indication that younger men, independent from the IRB, had now assumed control. The tensions generated by this also seem to have been behind the founding of the *Mayoman* newspaper by the Castlebar reporter of the *Mayo News*.[1]

Although the general election results gave the police the impression that SF and the IRA were lying in wait to strike, it was labour that first came to attention in post-war Mayo. In January 1919 the CI was concerned that the ITGWU was 'busy fomenting industrial unrest. The out of work donation scheme has not helped matters, fostering the idea of getting something ... for doing nothing.' In an afterthought he showed his disdain for the local people whose 'sly cunning and mendacity are more predominant attributes than self-respect and independence'.[2] With the ending of the First World War, social issues had again become prominent. Wartime inflation had benefitted farmers but lowered the purchasing power of workers. The post-war boom now gave the latter a stronger bargaining position. The first signs of this came when the shop assistants in Westport went on strike on 10 February demanding 'a Living Wage', followed by the drapers' assistants in Ballinrobe in March. Both were supported by the union and other workers. This led to the formation of two new branches of the ITGWU, including one in Charlestown, bringing the total in Mayo to fourteen with 2,863 members. Employers reacted with the familiar accusations of extremism and Bolshevism, which were strenuously denied. Although a number of other strikes were initiated during the rest of the year, most of them fizzled out without much result. A long-standing strike in Ballina ended in December 1919 in a victory for the employers. ITGWU membership nevertheless continued to grow, reaching 3,316 by December 1919, a very substantial number for an agrarian western county.[3]

As most employers now supported SF, the strikes also caused some tension between the two organizations, which had been working closely together during the conscription crisis and the general election, with Labour even agreeing not to field any candidates in favour of SF. In other cases, this close working relationship alienated employers from SF, particularly in relation to the co-operative movement, supported by many republicans. In some rural areas, farmers and labourers united against local traders by setting up a co-operative shop to sell local produce.[4]

With the ending of the war the purchase of the remaining thirty per cent of land owned by Mayo landlords and the splitting up of grazier farms by the CDB again became an issue. Tenants of unsold estates resumed agitation, while all farmers wanted to make sure they would have first choice when grazing lands were divided. The RIC favoured this, as they still believed that tenants who had procured the land were less interested in politics and more industrious and contented.[5] The pressure to resume sales was raised during the summer. In June rents were withheld on three estates with another two added the following month, one owned by the archbishop of Tuam. As a result, cattle driving, intimidation and assaults were again on the rise.[6]

While these social struggles gained the headlines, republicans remained active behind the scenes. The first meeting of Dáil Éireann in Dublin on 21 January 1919, attended only by John Crowley as local TD, was reported in the local newspapers quite dispassionately. It was noted that proceedings were conducted with 'the greatest dignity and decorum' and attracted great attention from the international press. The *Western People* claimed to be happy if independence were achieved but suggested that 'a full measure of Dominion Home Rule would satisfy the great majority' in Ireland. It was afraid hopes were raised too high with the promise of a republic. The *Mayo News* gleefully reported that the British press had reacted very unfavourably to the creation of an 'Irish Constituent Assembly', and that this was the best proof that the prospect of Irish liberty was possible. The RIC noted that the proceedings of 'the Dublin Parliament' attracted little attention but was 'a source of great delight and satisfaction to a few enthusiasts'.[7]

The role of the various republican organizations was now a little unclear. After the conscription crisis, the Volunteers had gone largely underground everywhere and SF had taken the initiative. The growing dangers involved in being part of an organization that was largely functioning in illegality led to a decline in activity and participation. This concerned activists like Patrick Hegarty, an officer in the Crossmolina area, who observed that 'many Volunteers became lax and would not show up for drill ... too much reliance was placed on the political position and too little on the military'.[8] One of the few things that still brought people on to the streets was the release of imprisoned Volunteers. In January, Mayo County Council unanimously passed a resolution calling for the release of men whose only offence had been 'loving their country'.[9] Stephen Donnelly remembered how on their arrival in Ballina in March 1919: 'We were carried shoulder high from the station to the Central Hotel and entertained.'[10]

The main activity of IRA companies remained drilling: 'In 1919, we used to mobilize the Volunteers and do a small bit of drill, dodging the RIC who were intent on getting the names of those who were drilling, or trying to accuse them of some other offence.'[11] Most companies had places where they could drill safely.[12] This was, however, insufficient to maintain the interest of less motivated IRA men. In December 1919, an organizer from Dublin reported a general malaise: 'The men are sick of doing the same "form fours" all the time and the officers are not very willing either.'[13] Some moderate members who had never envisioned engaging in actual fighting were pushed into the political wing, while several resigned with the excuse that they did not have the necessary time and others left the organization and emigrated.[14] The Fianna sluagh in Ballina had been discontinued in 1918 as 'the parents of the younger members would not let their sons attend'.[15] In early 1920 it became clear that the IRA company in Louisburgh had become entirely inactive after some of its most prominent members had been arrested and others left the area.[16]

One of the ways to keep Volunteers interested was an increased attention to training in so-called special services, such as first aid and signalling: 'There was flags and all that thing going on, from hill to hill, what you should do and how you should transfer information.'[17] To compensate for the loss in membership, renewed attention was also given to (re-)establishing companies in unorganized areas. This had some success as the RIC detected a growth from nineteen units with 2,280 members in January 1919 to twenty-one units with 2,419 members in March 1919. Many felt safer joining non-military organizations like the Gaelic League which grew from sixteen branches with 649 members to twenty-one with 994 members in the same period.[18]

Although not very active, there was still a strong IPP following in the country. As most of their political organizations had remained dormant, the extent to which this was present in Mayo and neighbouring counties is difficult to measure but results in local elections showed they still had strong support. A majority of the influential priests were also still on their side. Fr J.P. Conroy of Ballyhaunis, one of the few clerical SF supporters, wrote in August 1919 that he was 'astonished at the number of priests I meet who do not think our way. So many of them are in the old groove. They simply laugh at us.' Archbishop Thomas Gilmartin tried to make sure the divided opinion of the people, and to some extent that of the clergy, would not lead to problems. In June 1919 he issued instructions during a sermon in Westport that 'a priest can have his views about [politics], but he is not to take an aggressive part on either side, because we belong to you and you are all belonging to us.'[19]

While the movement concentrated on finding a political way forward, the use of force was not encouraged by IRA GHQ: 'raids at that time were more or less forbidden officially by our headquarters staff. If you got away with it you got a pat on the back, and if you didn't get away with it you were disowned.'[20] This attitude allowed some to take a more aggressive line. The Soloheadbeg ambush in Tipperary on 21 January 1919, causing the first police fatalities of the post-war conflict, was the clearest sign of this. This directly involved Mayo as one of the policemen killed, James McDonnell, hailed from Belmullet, which was noted in the local newspapers. In Mayo the equivalent of this more aggressive line was the shooting of the resident magistrate of Westport, John Charles Milling, on 29 March. Several revolver shots were fired at him through the windows of his house, killing him instantly. The attack was probably a direct retaliation for his role in sentencing prominent Volunteers. During previous months he had received several threatening letters and in 1918 his yacht had been destroyed off Westport Quay. The killing of Milling had serious consequences. Westport district was declared a military area with various restrictions imposed. Westport UDC was also ordered to pay Mrs Milling and her children £8,472 compensation, paralysing it financially.[21]

The shooting of Milling did not have any sequel in Mayo. During the remainder of 1919 no further life-threatening incidents took place there. In contrast to almost all other counties bar Tipperary, where the Soloheadbeg ambush featured prominently, the beginning of the year was actually the most restless period in Mayo. In January eight arrests were recorded for rioting and posting SF posters in Louisburgh and Ballycastle, while Joseph Kelly received a twelve-month sentence for discharging a revolver in Ballaghaderreen. In subsequent months activity was confined to public meetings and illegal drilling. There were also a small but steady number of cases of threatening letters and assaults, but it is not clear whether these were agrarian or politically motivated. Some arrests for minor offences, such as possession of seditious literature or arms without a permit also continued to take place. Known activists, like Joe MacBride now formally an MP, seemed to be singled out for this as their houses were searched frequently.[22]

The important limiting factor for the IRA in Mayo remained a lack of arms. One Volunteer recalled that if 'a fellow had a bloody old .45 at that time he was something like Napoleon.' By the middle of 1919 the stock of arms in west Mayo consisted of a few rifles in the Newport Battalion and a small number of short arms in Westport. To participate in operations the possession of a weapon was almost a precondition, so acquiring one became an obsession among more eager men.[23] Raiding local farmers who often had shotguns was taken up vigorously again. Although they were given receipts, this was not voluntarily. But no one actually informed the police during 1919. One company claimed to have collected about sixty-six double-barrelled shotguns, but most companies had only a handful. This supply of shotguns needed ammunition for which buckshot had to be produced. To this end, Michael Kilroy acquired a mould to turn lead into pellets.[24] Only on a rare occasion were the men able to acquire a rifle. In Ballina, Patrick Coleman bought a single-shot Martini–Henry rifle from a former officer in the National Volunteers, acquiring 100 rounds of .303 ammunition through a brother in the British army and another 50 through two soldiers whom he plied with plenty of alcohol. Later his unit also took some gelignite and detonators from the county council stores, which were eventually used to make pipe bombs.[25]

The main source for rifles, however, remained IRA GHQ, but this required money and good contacts. In the summer of 1919 many units, therefore, established arms funds. In Westport, local shopkeepers were asked to donate £10 each. Money was also raised by organizing concerts, céilis, theatrical performances, and raffles. The dances, in particular, attracted people from a large area. Some Volunteers claimed to have cycled up to twenty-six miles to attend.[26] Local dignitaries did not always cooperate with these efforts. In Ballina the parish priest refused the IRA the use of the town hall, for which he had helped raise funds to build. The IRA wanted to make a point and one night held up the caretaker and had a dance there for thirty minutes. Afterwards, the IRA officer was warned to escape so as to avoid the wrath of the local PP, who apparently was known to carry a heavy stick with which he abused locals, but he stood his ground.[27] In this way the Westport IRA eventually collected about £500 after which their quartermaster, Tom Kettrick, went to Dublin dressed as a deacon to negotiate purchases. He eventually secured twelve rifles, which immediately made Westport the best-armed battalion in Mayo for the entire War of Independence.[28]

The underground activities of the IRA were largely irrelevant for ordinary people. To mobilize them, militant republicans diverted their attention to attempts to substitute British rule with their own alternative. In June 1919 the Dáil cabinet formally agreed to set up their own court system, an initiative eagerly embraced in Mayo.[29] In December the RIC noted that Fr Carney, curate in The Neale, was very active in the arbitration courts and that the local solicitor Conor Maguire, who was closely involved in the republican movement at national level, had returned to Mayo, where he unsuccessfully tried to be elected as county solicitor.[30] As an alternative to the RIC, the IRA sometimes acted as a police force at these court sittings and also during fair days.[31]

The attempt to replace the RIC was bolstered by a formal boycott of policemen and their families instituted by GHQ in August 1919 'in an effort to make them resign from the force. We cautioned traders not to serve them with goods and the people were warned not to associate or speak to them.'[32] The boycott worked a little haphazardly. The son of the local sergeant in Tourmakeady recalled that the only noticeable impact was the replacement of fresh with condensed milk. According to one Volunteer, the boycott nevertheless had the desired effect. When refused service the police helped themselves, and subsequently made the lives of the traders difficult by prosecuting them for every trivial offence. This caused attitudes on both sides to harden and local relations sour.[33]

Replacing the local authorities was not always popular. When some IRA took it upon themselves to enforce the licensing laws in Ballinrobe on a Sunday morning, they ran into trouble. In one public house they found two RIC men drinking. They took their names and that of the publican, and 'informed them they would be compelled to appear before a Sinn Féin Court'. In another pub they came across seven members of their own company, including the quartermaster and the company captain. What ensued showed the tension between theory and practice:

> We passed on all the names to have summonses issued, and the very next night we were called before a Company Council, and ordered to drop the whole lot. We refused to do so and were brought before a Battalion Council the next night, when we again refused to withdraw and were told, before we left that meeting, that we were not entitled to issue summonses, as we were not on the police section. Neither of us was ever asked to do police work afterwards.[34]

Another important initiative with local effect during 1919 was the introduction of the Dáil loan, intended to finance the alternative government.[35] This seemed to have been taken up vigorously in Mayo, unlike neighbouring Sligo and Roscommon where much of the effort had to be initiated by Mayoman

Patrick Hegarty.³⁶ The Mayo police first detected house-to-house collections for the loan in November 1919, for which Conor Maguire was charged. They argued the collection was done 'by persuasion or where that failed by intimidation', and in December by the actual use of 'terrorism'.³⁷ Volunteers admitted to pressurizing people into subscribing. As one of them put it, we surveyed the area and 'made everyone who had any means at all subscribe at least one pound'.³⁸ Dealing with these large sums of money created particular challenges. The police were actively trying to confiscate the funds by searching the houses of local activists, leading to a number of narrow escapes. On one occasion, a bag with a large amount of money and other important material was smuggled out of Dick Walsh's house during a police raid. Subsequently, a secret chamber was constructed in the house 'so that on a sudden swoop by Crown forces nobody would be taken unawares'. To ensure safe transfer of the money, priests were asked to take it to Dublin.³⁹

All of this had little impact on everyday life during 1919. Police records in Mayo remained more concerned with social problems than republican activity. After an initial decline due to high prices following the end of the war, the incidence of drunkenness and poteen-making had increased considerably by the autumn. More striking were a few cases of rape or attempted rape reported at the end of the year. In August one prosecution was pending upon a possible marriage settlement. Apparently, pressure was being put upon the victim to marry her assailant. Two more cases were recorded in the following months. This issue had rarely featured in the police records before 1919. It has become clear that cases of sexual violence were more widespread during this period than previously thought, but evidence is hard to find as such incidents were usually hidden from view. The only other remarkable occurrences were two attempted suicides, but these do not seem to have been associated with the rape cases or politics.⁴⁰

Apart from the military preparations by a small group of Volunteers, politics occupied the minds of most people at this time. SF had organized a large number of meetings, particularly in the west and south of the county, but in the absence of pressing issues, enthusiasm was limited. Recorded SF membership in Mayo declined somewhat at the end of 1919 from 7,208 in August to 7,107 in December. The only public campaign that republicans were engaged in was to persuade car drivers to refuse to take out permits, which had been introduced in November to prevent the IRA from using automobiles. This campaign did indeed cause widespread disruption. Most attention, however, turned to the elections for the UDCs set for 15 January 1920. This was a good test of the relative standing of the various groups in society with representatives of all parties, including Labour, up for election.⁴¹

The result was not especially impressive for SF. The CI recorded that: 'Sinn Féin met some nasty rebuffs in the late Urban Elections in Castlebar and Ballina.' Joseph MacBride did top the poll in Castlebar, but Labour and the

Ratepayers' Association picked up most of the seats. The success of two female candidates in Castlebar was notable: 'The Lady candidates were of course first favourites, and were favourably met by all voters'. The role of the newly enfranchised women was so large that male candidates felt forced to be especially attentive to female voters, who had come out in large numbers. The female candidates, nevertheless, topped the polls in both wards, with only MacBride doing better. In Ballina, four out of six Labour candidates were elected, while only three out of seven SF candidates were successful. These were supplemented with five members of the Ratepayers' Association and two representatives of the Comrades of War, an army veteran body.[42]

The elections in Westport were an overall disaster, as almost nobody wanted to sit on a council that would have to raise the rates substantially to cover the compensation to Mrs Milling. Only three people had put themselves forward for the twelve seats. In such cases, sitting members were to continue but these were also mostly unwilling to do so, making the running of the council almost impossible.[43] The relatively poor results for SF in the three UDCs was partly due to the change in the electoral system from first past the post to proportional representation, introduced after the 1918 general election to prevent republicans taking total control of local bodies. Special interest groups like workers, employers and ex-soldiers concentrated in urban areas would now elect their own politicians to represent them. The large presence of police and military in urban areas also hampered republican propaganda.[44]

The situation in rural areas, where small farmers and the landless had a common enemy in the landlords and large graziers, was more favourable to SF, but this presented its own problems. Agrarian agitation exploded in early 1920 as it did in neighbouring Galway, Roscommon and parts of southern Sligo. As Conor Maguire put it: 'our Courts were rather unexpectedly resorted to for the purpose of considering claims between landlords and tenants and also between owners and "landless" men.'[45] The latter, in particular, scared the national republican leadership, afraid of the possible implications of a take-over of land and the consequent threat to social stability. Up to now, the arbitration courts had been able to deal with local disputes, but they were not equipped to resolve cases of land occupation as locals were not always willing to abide by the rulings of neighbours who ran the courts.[46]

This came to a head in a case involving a farm near Ballinrobe, which became the driving force behind the formal establishment of special Dáil Land Courts in May 1920. Fountain Hill, a 110-acre grazing farm rented by two local farmers, John Hyland and John Murphy, had been occupied by other tenants from the same estate who only had small holdings and demanded that the farm be divided between them. Hyland and Murphy refused to accept arbitration by a local SF court as they feared they would be unfairly treated and they called in the aid of the local parish priest. Fr Healy went to Conor Maguire and pointed out that the two would submit to arbitration if there were judges brought in from outside, who would 'easily give their decision independently of any local influence'.[47]

Maguire went to Dublin and spoke to Arthur Griffith, then minister for home affairs in the Dáil cabinet. He was initially hesitant, 'afraid that the tribunal would not be able to enforce a decision unfavourable to the agitators', but Maguire convinced him that the local IRA would be capable of doing so. The Dáil cabinet then approved the decision but asked those with influence, especially the local clergy, to ensure the decision of the courts was accepted. Kevin O'Shiel and Art O'Connor, two leading jurists in the movement, were sent as judges.[48] The case, which was recorded in the *Western People* as the 'first public Arbitration Court in Ireland under the auspices of Dáil Éireann', attracted a lot of attention and aroused considerable emotions. At the last moment, the proceedings were almost scuppered when the solicitor representing Hyland and Murphy pulled out, possibly afraid of the consequences. To save the day Fr Healy stepped in and pleaded their case. Within a week the court came to a decision which favoured Hyland and Murphy. The claimants, represented by Conor Maguire, 'stamped out of the hall in an arrogant temper, proclaiming, in loud and angry tones, that "we were no Sinn Féin court" (which, of course, we did not claim to be), and that we were "worse than the British".'[49]

The indignant claimants also proclaimed their intention to ignore the ruling, despite having signed an agreement to abide by the court beforehand, and continue the occupation of Fountain Hill. O'Shiel argued that if nothing was done this would make the assertion the Dáil formed the legitimate government unworkable. Although the IRA was hesitant to get involved, Griffith approached Tom Maguire who arrested the sons of some of the most prominent opponents of the court ruling and carried them off to an island in Lough Corrib. The family of the men then promised that if they were released, they would abandon the occupation and abide by the ruling of the court. In O'Shiel's and Maguire's eyes this saved the working of the land courts and ensured a successful boycott of the local assizes. This seems to have deradicalized the land issue somewhat in Mayo unlike Roscommon where a first case came before a land court later in May at which O'Shiel also presided. He later claimed 'there was an aggressive, "bolshie" spirit about the Roscommon litigants that was ... not so obviously present in the other counties'.[50]

The kidnapping of these dissenting tenants highlighted another problem associated with running an alternative court system, namely the need for a police force and a prison system. During an earlier case at Louisburgh in October 1919, a man who refused to abide by the ruling of a SF court was taken by local officers to commandant Tom Maguire who brought him to a farm in the Castlehacket area outside Tuam. There, the man was put to work as a labourer and warned that if he returned home prematurely, he would be shot on sight.[51] Although a makeshift prison system was subsequently established, holding people was dangerous. 'Prisoners were detained at specially selected places, usually out of the way – houses in bogs and so forth.' If such a person escaped and went to the police, this put the IRA and their supporters at risk. As an alternative, those convicted were fined or in a few cases deported, sometimes having their boat tickets paid. In most instances, however, a threat of deportation was enough to prevent trouble.[52]

Another implication of setting up their own court system was the deliberate attempt to frustrate the operation of existing courts. Cahir Davitt, a solicitor who acted as a judge in the Dáil courts, remembered a meeting of the official Swinford quarter sessions in which all participants – counsel and solicitors, the customary complement of court officers and police – were assembled but no litigants or witnesses showed up. 'Everyone knew that the cases had gone to another jurisdiction, but the Republican Courts were never mentioned.' It quickly became clear that this was not entirely voluntary. All roads leading into Swinford were picketed by Volunteers who prevented anyone attending. In the end, one litigant was let through and eventually made his way into the court. He was a publican who wished to submit an application in connection with his licence. 'He had, apparently, after considerable argument, been allowed "in the public interest" to pass the pickets.'[53]

The growing success of the alternative government had already caused the suppression of the Dáil and other republican organization during the autumn of 1919. At the same time, attempts to secure Ireland's independence at the Peace Conference in Paris faltered. This apparent failure of political means gave the militarists in the movement a freer hand. In January 1920 IRA GHQ endorsed open attacks on the Crown forces, which had already started in some areas. In districts where the IRA was not yet capable of staging such attacks, GHQ ordered an assault on 'lines of communication', including telegraph wires and post offices, and attacks on minor police barracks and military posts.[54]

In Mayo, this policy was taken up very slowly. During the early months of 1920, just a few politically motivated minor offences were reported. Apart from the usual threatening letters and notices, incidents in the first months included firing at the prison and a house, and a malicious use of explosives.[55] Such minor confrontations did bring a few republicans, somewhat hesitantly, into conflict with the police. On one occasion, 'an RIC man from Foxford refused to give up his bicycle until a shot was sent off by his ear.' Patrick Hegarty from Enniscoe recalled how after leaving a meeting by car:

> a sergeant and three RIC men tried to arrest the driver, Farry, myself and a young man from Dublin. By this time I had secured a .38 Colt revolver from Tommy John Conlan. My Dublin friend also had a gun. I advised the sergeant to have sense and quit or, if not, to double his insurance as there would not be a next time.[56]

Such willingness to engage the police was, however, still rare in Mayo. One officer from Kiltimagh, who wounded a policeman during an arrest attempt, fled on a cargo boat to England as republicans had generally done in the past in such situations. The IRA leadership was unsure whether they should allow this. Another Volunteer who emigrated of his own accord was abducted from a train and brought up for desertion.[57] Most wanted men, however, refused to quit and were thus forced to avoid the police. This still had an innocent quality in Mayo: 'My house was raided a few times and I went on the run, that is to say, I did not sleep at home at night but otherwise I performed my normal duties'.[58]

The more violent conflict that developed elsewhere in Ireland did have consequences locally. In response to some successful attacks on police barracks in other counties, up to 500 isolated police posts were evacuated throughout Ireland, including 42 out of 68 police posts of various sizes in Mayo, starting at the end of 1919. This allowed open drilling to resume in many rural areas and republicans now felt safe to enforce adherence to their alternative government more diligently.[59] To aid in what could be called the blooding of local Volunteers and to show publicly that the Dáil was taking control, GHQ ordered the mass burning of courthouses and evacuated barracks at Easter 1920. Another target was local tax offices; they were to be raided and their records burned to prevent the authorities from operating government services.

For many Volunteers in Mayo even this bloodless open challenge to the authorities was difficult to engage in. In Aughagower, only three Volunteers actually showed up for this duty. In most of the few attempted cases, the burnings proved to be a simple affair, but sometimes the inexperience of the men was exposed. In Drummin, 'the door of the barrack was forced open and petrol sprinkled inside the building. Captain Peter McDonnell climbed up to a window and applied a lighted match. The resultant explosion scorched his face and hands and the marks were noticeable for many days after.'[60] In a similar incident near Bohola, two leading Volunteers had to be brought to hospital with significant burns. One raider recalled how after the incident, one of their comrades had said: 'We should shoot them to take them out of pain as they can't live'.[61]

Not all of the many empty barracks were destroyed. A second order to burn evacuated barracks, including those that had continued to serve as homes for sergeants and their families, came in May. Consequently, eleven more vacant barracks were destroyed in Mayo in July and ten in August (see map 4). In Ballycroy, the local sergeant was put out of the barracks with his family and two other policemen. During the destruction of the RIC barracks in Shrule on 16 July 1920, Volunteer John Joe Keleghan was burned and subsequently died in hospital. The shock of this experience caused some local Volunteers to leave the IRA.[62]

Participation in these burnings and the growing number of raids for arms and on the mail in 1920 generated activity in local companies that had been practically dormant during 1919. This became evident in a significant increase in the number of indictable offences, from eleven in January 1920 to sixty-six in May. Besides illegal drilling and minor attacks on the Crown forces, these included the first recorded ambush of a police patrol, which was forced to give up all arms without causing any casualties. The real level of lawlessness was probably even higher. As the CI argued in June, 'there is an improvement in the numbers of actual crimes reported, but we are not so certain that there is a real reduction as people intimidated are afraid to report to police now, and the number of secret intimidation has certainly increased.'[63] Much of the activity was aimed at the civil population, showing the inclination of Mayo activists to concentrate on their position in local society rather than seeking confrontation with the authorities. Besides arms raiding, this involved threatening notices backed up by intimidation to force the people to boycott the British institutions and use republican alternatives. Agrarian agitation also became more prevalent and aggressive, with about a third of the offences falling into this category. In early June two men who had continued to work on a boycotted farm in Clogher were stoned and beaten to death. In this charged atmosphere, SF was able to force the CDB to split up a farm in the Westport district.[64]

Prosecuting those responsible for these offences through the existing legal system also became increasingly difficult. Summonses for the Crown courts were taken forcibly from the police, proclamations were issued by the SF courts and people were arrested by the IRA. The CI acknowledged that this had practically put an end to quarter and petty sessions. In July only twenty-five out of 140 jurors attended the regular courts and, consequently, no jury could be formed. Most of the cases listed had the day before been disposed of by 'a Sinn Féin tribunal'. The proceedings in these Dáil courts were fully reported in the papers, where it was announced that their decisions would be enforced by 'the military forces of the Irish Republic'. Indeed, the police noticed that seven men had been arrested by the IRA, two for larceny and three for failure to comply with orders of the SF court. The boycott of the police and their families also received a lot of attention, with the RIC reporting that the refusal to sell them goods or even speak to them was widespread, made possible by the very high membership of SF, the IRA and associated organizations in Mayo.[65]

Events in early 1920 had thus given the IRA a new lease of life. Between January and July seven new companies were identified by the RIC, and membership almost doubled from 2,362 to 5,564. During the same period, SF saw comparable growth from 7,107 to 11,090 members, which made Mayo among the best-organized counties in Ireland, showing the widespread acceptance of republicanism there.[66] In July the CI reported his increasing alarm over the situation:

> The closing of the police stations has proved a most disastrous and dangerous expedient whilst the lack of men, of transport and of effective military cooperation have only added to the mess. Sinn Féin given a free hand has grown more and more active and aggressive and intimidation is much more general and effective. The countryside left without protection now bows the knees to Sinn Féin. Drilling by Volunteers has again come into vogue, Sinn Féin courts openly arrogate themselves the function of courts of law. Traders no longer dare furnish the police with necessaries nor in any way assist or hold conversation with them. Police when opportunity offers are waylaid, robbed and murdered.

He saw no benefits in the accommodating government policies and was apprehensive that 'few police will ... remain to face the coming winter'. In his view, 'if the police with their local knowledge go, farewell to civil government'. That the police could still function in Mayo without fear for their lives meant they still had a reasonably good knowledge of what was afoot locally, even though many incidents remained out of their view.[67]

Slowly the character of the conflict had changed in Mayo. A small, but growing, number of Volunteers had been radicalized by their involvement in minor operations mostly connected with taking control over aspects of civilian life and were now increasingly prepared to engage the Crown forces directly. This was exacerbated by the large-scale nationwide arrest of IRA activists at the beginning of 1920 and their subsequent release in May following a general strike. The growing republican power in the countryside caused by the evacuation of many RIC barracks was demonstrated in the local elections for RDCs and the county council in June 1920. The poor results in the January urban elections had caused republicans to prepare more diligently. The extra effort, which involved some illegal practices, paid off as SF doubled its share of the vote nationwide. In the whole of Connacht, 97 per cent of seats went to SF, including all on Mayo County Council. At its first meeting, it swore allegiance to the Dáil, just before the meeting was raided by the police, which hoped to arrest a number of its wanted members. Many months after military conflict had developed elsewhere, it now also became a defining feature in Mayo.[68]

6 'Sinn Féin agents were reported visiting the county to foment trouble': violence comes to Mayo, 1920–1

In contrast to the violent conflict that characterized southern parts of Ireland, in particular, during the early summer of 1920, the small number of full-time IRA in Mayo had focused on making regular government impossible and supporting the republican alternatives. Open conflict with the police remained comparatively limited, and GHQ was still ambivalent about pushing a full-scale war. On the one hand, it desired 'that any operation, such as a barrack attack or a serious ambush, should not be attempted or carried out until all the information that was available locally should be submitted to G.H.Q. for their approval'. On the other, it had issued blanket orders in January 1920 to shoot 'all Black & Tans and vicious RIC men' on sight. The requirement to obtain permission before an operation inhibited many in Mayo, unlike other places.[1] On 1 July 1920 Louisburgh IRA, who patrolled the town during fair day, were presented with an opportunity to rush the barracks after overpowering a police patrol during a scuffle. Nothing transpired as the local IRA officer believed he did not have GHQ sanction to start such operations.[2] Nevertheless, Mayo remained resistant to attempts by GHQ to take more control of local affairs, and thus did not fully conform to the three phases of the War of Independence postulated by Townshend.

The Mayo IRA, like neighbouring counties, was only slowly drawn into taking more direct action against the authorities, although in Roscommon there had been more consistent agrarian-based violence throughout 1920. In July 1920 alone, there were four cases in which policemen were robbed and a couple of shooting incidents. In general, a spirit of what was called lawlessness can be detected in the months that followed with rising numbers of threats, larcenies, intimidation and malicious damage reported. The RIC acknowledged that more offences were committed than reported.[3] Sergeant Thomas Armstrong became the first (unintended) police fatality in Mayo when he was killed in Ballina on 21 July when the local IRA attempted to disarm a small police patrol. When they rushed the patrol from an ambush position Armstrong pulled his gun and was shot. The attackers were somewhat shaken by this and let the rest of the patrol go even though one of them had made clear he recognized some of his attackers, leading to three subsequent arrests.[4]

Direct attacks on occupied barracks were now also contemplated. In August a failed attempt, sanctioned by GHQ, was made to gain access to Cross barracks. The plan involved some Volunteers dressed in British military uniforms driving

75

up to the barracks in the hope the police would open the door, after which another IRA party was supposed to storm it but this group did not turn up and the operation was aborted, causing significant disappointment.[5]

The most daring operation was the taking of Ballyvary barracks in August. This was a well-planned operation with the Mayo Brigade officers Michael McHugh and Dick Walsh in charge. The Bohola company executed the attack with the support of battalion staff. Neighbouring companies blocked roads into the village. The attack was planned while most of the police were attending 11.30 Mass, a mile from the barracks. The backdoor of the barracks was left open by a friendly constable, allowing the IRA to surprise the small garrison inside and there was no resistance. Arms and ammunition were seized, including about fifteen rifles, the first to become available to the east Mayo IRA. Afterwards, the military searched all houses within a mile radius, showing their anger when they fired a volley over the heads of some local boys and girls who shouted 'Up Sinn Féin'. The barracks was subsequently closed and later burned by the IRA.[6]

On 30 August men from north Mayo were also involved in an attack on the coastguard station in Enniscrone, County Sligo. The attack was planned during a busy evening hour when many people were bathing around the station. Six coastguards returning from the town were held up, after which a small group of men armed with revolvers stormed the station using two coastguards captured in the wash house as cover. A substantial amount of arms, ammunition and other equipment was captured and removed by car. The station was then burned and the coastguards released.[7]

Escalating conflict throughout the country prompted the government to stop its somewhat conciliatory policy introduced after the public protests of May 1920, and introduce the Restoration of Order in Ireland Act on 9 August 1920. This allowed for harsher measures, including internment, official reprisals and court martial of civilians. The deployment of additional police during the summer of 1920 made the execution of this new policy possible. These forces, which became known as Auxiliaries and Black & Tans, consisted mostly of ex-soldiers recruited in England. In Mayo, only a few Black & Tans supplemented the depleted police numbers in the early summer, while a small contingent of Auxiliaries arrived in Westport in October 1920.[8]

The most visible expression of the new approach was the order to arrest all known IRA officers and republican activists. The relatively open functioning of republican institutions in Mayo meant many arrests could be carried out. In October twelve IRA officers were taken from their homes, followed by another eighty-two in November and twelve in December. Further arrests followed in early 1921; thirty-three in January and forty-four in February. Nine IRA were arrested in Ballyhaunis when a IRA meeting was discovered, and six apprehended following the capture of an IRA despatch by the police in Hollymount. Reasons for arrest also included cases of illegal assembly, carrying despatches, signing bonds or possession of arms.[9]

Violence comes to Mayo, 1920–1

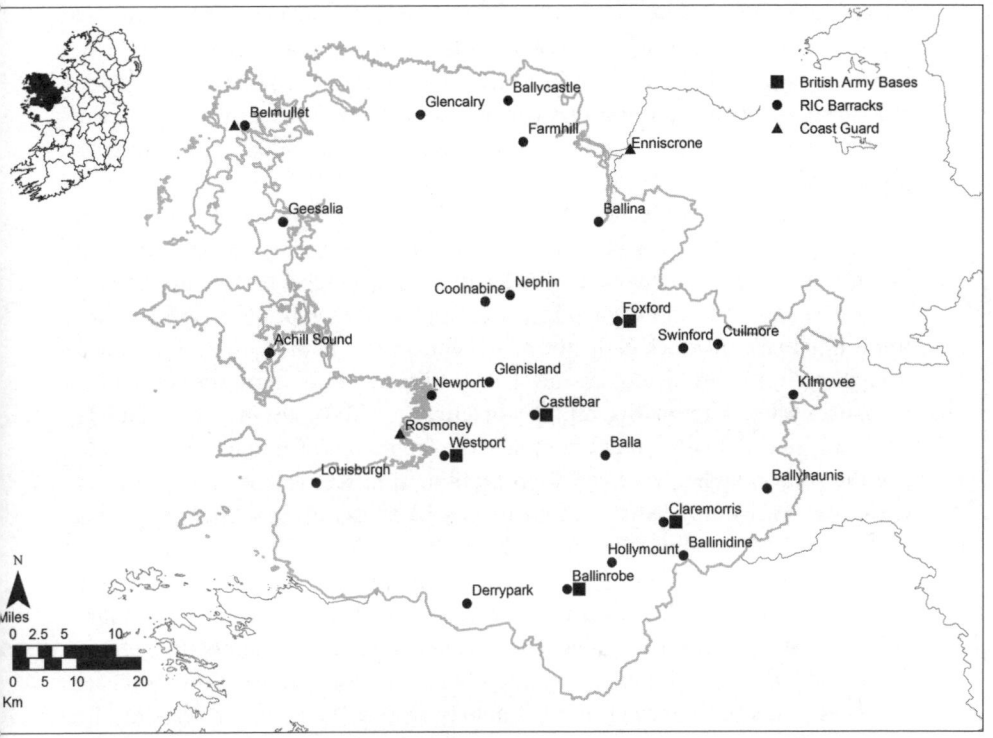

4 Police and British army distribution, 1920–1

The large number of arrests in Mayo contrasted sharply with other counties, where comparatively few were recorded in this period.[10] This and the closer co-operation between the police and military made CI Steadman more optimistic. In October he reported that 'if quietly and systematically continued [the new measures] will knock the bottom out of the Sinn Féin movement in a short time.' He suggested that SF 'have become much exercised in mind and body at the very suggestion of the application to themselves of a little of their own ointment.' The attitude of the population was considered crucial in this new found optimism: 'The threat of reprisal makes people exercise their influence to prevent anything occurring in their midst that would likely bring such in its train. This is rather a novel feature in Irish psychology'.[11]

In November Steadman cautioned that the new measures 'will duly scotch[?] the [republican] snake however not kill him and in his scotched[?] condition he may become even more venomous and dangerous.' He also brought the lack of personnel and transportation to the attention of the inspector-general, claiming that the fixed strength of the Mayo police had been reduced in 1920 from 436 to 348 but that there were still 67 vacancies. Furthermore, only one of their four Crossley tenders was operative, seriously reducing the mobility of the police. His appeal was effective as new recruits and four Crossley tenders and five Ford cars arrived in December. A steady stream of additional police arrived in 1921: 10 in February, 29 in March and 20 in April. Besides this, barbed wire was made available to protect the remaining barracks and the train strike preventing the transportation of military equipment was ended. All this enhanced Steadman's optimism.[12]

The arrests certainly depleted the IRA ranks but also had unintended escalating effects. Some Volunteers conformed to the RIC's expectations and became extra careful. Officers in Castlebar refused to allow further operations: 'We were stopped each time on our way in to attack by senior officers who didn't want us to make an attack in the town.'[13] Commandant John Hoban even handed over the gelignite in his possession to subordinates, essentially abrogating his responsibilities. The relative military inactivity of Mayo annoyed IRA GHQ, which expressed its disappointment over the failure of the men in west Mayo to use the rifles they had received from Dublin. Tom Kettrick recalled Gearóid O'Sullivan exclaiming 'what the hell are you losers doing' and Michael Collins asking 'why the hell don't you use the arms'.[14]

To improve matters GHQ instigated a reorganization of the county in the hope that smaller local units with more determined leaders would react more coherently to the new pressures. The brigade staff was still led by the ageing Joseph MacBride, while in spring 1920 both the vice-commandant, Michael McHugh, and the quartermaster, Thomas Derrig, had been arrested. The responsibility for running the brigade was effectively in the hands of Dick Walsh, the brigade adjutant, then 32. After discussions with GHQ and consultations with local officers a brigade convention was convened in September 1920.

This meeting, presided over by MacBride, was held in the county asylum grounds in Castlebar, with members coming together under the guise of the annual athletics competition held there. Éamon Price was present as a GHQ representative. It was decided to divide the county into four brigade areas: East under Seán Corcoran, West under the recently released Derrig, North with Tom Ruane as commander and South under Tom Maguire (see map 5). Each brigade was instructed to form its own complement of battalions and companies covering their entire area. Even in February 1921 there existed unorganized areas. Charles Gildea recalled how he tried to set up an IRA outpost in Gleneask near Charlestown, but none of the invited locals showed up. Eventually, each brigade created four battalions, except for North Mayo, which comprised seven, including Belmullet, Ballycastle, Ballina, Foxford, Crossmolina, Bangor and Corbally in Sligo. The south Mayo battalions were Cross, Ballinrobe, Claremorris and Balla, while the West Mayo Brigade had four battalions: Castlebar, Newport, Westport and Louisburgh. East Mayo contained Swinford, Kiltimagh, Ballyhaunis and the area in Roscommon around Ballaghaderreen. One of the considerations in establishing internal borders was to ensure a direct

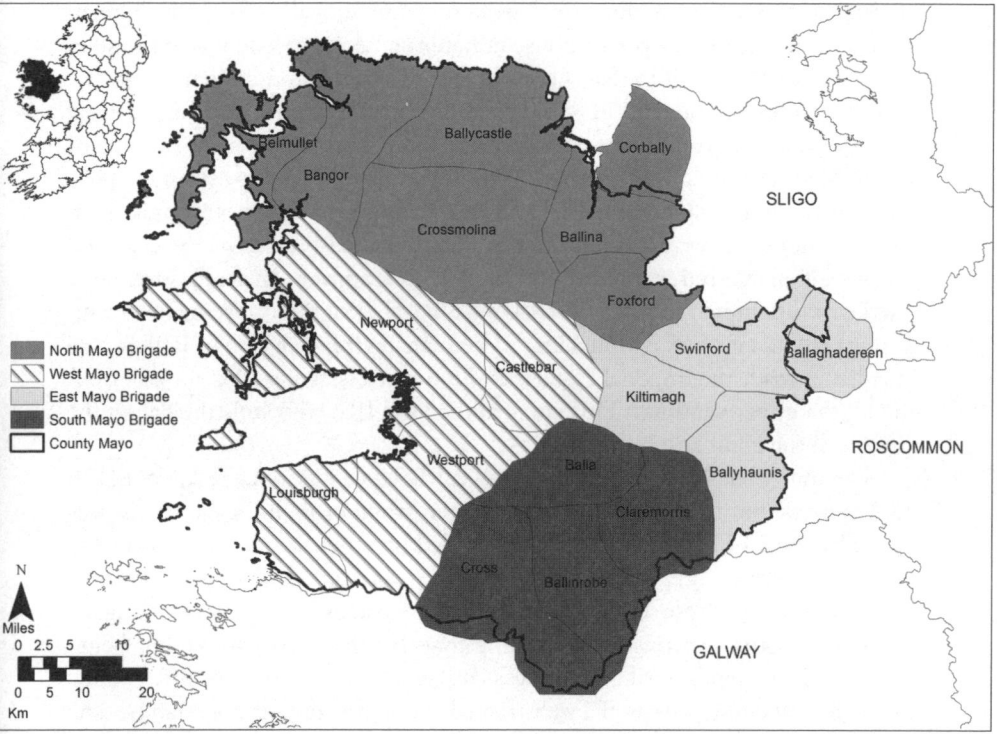

5 IRA battalion areas

railway connection between each brigade and Dublin. In this way, against local wishes, Ballyhaunis was made part of the East Mayo Brigade.[15]

A second unintended consequence of the new government measures was the forming of flying columns or Active Service Units (ASUs). Contrary to what had occurred in many southern counties, most active Volunteers in Mayo had remained living at home during 1920. Even those who had been forced to go on the run after involvement in the few violent clashes, like Patrick Hegarty in north Mayo, generally stayed locally and frequently returned home. On one such visit he awoke 'to find rifles pointing at my chest'. Hegarty was arrested with his three brothers, who were released after a court martial, but Patrick was given two years' hard labour.[16] His colleague in east Mayo, Seán Ruane, was more fortunate when visiting his home. He was able 'to cross over the wall into a neighbour's yard, where, dressed in woman's attire, he crossed the street, cordoned off [by] the military, got into a house, left the disguise there and escaped'.[17]

The threat of arrest changed this somewhat lax attitude. Although the police apprehended many known activists, others evaded arrest, sometimes after having been tipped off about an impending raid. In Westport, the men were warned by the DI, who regularly passed on information to the local IRA intelligence officer through a local priest.[18] Other warnings were unintentional. A friend of Stephen Donnelly overheard in a public house in Ballina a 'sergeant who was in the snug at the bar tell the publican that there was going to be a round up that night'.[19]

The impending arrival of some Auxiliaries in Westport also forced local Volunteers on the run. Their notoriety had clearly preceded them, as some of the IRA congregated on a nearby hill-top. Waiting all night in extremely poor weather without instructions was a disheartening experience, and most men returned home the next morning. When the Auxiliaries did arrive, the expected convoy of armoured cars and lorries did not appear. Instead, just three Auxiliaries attempted to make the IRA 'look foolish. But these 3 were not violent. It was really a bit of swash-buckling more than anything else'.[20] In Ballina, the Auxiliaries made the Imperial Hotel their headquarters, flying a Union Jack from one of the upper windows. This enraged the local IRA who stole the flag in the middle of the night and burned it.[21]

The initial result of the increased police vigilance was a marked decrease in IRA activity, but it also led to a much larger group of men on the run as was noted by the CI in November.[22] They banded together for reasons of security and comradeship, but also because the 'safe areas' were few. To provide these men with some purpose, GHQ had ordered the formation of ASUs in all brigade areas in October, optimistically arguing that: 'In this way – instead of being compelled to a haphazard and aimless course of action – they would become available as standing troops of a well-trained and thoroughly reliable stamp'. The ASUs were to support individual battalions but had to instigate independent action as well, including confiscation of enemy goods, attacks on minor police stations and patrols, and cutting lines of communication.[23]

It took some time before these instructions were implemented. West Mayo was the first to act. In November, following a brigade council in Brockagh, Derrig instructed the quartermaster to order 'twenty sets of breeches, leggings and suitable shoes'.[24] The actual start of ASUs was delayed by the arrest of Derrig and other officers. In its diary of operations for March 1921, about four months after the men were forced on the run, the West Mayo Brigade reported to GHQ that the Westport Battalion had formed an ASU and that two other battalions were in the process of organizing one.[25] In the Newport Battalion ASU members were recruited from the ranks of each company who were informed that 'a Volunteer who agreed to join had nothing to gain from it but an early death, and that anyone who did not feel he could see it through would be thought none the worse of it if he stood down.'[26] Eventually, Michael Kilroy picked a certain number of men from each company and gave them the arms on hand. In the Castlebar Battalion, the formation of the ASU was a chance for those frustrated by the inactivity of the somewhat older Hoban, then 39, who had fled to England, to act. Although armed with about seven or eight rifles, some of them purchased from the local army garrison, this ASU stayed mostly in the nearby village of Doogary and initially did not even carry their arms.[27] In Ballaghaderreen Battalion, a unit was also constituted from the disparate men on the run, but both arms and men were much less numerous. Aside from shotguns, they had just one service rifle, two Martini rifles and three revolvers.[28]

Initially the haphazard formation of the ASUs meant they made little impact. Most of them simply stayed out of harm's way and did not directly engage the Crown forces, the stripping of two British soldiers being a highlight.[29] The inexperience of the men was also evident. When Tom Kettrick, the quartermaster in west Mayo, visited a shop to get supplies, he had 'his hand on his automatic on account of the soldiers being outside and it went off accidentally; the bullet passed under his kneecap and out in the side of his shin.'[30]

The pressures on the Mayo men to act mounted. In February 1921 the police became aware of GHQ's demand for a western offensive to relieve the pressure on the southern IRA: 'Sinn Féin agents were reported visiting the County to foment trouble, and organize parties for ambushes.'[31] Intelligence on police movement was limited, so the ASUs had difficulties engaging them. To improve their chances, diversions were instigated to draw the Crown forces out, as occurred in the Liscull area: 'We raided the local Post Office and fired shots, and got a man to go to the barracks and report us as being in the area, to try and get them out but to no avail – they would not oblige.'[32] In the eyes of the police the reverse took place: 'Several cases of anticipated ambushes where rebels were seen lying-in-wait, were reported during the month, and the places were immediately visited by the Crown Forces, but nothing was discovered.'[33]

The start of the ASUs also changed the role of the rank and file, which potentially involved a large part of the population in Mayo, although most did not actively participate in operations. In June 1921 the RIC estimated that there were 6,608 Volunteers, accounting for seven per cent of all Catholic males, about three times as many as in an active southern county like Tipperary, which mobilized only 2.2 per cent, and a much higher rate than in the quiet counties of the east and north, such as Wexford with 1.9 per cent and Derry with 1 per cent. There were also clear concentrations of support. Contemporary parade reports show the South Mayo Brigade had a total of 890 men enrolled, while a single battalion in west Mayo recorded 773 members. The rolls of the Owenwee company show that more than a third of Catholic males between fifteen and sixty in the area were members, including almost all male members of certain families. It is not clear how active all these men were, but the IRA in Mayo could potentially call upon a very large proportion of the population, including many women.[34]

All companies were now ordered to form intelligence sections capable of warning the ASUs of enemy movement and gathering local information, in particular on 'cars in the battalion area with their numbers, names of owners and so on', houses that were safe, and 'a list of all those who possessed arms'.

Messages were transferred by signalling with flags or on bicycles, often by members of Cumann na mBan or young boys.[35] More direct information was obtained from post office workers, but the best source was an employee of Castlebar barracks who copied all coded messages and passed them to the IRA. Involvement in actual operations by local Volunteers was limited and might not have exceeded road-cutting in preparation for an ambush. To rouse local Volunteers, GHQ issued instructions on 30 March to isolate enemy posts with a systematic road-trenching campaign. This was taken up but proved of little military value because the 'enemy usually rounded up the men in the vicinity and made them clear the roads again and fill in the trenches.'[36]

Although membership of and support for SF and the IRA was thus extremely high in Mayo, opposition was encountered from

> a big section of the landed gentry, most of the monied [sic] and influential people of the country, as well as the friends and relations in most cases of all whose sons were in the British Army, Navy, RIC intelligence, and all the other sections of the people who had contact with or were earning a livlihood [sic] from any Government source.[37]

By 1920 few of them would oppose the IRA actively and as their number was relatively small in Mayo, speaking up had its dangers. The few dissenting voices were silenced, sometimes by intimidation and threats, but actual force was rarely necessary.[38] There were people who did provide the RIC with information. Although they often were ordinary members of the local Catholic community, those associating socially or economically with the authorities were often suspected more easily. The local gentry were top of the list in Westport. We 'had our agents working in and near the big houses and, as a general rule, we were always able to render them useless without actually proceeding to extremes.' When suspected, such people were harshly dealt with. In Srah near Bunnahowen, the nightly training of the local company was observed by two local men, an ex-soldier and a member of the ascendancy. They were held up 'taken to a disused house, court martialled and ordered to leave the country for four years.'[39]

Being observed speaking to the police could potentially have lethal consequences as in the case of two men from Carracastle. Patrick Cassidy, the local IRA leader, tried to draw them out by approaching them dressed as a British soldier. It became clear the men were keen on talking about the actions of the IRA, but Cassidy concluded that 'their action was more from ignorance than being desirous to hurt us. We took them out and tied them to a tree and gave them a good beating, and warned them that, if they gave any information to the British or ever went into the town again, they would be shot'. Shortly afterwards, Cassidy met another IRA party on their way to shoot the same men:

'I forbade them to do so, and told them, if anyone was shot without orders, I would have themselves shot, and that stopped that.'[40]

This relatively limited application of force against civilians compared to that used in other counties was generally sufficient to control the local population. Among Mayo IRA there was also a certain reluctance to act against civilians, and no non-combatants were killed as suspected spies or informers in Mayo. This concentration on combatants and those who had a direct association with the government can also be found in neighbouring counties, although there were a couple of outright killings of civilians accused of being spies or informers by the IRA in Galway and Roscommon, some of them agrarian related.[41] In the absence of hard evidence, suspicions were not acted on in a lethal sense. Those found to be transgressing IRA rules were intimidated. One farmer in Carracastle was taken out, beaten up, and left tied up with a sign saying: 'Spies Beware; death penalty – IRA'.[42] Some Ballina Volunteers even refused to execute a man convicted of informing by an IRA court because they doubted his guilt.[43]

The attempt to function as a regular government also put strain on the relationship with the local people. In 1920 SF had declared a campaign against the distilling of poteen, the consumption of which created 'havoc'. In the Ballina area, six poteen stills in four villages were confiscated by the IRA. The equipment was taken to the chapel yard and destroyed in the presence of the community. To make an example, one man was tied to a tree and a note pinned to his coat read: '"Poteen" painted in big type, so that everybody who passed the way would see him, and at the bottom of the card we wrote the following "This is the treatment for all offenders in future".'[44] By November 1920 the RIC confirmed that poteen-making had been choked off by SF.[45]

Ordinary people often found themselves caught between the two parties not knowing who to answer to and liable to be punished by one if they adhered to the directives of the other.[46] On 7 January 1921 local solicitors received a letter informing them 'that barristers and solicitors attending SF Arbitration Courts, Republican Courts or any such assembly purporting to be held under the authority of Dáil Éireann are liable to prosecution'.[47] In December two men had been arrested by the RIC for acting and signing writs as justices of the peace for the Irish Republic.[48] This pressure made maintaining the republican court system problematic. In January 1921 the RIC claimed not to have heard of any arbitration courts for some time, while in February they reported 'a vastly increased tendency on the part of the people to come to the police for assistance and protection, they ceased to have any faith or reliance on the SF courts which now have ceased to exist.'[49]

Often unable to get to the IRA, the authorities sometimes took their frustration out on their sympathizers. In Ballina, shopkeepers who were known to have supplied the ASUs, either voluntarily or under threat, were targeted following the shooting of the local DI, Captain White, in May 1921: 'several prominent merchants in Ballina were arrested, brought to the Auxiliaries headquarters. They were marched through the town at revolver point, made carry Union Jacks and, at the Market Cross, go down on their knees, kiss the Union Jack and shout "God save the King".[50] In Newport, the IRA claimed the new DI had instituted a reign of terror: 'This man seemed to have run amok and was out night after night hanging people until they were almost dead, tying men on cows and putting shovels in their hands and endeavouring to stage a mock combat, going into houses accompanied by some lady and shooting up the houses.'[51]

Family members of active Volunteers had their houses smashed up and were physically abused by some members of the Crown forces, in particular after successful IRA operations. What actually transpired on these occasions is hard to establish, but in the minds of active Volunteers, this was real. Seán Gibbons related what they perceived to be the modus operandi of soldiers and RIC in Castlebar: '[They] took out the father, brought him to the barn, fired a shot, told him to lie down, threw a bag over him and came back to the house, saying they had him shot and the best thing for the remaining people to do was to give any information in their possession with regard to the IRA'.[52] In Newport, a local Volunteer suffered particularly badly:

> He was a comical sight. Half his moustache was cut off, half of his hair was clipped bare, his shirt was torn in ribbons, and he had no trousers. Seemingly a gang of RIC under Dist. Inspector Fudge and Sergeant Butler had raided the house just before we arrived. They brought a cow into the kitchen and put Michael sitting on her back, whipped her around the kitchen and out the front door.[53]

The IRA tried to pick out the men involved in such ill-treatment, but with limited success.[54]

The clergy played an important part in shaping local responses to the conflict. As in most other counties, their reactions were divided, ranging from outright condemnation of republicanism to membership of SF and in an odd case even the IRA. Relatively speaking, public condemnations of IRA actions by clergy in Mayo was among the rarest in the whole country, with only one out of 243 such instances found in the national newspapers. Mayo priests were among the most supportive of republicans after Galway, Longford and Sligo, with five of them found to have given actual material support to the IRA from a total of seventy-one cases nationwide. Consequently, Mayo priests suffered more than their fair share of intimidation, 7 out of 80 cases nationally, and arrests, 5 out of 43. This included Fr Meehan from Castlebar who was arrested in October 1920. His home was raided in the evening and, according to the archbishop of Tuam, he was left undressed while they searched his house.[55]

Most of the opposition from the clergy to republicanism was expressed from the pulpit or in the confessional.⁵⁶ One priest tried to induce a local Volunteer to leave the movement: 'Father, I came to Confession, not to be lectured. I am going out to fight the enemy of my country. I came here on good intentions and if you cannot give me Absolution I must go'.⁵⁷ When Stephen Donnelly went to confession after an attack the priest told him that 'although he was sorry and sympathized with our movement, he had instructions from the Bishop that anyone implicated in the attack would have to go to His Lordship'.⁵⁸ On the other hand, GHQ was asked for permission to shoot a local parish priest who was passing on information to the authorities. This was refused.⁵⁹

Many tried to play a balancing act. In May 1921 a priest in Knock described the IRA as 'a magnificent body of men' but as they had no hope of winning their actions were useless and destructive, and could therefore not be supported.⁶⁰ In the same month, the parish priest in Ballinrobe, who had to bury the casualties of the Tourmakeady ambush, a Volunteer and two RIC men, placed the body of the IRA man before the high altar and the two RIC before side altars. Although this led to protests from the RIC it was kept that way.⁶¹ Such approaches could confuse. A Volunteer who was shot in the leg, found refuge in a parochial house occupied by a priest who had only recently denounced their methods from the pulpit, but now treated him with care: 'That was the first time in my life a hot water jar was placed in my bed.'⁶²

Some clergy were more openly supportive. A number of them heard the confessions of ASU members.⁶³ When a Volunteer admitted to shooting three policemen, one priest responded: 'You're no bloody good if that's all you have shot'.⁶⁴ Fr Patrick MacHugh from Aughagower was reported as having told a Volunteer that 'as long as he got orders he was not responsible' for the deaths of policemen, reassuring him that depending on the circumstances such killing was not a sin.⁶⁵ Fr Cunningham in Leenane actually allowed the use of the parochial house for storing arms, while a local priest in Enniscrone claimed to have been in charge of the burning of the local coastguard station.⁶⁶

Such active support, especially by junior clergymen who tended to be more radical than parish priests, could be dangerous as they were not only confronted by the government forces but also by their church authorities. A small number of priests were arrested for acting as judges in the Dáil courts, Fr John Meehan from Castlebar for possession of ammunition and seditious documents, while MacHugh was informed on and barred from the parochial house by the parish priest.⁶⁷ A priest from Partry was threatened with guns when he visited the site where an ambush had taken place, the soldiers claiming he was responsible for it. A local priest in Claremorris who complained to army headquarters about the mistreatment of local citizens was later visited by some British officers 'plainly bent on murder'. One of the few times such behaviour was dealt with was when two Black & Tans forced the local bishop to kiss their revolvers. The two men were transferred after John Dillon and the bishop complained about this and a court of enquiry was held at which General Tudor, the head of the RIC, was due to attend.[68] However, his party was ambushed on the way and the enquiry was never held.[69] The bishop had one of the more radical priests moved to the US to 'visit his brother for purely *ecclesiastical* reasons'. The new CI, a Major Foley, appointed in March 1921 upon Steadman's retirement, was happy that 'one of the strongest supporters of SF' had now gone, adding that another known IRA supporter, Fr Carney from Cong, was preparing to follow him.[70]

Despite the removal of more extreme voices among the clergy, support for SF was almost universal in Mayo, while those opposing them were unwilling to express their sympathies as was clearly shown in the May 1921 elections for home rule parliaments for Southern and Northern Ireland respectively. This was an attempt by the government to follow up on the 1914 Home Rule Act that was on the statute book and also a way to isolate the opposition in the northern unionist-dominated counties, thus enabling some sort of settlement with SF. For this election, proportional representation with multi-seat constituencies was used. Mayo was included in three new enlarged constituencies of Mayo North and West, Mayo South-Roscommon South and Sligo-East Mayo (see map 6).

The elections generated 'practically no interest' in Mayo. As in all other southern counties SF candidates were unopposed and declared elected without any votes having to be cast. It was lamented in the local papers that it was impossible to have 'impartial elections' but they united behind SF by adding that it was 'the intension of Nationalist Ireland to make the one for the South unworkable, and, if possible, also that for Ulster'. Some attention was given to the contested elections in the new Northern Ireland, but in relation to the Mayo elections the papers simply reported on the nominations and carried notices of those who had been elected. Most of the Mayo candidates were leading local IRA and SF men, including Tom Maguire, William Sears, Joseph MacBride and Thomas Derrig.[71]

The escalation in the conflict between IRA and the Crown forces increasingly affected civilian life, but actual fighting remained limited. As a result, the third phase of the conflict as defined by Townshend started very late in Mayo. The CI could still note in February 1921 that 'Owing to the continuous searches and raids that are being made by the combined forces of the Crown, the evil disposed are kept in such close touch that they are unable or unwilling to venture far in the way of outrages.' At the same time he realized that republicans were not going to abandon their hold without a struggle and were preparing a new offensive.[72]

The main obstacle remained a lack of arms. The frustration over this spilled over in the April 1921 report from the South Mayo Brigade, in which it argued they had enough men, including an ASU of twenty-five men, 'to make the place as hot as H——', but they had no arms. For the £300 they deposited with GHQ,

1 John Dillon MP, *c.*1915.

2 Joseph MacBride at Fairford, Glouchester in 1917 after his deportation.

3 Thomas Maguire, South Mayo IRA.

4 Bridget Walsh, member of Westport Cumann na mBan.

5 Cushlough Fife and Drum Band, 1910s.
6 Westport Sluagh – Fianna Éireann, Easter 1915.

7 Poster advertising concert in aid of arms fund, on Easter Monday night 1916.

Óglaiġ na h-Éireann

(IRISH VOLUNTEERS).

A GRAND

CONCERT

In aid of the

EQUIPMENT FUND

Of the

WESTPORT CORPS

Will be held in the

TOWN HALL, WESTPORT

On Monday Night, April 24th, 1916

Liam Mellows has been banished from Ireland, without charge and without trial. Why? If you are Irishmen do your bit for Ireland y supporting the Irish Volunteers. They have saved Ireland from Conscription and they will save it from Militarism

Admission: 2s. 1s. 6d. Concert commences at 8 o'c

A Ḋia Saor eir

Mayo News

8 (*below*) RIC officers, Westport.

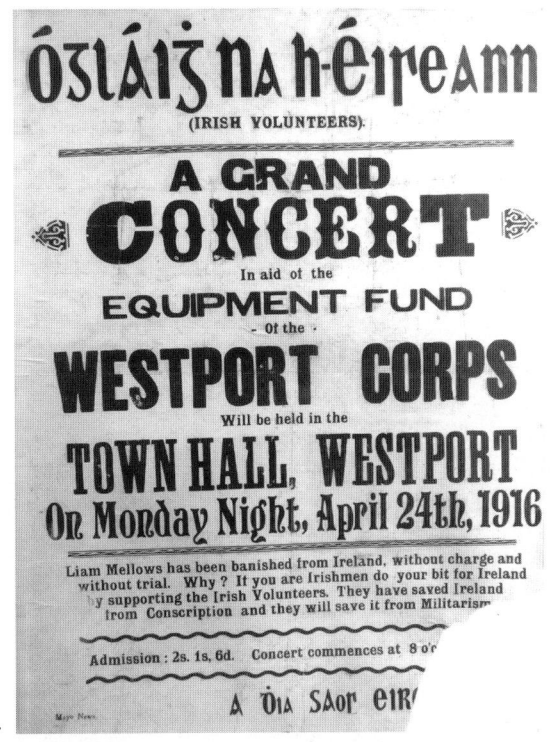

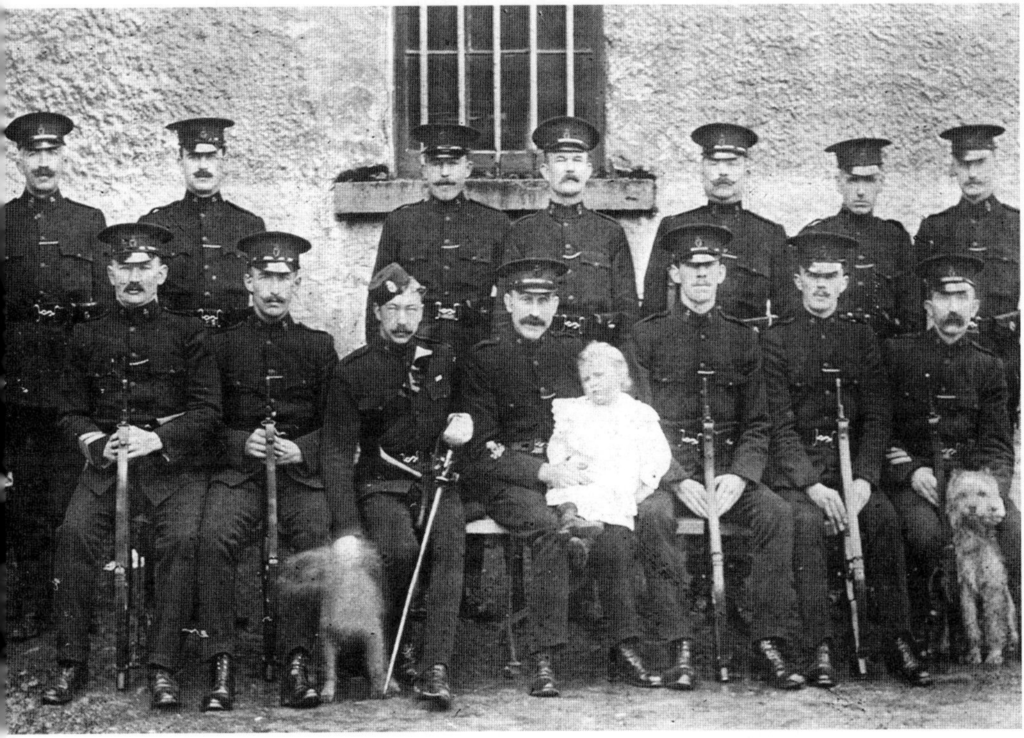

9 Auxilliaries based in Westport.

10 Castlebar Jail.

11 West Mayo Brigade Active Service Unit.
12 Bristol Fighter F4351 at Castlebar Aerodrome.

13 Broddie Malone, Rick Jones, Paddy Duffy and Butch Lambert.

14 Edward Moane, Jimmy Flaherty and Michael Kilroy with Lewis machine-gun captured at Carrowkennedy.

15 National army officers, including Joe Ring, with armoured car.

16 Funeral procession with National army soldiers for Joe Ring.
17 Home-made armoured car, named 'Queen of the West'.

all they had received were five Mauser rifles with 50 rounds in all. Furthermore, the brigade had no explosives to mine roads or to attack vulnerable police barracks. This prompted the question: 'Under the circumstances how can GHQ expect big results here?' Shortage of ammunition was so pressing that the West and North Mayo Brigades ordered their men to ensure that every operation returned an amount of ammunition at least equal to that expended. In one of the ambushes of the West Mayo Brigade ASU, some men were even forced to throw stones when their ammunition ran out.[73]

In autumn 1920 the IRA had already initiated another concerted campaign to collect any remaining arms in civilian hands. This followed information received by GHQ of an impending effort by the Crown forces to ensure no arms were left in civilian hands.[74] Until then arms were mostly taken from those who were friendly to the movement, but now the IRA became more forceful and the operations more risky. The houses of the local gentry became a target as they were often 'the property of men holding fairly high rank in the British Army'.[75] Opposition was encountered in some houses as Paddy Kelly related:

> We had good fun raiding two loyalist houses. The occupants barred all doors, so that we had to improvise a battering ram to force the door of one, and another, who lived very near and in sight of the RIC barracks, would not admit us. A ladder was procured and entry made through a window when, after a swift search, his gun was collected.[76]

In another case a Volunteer was shot in the stomach when raiding a house near Tibohine in the Ballaghaderreen area, later dying of his wounds. 'We informed the owner of the house that we were going to shoot him for this, but he accommodated us by clearing out of the country shortly afterwards'. Other owners asked for assurances that the guns 'would be returned to him when the Trouble was over'. Inexperience again posed present danger during these raids. During one search a Mills bomb was found and a Volunteer, unaware of what it was, put it in his pocket until informed of the danger by a comrade who was an ex-soldier.[77]

The number of arms acquired through raids was meagre so other avenues were pursued. In September 1920 the Mayo Brigade sent a deputation to Britain to buy weapons there. A quantity of rifles and revolvers was acquired but getting them to Ireland was difficult. When they attempted to use the smuggling line setup by GHQ, called the 'headquarters route', Michael Collins was 'enraged at our going independently to England without permission from Headquarters as he maintained this would upset the market and our channels of supplies.' He duly confiscated the arms, none of which ever went to Mayo. A second attempt, with permission from GHQ, ended similarly when the arms procured were 'borrowed' under duress for some operations in Cork but never returned, causing angry protest from the Mayo officers. A small number of arms were bought by individual Volunteers going abroad and smuggled home successfully.[78]

Many local units tried to supplement their limited supplies with military equipment of their own making. Most made buckshot for shotguns and some tried to make .303 rifle ammunition. Others assembled grenades or mines. In east Mayo 'road mines were filled with gelignite, or rather provision made for that purpose'. Due to a lack of explosives many of the mines were actually dummies, but this could still be effective: 'We cut a trench across the road at Tullyhill and placed dummy mines in the road. The Tans came along to this and spent several hours there before they discovered that the mines were dummy'. In west Mayo they only made grenades. As Kettrick put it: 'We did not go in for mining the roads or making land mines. Our strategy was a hit and run affair.'[79]

The most effective way to obtain arms was to take them from the police. Overpowering a police barracks was, however, increasingly difficult. Vulnerable posts had been abandoned and the defences of remaining barracks were reinforced. Sometimes this amounted to barbed wire and sandbags but in other cases, such as Partry, the windows were fitted with steel shutters and a wire net to keep out grenades. The RIC also made access to adjoining buildings possible as a means to escape when under attack, and sawed the floorboards on the upstairs to enable them to drop grenades.[80] Efforts to protect police barracks were frustrated when building materials were prevented from arriving. In Ballina, the IRA removed shutters from the train station store and dumped them in the River Moy.[81]

Bringing mines into operation against these increasingly well-protected barracks was a challenge. A large mine consisting of a beer barrel filled with gelignite and concrete was prepared for an attack on Ballaghaderreen barracks in February 1921 by a combined force of the Sligo and East Mayo Brigades. The bomb was hidden in a cart of hay and placed opposite the barracks, to be pushed against it that night. There are conflicting versions of what happened next, but the operation was called off at the last minute as contrary to expectations, the police were patrolling the town. When the bomb was later detonated by the police in a bog it caused an explosion so powerful it was felt up to ten miles away.[82]

Despite the lack of armaments, the institution of ASUs did eventually lead to more open confrontation. Initially, the main concern had been staying safe. In south Mayo, the ASU 'camped out in the woods in felt tarred shelters to keep out the rain, straw beds with bed clothes given to us by the people.'[83] In less supportive areas, such as around Balla, men on the run spent much of their time in dugouts, but most ASUs tried to evade the police by moving from one safe area to another.[84] Local people provided the ASUs with supplies and entertainment in the form of music and dance, some made them feel particularly at home:

There was a great house, Pat Joyce's of Durlis at the back of Croagh Patrick in Drummin, and they'd kill a sheep each the Joyce's and a few ducks whenever we came, for there [were] no women in the house. Kettrick was in bed one morning and he walked to the door 'It's a great house he said you can have a piss from the door'.

Although the brigade tried to pay for supplies, the needs of the ASUs could be onerous: 'The county people are being weary of the Flying Columns as they eat everything they have.'[85]

The main preoccupation of the ASUs soon became staging an ambush. The successes of the IRA in other counties and stories of maltreatment of family and friends during police searches, although sometimes exaggerated, inflamed some column men. We 'asked to be allowed into Ballina to see if we could do anything in the line of having a pot-shot at members of the RIC who were continually raiding our homes and abusing our people.' The local Volunteers were considered too well known to engage in this, so men from another battalion were brought in to attack the police. However, RIC patrols numbered about sixteen and marched in extended formation, which made IRA officers consder it too dangerous to hold them up or ambush them.[86]

The inexperience of the men also hampered open fighting. A number were put out of action by accidental shootings. Before ever engaging the enemy, the Westport Battalion ASU killed two of their own. Several ambushes failed when men accidently fired their weapons prematurely, or sometimes deliberately to prevent reprisals on local people. A member of the Beakin company inadvertently shot his officer in the face at the ambush site, while an ambush attempt in the Louisburgh area was cut short when, as Paddy Kelly recalled, 'a revolver was discharged accidentally, the bullet passing through A. Harney's stomach and lodging in my arm.'[87] Fear also affected the men during ambushes. Some forgot to fire altogether and started praying, while one swallowed his cigarette in the excitement. A former policeman, who had joined the South Mayo ASU with a supply of Mills bombs, showed his anxiety during the Partry ambush: 'The ex-RIC man ... must not have known to remove the pin because they [Mills bombs] were rolling down the road like pebbles and not exploding.' In extreme cases men deserted. According to Ernie O'Malley, this happened three times during operations of the West Mayo ASU. Only the strong bonds of friendship that evolved in the columns, he argued, prevented the court-martial of those concerned.[88]

There were ways to overcome fear. Some sang songs as during the Carrowkennedy ambush when 'Kelly the boy from Killane' sounded during the fighting. It was also fairly common to resort to alcohol before and after going into action. Michael Hughes recalls how after picking men for a raid in Castlebar, they arrived at Mickey Walsh's pub on the Newport Road and in we went. I ordered 13 pints of stout although I had no money to pay for them. He understood who we were. I said to the men that we might never be together again and to enjoy a drink. Most of these lads never put a glass to their lips before but on this occasion each man drank his pint.

Not all officers approved of this approach: 'Michael Kilroy had an antipathy towards us Westport fellows. We were a bit too tough, Rabelaisian and irreverent for Michael's puritanical mind. In fact, some of them even drank, and in Kilroy's sight nothing could be expected from a drinker.'[89] Kilroy was indeed widely known to be somewhat puritanical and was also older than the other activists but was not able to enforce a ban on drinking. It took an incident, afterwards named 'the night of the long bottles', in which alcohol abuse seriously endangered their lives, before he could accomplish this. Although all ASU men then took the pledge, their hearts were not in it: 'Someone asked what was to be done with the whiskey now that all had the pledge, when in a fierce whisper from Kettrick came the words: "Give me that bloody bottle".' Kettrick was also responsible for organizing having meat on Fridays to tease Kilroy.[90] In general, Kilroy stood out for his particularly serious and diligent approach to the fight and the fighting.

Slowly the number of violent incidents increased in 1921 and involved some minor attacks on policemen, primarily in south and west Mayo and the area around Ballina. The first ambush that resulted in fatalities took place on 7 March in Partry, where the south Mayo men under Tom Maguire engaged a military patrol that they practically stumbled on, killing one soldier and wounding three.[91] The first engagement in west Mayo, on 22 March, was also the result of coincidence. Three brigade officers, who were walking along the Oughty road, were approached from the rear by some unsuspecting policemen on bicycles. When they came close the IRA turned around and fired, resulting in the wounding of two policemen, after which the others surrendered. This small 'victory' gave a great boost to ASU morale, but no further engagements took place for a while: 'All our planning, debating, marching and counter-marching had seemed so much waste of time.' Keen to start a fight, some Westport ASU members wanted to go into town to attack the police or military there but this was opposed by some officers as 'it flavoured too much of Dublin tactics'.[92] In east Mayo, an ASU did go into Ballaghaderreen two or three times to snipe at the police barracks, but with no results.[93] The ASUs in north Mayo were more reluctant to act given they had 'the worst fighting ground in Ireland, flat country, dominated by two hills, no cover, not a solitary bush.'[94]

In May a flurry of successful ambushes finally occurred. The first took place at Tourmakeady where sixty Volunteers from the local Ballinrobe Battalion and the South Mayo ASU occupied the village on the morning of 3 May, rounded up all the (mostly Protestant) villagers, and awaited the arrival of a police patrol.

The ambush itself was relatively successful. The patrol was overcome after four policemen were killed and two wounded, but the aftermath was disastrous. A post office worker who had been left in his post to prevent suspicion, immediately wired Ballinrobe and a big counter operation followed with military units moving in from Ballinrobe, Castlebar and Westport. To prevent the men from being captured, ASUs from north and west Mayo and Galway were called in to break the encirclement. They came too late to make a difference, as an army patrol caught up with the South Mayo ASU on the Partry Mountains. In the subsequent shoot-out Michael O'Brien, brigade adjutant, was killed and Commandant Maguire seriously wounded. This loss of leadership meant that no other serious attacks were attempted in south Mayo before the truce.[95]

Despite a head-start in terms of early activity and armaments, the west Mayo men did not conduct a successful ambush until early May. First, an attempt near Islandeady ended in disaster. A local party digging a trench after a military patrol had passed, to prevent reinforcements coming from Castlebar, were surprised when the patrol suddenly turned back. In the ensuing engagement, two local Volunteers were killed and two others arrested.[96] To force an engagement three ASU members were subsequently allowed to go into Westport to stage an attack. On 8 May they positioned themselves on the railway bridge over Mill Street 'armed with short-arms and a good supply of bombs'. Eventually, a patrol approached from McGreal's public house on the Westport side of the bridge:

> I went to the other side of the bridge, where they would emerge, let the first pair go on about 20 yards and then dropped the first bomb. It seemed an eternity before it went off but it did. The explosion was soon drowned in the sound of the other bombs going off. The night was made hideous by the shouting of wounded police and windows being broken in the houses.

In the attack six policemen were wounded.[97]

This incident was soon followed by two more ambushes. On 19 May a part of the ASU took up position at Kilmeena, while a few men were sent into Westport and Newport to stage a diversion. It was hoped reinforcements would be sent from one town to another if an attack succeeded. In Newport, Sergeant Butler was shot from long range after which reinforcements were indeed sent from Westport. When they reached Kilmeena some of the ASU had fallen asleep, tired from a long night's march and having waited in position since early morning. The results were disastrous; although one constable was killed and a head constable wounded, the machine-gun used by the military caused havoc, killing four Volunteers and wounding several others. Although six Volunteers were arrested and seven rifles were lost, most men got away: 'We commandeered any available horses, strapped our wounded on them and started the long trek across country through very rough terrain to Nephin Mountain'. Hiding from their pursuers, the dejected men ended up in Skirdagh where the ASU was again surprised on 23 May. Although most again got away safely, one Volunteer and a policeman were killed.[98]

The ASU had more success a week later, when Volunteers noticed two RIC lorries going towards Galway, which presented an opportunity to lay an ambush on their return journey. The ASU lay in wait at Carrowkennedy. When the first lorry arrived, it was stopped by shooting the driver. After some exchange of fire a grenade went off inside this lorry, and the men surrendered, leaving six constables and DI Stevenson dead. Those in the second lorry had taken cover in a nearby house, but they also surrendered when threatened with machine-gun fire and the shooting of their wounded comrades. The lorries were subsequently burned, but a machine-gun, several rifles, revolvers and a great deal of ammunition were captured.[99]

In north Mayo the local unit was less successful in encountering the enemy: 'We knocked around Crossmolina, Dooliage and Bangor hoping to contact lorries of British forces going to Belmullet.' The most memorable action was an attempt on the life of DI White in Ballina on 25 May. The men in command of police units like sergeants and DIs were often deemed responsible for anti-IRA operations or the abuse of their sympathizers and were consequently often targeted by the IRA. White had been observed going off towards Enniscrone in a car with his wife and a RIC driver. An ambush was quickly laid in which an exchange of fire ensued, wounding White. The attacking party subsequently stayed the night locally due to curfew, and were surprised the following morning by a police search party. Rather than surrender, the IRA ran out the back door. Two got away but Thomas Hawley, a local shop-assistant, was seriously wounded. Soon afterwards, the activity of the ASU was effectively ended, when they were surprised in bed by the police, resulting in one dead Volunteer and six men captured.[100]

Apart from a failed attempt at taking the Ballaghaderreen barracks in February, no major operations took place in east Mayo either. Volunteers on the run appeared to have mostly remained locally. The small ASU brigade became largely inactive after their commandant was killed while surveying an ambush position at Crossard, but also as a result of infighting following disciplinary measures against one of them.[101] The most telling activity consisted of a number of sniping attacks, including one in which they commandeered a train under steam and drove past the barracks in Ballaghaderreen twice while shooting. Two policemen were believed to have been hit in the attack, but two Volunteers were arrested later that day. In fact, the situation in north and east Mayo was considered so safe the police reopened four barracks that had been closed earlier.[102]

The sudden burst of violent conflict in the spring of 1921 forced the ASUs to wind up. The countermeasures of the military, including the arrest and killing of leading officers, combined with the lengthening days, had made their existence increasingly dangerous. Activity by the Crown forces after the Carrowkennedy ambush included search parties of military that for the first time used spotter planes. This forced the ASU to hide in the quiet area around Bohola in the East Mayo Brigade area. On returning to west Mayo, it was decided to disband the unit for safety reasons. Although the search parties continued, none of the men were caught.[103] As a result, there was effectively no ASU in operation in Mayo from about mid-June 1921, and no more major incidents took place.[104]

Before a new form of activity could be found for the men on the run, the conflict came to an end when a truce was called for midday on 11 July. Local activists were informed about it by a courier from GHQ in early July, after which they decided to suspend operations totally as 'it would be next to dishonourable to attempt' any.[105] Although rumours had circulated for some time in the local press, most men were surprised: 'No one ever thought that the mighty England would sign or agree to a Truce with a band of practically untrained and almost non-armed men whom previously they had always referred to as robbers and murderers.' The men on the run were 'glad for the respite – glad to get home to see our people and to get proper rest and regular meals once again and to fall asleep without a "gun" in our hand.'[106]

Despite the late surge in violence, the conflict had been of relatively low intensity in Mayo. The county came tenth in the numbers of fatalities per county with forty-five people dying by violence in the course of the entire conflict between the beginning of the Easter Rising and the end of 1920, well ahead of Sligo with eighteen, but substantially behind Galway and Roscommon with sixty-two and sixty-five respectively. More specific figures for the period from January 1920 until the truce showed that there were forty casualties among the Crown forces, either killed or wounded, and twenty-two in the IRA. This compared to 163 losses among the police and military in Dublin city, and 114 in a more active county like Tipperary. In Mayo twenty of the twenty-two IRA and half of the Crown force casualties occurred in the last three months of the conflict, unlike elsewhere where casualties were spread out over the entire last year. Mayo also stood out in terms of the absence of civilian casualties. Newspapers reported the wounding of just six civilians and no fatalities, except among a number of men closely associated with the authorities, while in a county like Tipperary eighty-three non-combatants fell victim of the violence.[107]

7 'Glad for the respite – glad to get home to see our people and to get proper rest and regular meals': the anti-Treatyites take control, 1921–2

The truce conditions provided the opportunity for ASU members in Mayo and elsewhere to go home without fear of arrest and they were generally well received. The *Connaught Telegraph* observed that they 'looked remarkable well after their trying experiences.'[1] Celebrations were widespread but joy was mixed with uncertainty about the future. In many places bonfires were lit but mostly by children. As the *Freeman's Journal* put it: 'the truce has been received with joyousness, subdued by the knowledge that the nation may yet be called upon to suffer still more if the people's aspirations are to be realized.'[2] The late flurry of activity and the handful of successful ambushes had imbued the Mayo IRA with confidence and earned them local admiration. They built on this by enforcing their control, aided by the large-scale support for the movement in the county. Ultimately, this facilitated a take-over by opponents of the Anglo-Irish Treaty signed in December 1921.

Apart from the absence of violence, there were many practical benefits to the truce. As soon as it came into operation, the prohibition on fairs, markets and public meetings, and restrictions on the use of bicycles ended. On 13 July 1921 a fair was held in Castlebar which was well-attended and recorded a good trade in cattle and sheep, including one sale of 700 lambs for export. The economy picked up quickly. Although unusually dry weather affected most harvests adversely, the potato crop was a bumper one, leading to low prices and rumours of farmers refusing to bring their potatoes to market. The newspapers also contained many announcements of sport events, marriages and other expressions of a return to normal life.[3]

The local authorities attempted to resume regular business, even though they were still torn between their allegiance to the Dáil, declared after the local elections in 1920, and the need for British government funds. Money was a major problem. Much of the regular council work had been suspended during the fighting and a lot of the rates had not been paid as was made clear in the county council proceedings:

> This is most disappointing and unpatriotic, and those who take advantage of a crisis in our country's history to avoid their liability will soon find that it will not be to their advantage to have acted so cowardly at a time the popular public bodies were straining an effort to throw off the yoke of foreign rule.[4]

The problems for local government had become pressing. The success of SF and Labour in the 1920 elections led many councils to recognize the Dáil as the legitimate power in Ireland, which meant they lost their Treasury funding that made up nearly one-fifth of their revenue. Furthermore, they were often denied access to their funds in local banks. The IRA had to force the secretary of the Castlebar RDC, who had refused to recognize the authority of the Dáil, to hand over the council's money and books. Seán Gibbons, the IRA officer in charge, later argued that there 'were no threats of any kind and Mr Quinn, seeing I was firm about the matter, agreed to get the books and give me a cheque.' That armed men accompanied Gibbons may have proved decisive though.[5] The non-payment of rates added to the issues facing local government. In Sligo, the problem was alleviated when the IRA oversaw the collection but this was less successful in Roscommon and Mayo. Much local authority funding had to be used to compensate victims of the conflict. After the truce, the pressure was alleviated when Mayo County Council received a grant of £1,800 from the British War Department as compensation for damage done to the roads during the fighting.[6]

The main issue that confronted the county council was the amalgamation of eight previously abolished workhouses with the county hospital into one county home. This was ordered by the Dáil as a way of doing away with what was seen as a vestige of imperialist rule associated with the Famine. Mayo was the first county in Ireland to take this action. Under the scheme, all local workhouses were to be closed and the inmates, of whom there were 850 in 1911, concentrated in Castlebar. This, however, met with strong resistance from local guardians, particularly in Ballina and Swinford. They objected to the choice of the county as the unit of care, which meant that those in need living near the county border would have very far to travel.

A more serious issue with long-term detrimental implications for the whole of Ireland related to what was referred to as the future of unmarried expectant mothers and unmarried mothers who often ended up in the workhouse. It was claimed that the 'presence of this particular class would be a stigma on the status of the Central Home'. The suggested solution was to transfer these 'undesirables to some provincial or national institution, where their maintenance will be paid for, as far as possible, by their own labour'. In a move foreshadowing future scandals, the Magdalene asylums were suggested for this purpose. After long debate, the amalgamation scheme was implemented and all workhouses except that in Castlebar closed on 1 October. As soon as they were vacated, the IRA took control of most of them as local barracks.[7] On a lighter note, a request from the RIC to the council to be allowed to use the Castlebar courthouse for their New Year's dance was refused, although a suggestion was made to reconsider if they resubmitted the request in Irish.[8]

One of the immediate benefits of the truce for the IRA was the withdrawal of some of the additional Crown forces stationed in Mayo. For example, 500

Lancers, based near Swinford, were urgently ordered to relocate to Galway through an order delivered by 'airship'. Before their departure, the men enjoyed themselves in Castlebar where 'rather a remarkable scene' ensued when about twenty of them sang 'Slievenamon', 'Wrap the Green Flag Round me', and 'A Nation Once Again'.[9] When a party of Auxiliaries subsequently passed through Castlebar on motorbikes, they were heard to shout, 'Up Ireland. Up Sinn Féin'.[10] Not all the members of the Crown forces were so positive or probably ironic. The same Auxiliaries held a mock wake before leaving Ballina, following an impromptu open air concert by the local RIC, and objected to the display of SF flags as a breach of the truce. After consultation, the flags were removed.[11]

Many of the men involved in the recent spate of ambushes and other violent incidents before the truce were unsure what was to happen next. Tom Kettrick remembered feeling bewildered and Peter McDonnell recalled that the men did not go 'wild at the news. To say we were stunned would be nearer the mark'.[12] During the first days of the truce the two sides were stand-offish but also curious. When the ASU from Westport came home the local police were keen to check them out: 'The Auxiliaries, a Company of which were in Westport – all ex-British officers – were anxious to ascertain what kind of men they had been sent to oppose and, from the reports I gathered, were extremely annoyed when they discovered how young the members of the Flying Column were.'[13]

Generally, the fighting men were optimistic. The ASUs in west and south Mayo had successfully evaded the large-scale searches of late June and early July, and the west Mayo ASU had greatly improved their stock of arms, including the capture of a machine-gun, enough for arming a second brigade ASU. It was widely assumed there would be another round of fighting: 'None of us took it that the war was over for long and assumed that the peace would be only temporary.'[14] Their experiences also gave them a lot of confidence: 'Man for man we believed we could match and beat any force the British might send against us and outwit them at their own game.'[15] This optimism even extended to the less successful men in east Mayo:

> We believed that, given any kind of a decent chance, even when the odds were very much against us, we could beat them every time; our men were hardier and more wily, and we had a tradition of suffering and hardship behind us and had all to gain and very little to lose. We were fighting for an ideal on a voluntary basis while they were professional soldiers only.[16]

Remarkably, the truce was initially well observed, despite the feelings generated by the conflict and recent loss of comrades. The IRA was seen drilling in remote places throughout the county, but the only indictable offence in July after the truce was the kidnapping of three men by the IRA, probably on suspicion of cattle stealing.[17] Even the regular assizes operated again with enough people turning up for jury duty despite the earlier ban on it by the Dáil. To keep the peace between the two sides, liaison officers were appointed by the IRA for 'securing the observance of the Truce and carrying out the "cessation arrangements".' For Mayo and Galway this was the Dublin GHQ officer and TD Michael Staines, who subsequently asked the Mayo men Joe Ring and later Seán Gibbons to be his assistants. The liaison officers were to stay in constant touch with their counterparts in the Crown forces to avoid escalation by investigating any breaches of the truce. During the following months, these ranged from serious outbreaks of fighting to petty incidents, like the confiscation of a shotgun and an air rifle from a Volunteer when the RIC came to collect a fine for riding a bicycle without a light while engaged in IRA work.[18]

The co-operative attitude was aided by the release of the high-profile interned and imprisoned men. In early August the Mayo members of the Dáil, including Dr John Crowley, Patrick Joseph Ruttledge, Joseph MacBride, Thomas Derrig, and William Sears, were put on a train to Dublin still in their prison gear of 'Hamar' suits and heavy awkward boots.[19] Ordinary Volunteers, however, remained imprisoned. Early in September at least eight of them escaped from Rath prison camp in the Curragh, with some Mayo men among them.[20] In early October there were consistent calls for the release of these internees. The county council, which had six of its members still in prison, called on de Valera to withdraw the plenipotentiaries negotiating a peace in London unless all political prisoners were released unconditionally, but the British authorities wanted to wait until after an agreement was reached.[21] The first releases eventually came at Christmas time after the signing of the Treaty, when fifty men were welcomed by parades, torchlight processions and marching bands.[22]

The uncertain outcome of the negotiations started after the truce clearly affected local conditions. In August the Killala branch of the Irish National Teachers' Organization unanimously decided 'to leave matters in abeyance pending the negotiations of the Peace Conference', as 'in all probability when a settlement comes there will be a reconstruction'. As a result, no resolutions were brought forward or discussed.[23] By mid-August, when negotiations between de Valera and Lloyd George were making little progress, some desperation entered the previously optimistic tone of the local press. The *Western People* spoke of 'profound disappointment' among 'the people of this country, who were led to expect that considerable progress had been made towards rapprochement'. The offer of dominion status for two separate parts of Ireland was seen as the stumbling block at this point. During the following weeks the desire for peace and some anxiety were defining features of local newspaper editorials. After the two sides agreed on a formula for negotiations at the end of September, there was renewed optimism about the likelihood that a settlement would be found.[24]

During the Treaty negotiations virtually no large-scale political rallies were organized in Mayo. Local TDs made few addresses but they were actively involved in organizing the IRA and running the Dáil institutions. Derrig toured his constituency and spoke at different meetings of local bodies. He did not reveal his preferences for the outcome of the negotiations. Instead, he encouraged the continuation of the boycott of Belfast and British products and promoted the use of the Irish language and Irish products. In this, he laid great stress on the important role of women. To ensure the nation was united behind the delegates whatever the outcome of the negotiations would be, he called on everyone to (re-)join the local SF branches, which he claimed had collapsed due to the emphasis on the IRA. The largest congregation of Mayo TDs was at an aeridheacht in Castlebar on 15 October when six TDs attended. The speakers lauded the role of the Mayo IRA who they claimed had played their part in forcing the British to the negotiating table. Apart from calling for the establishment of a free and independent Ireland that would be friendly to England, no political position was taken.[25]

The lack of progress in the negotiations caused some tensions in the IRA. Although the population enjoyed the new freedoms and were, according to the authorities, generally in favour of peace at any price, the IRA generally observed the truce but prepared for the possible resumption of war. In August it restarted the destruction of vacated RIC barracks; set up training camps, initially near Ballinrobe and Newport; and supplemented its depleted funds by house-to-house collections and dances. By September all parts of the county sported an IRA training camp to accommodate the large influx of new members and teach them basic drill and musketry. Although the RIC thought this was largely under compulsion, in the short term they felt it was positive as 'in out of the way places they [the young men from the towns] do not cause us much trouble.'[26]

Part of the preparations was the decision, taken at a meeting of all IRA brigade officers in Dublin immediately following the truce, to introduce a full divisional structure in the country.[27] The divisions, which were already functioning in the south, were meant to operate as a co-ordinating unit between the brigades and GHQ. The most successful military leaders in the region, Tom Maguire and Michal Kilroy, were respectively appointed commanders of the 2nd Western Division, which included the South and East Mayo Brigades as well as West Galway and South Roscommon, and the 4th Western Division, incorporating North and West Mayo as well as the Connemara Brigade. Both leaders had dedicated their lives to the movement and were locally acknowledged as particularly serious and dedicated men. Part of this reorganization was the decision to divide in two the North Mayo Brigade, which covered a very large area, by the creation of the Northwest Mayo Brigade. The influx of recruits during the truce gave these units at least the numbers to contemplate a new fight. In the autumn Maguire reported a strength of 2,420 men, rising to 3,507 by December. By then Kilroy could depend on 3,271 Volunteers. Arms were, however, still very limited. In September the various brigades claimed to have fewer than twenty good rifles each at their command, except for West Mayo, which possessed forty-six Lee Enfields and two machine-guns. Their munitions were supplemented with about fifty grenades and a stock of shotguns.[28]

This picture of active preparation did not apply to the East Mayo Brigade, which was riven by an internal split. The discord was serious enough for two officers from GHQ to be dispatched in August to investigate the matter. Two issues divided the men. One had arisen after the Kiltimagh company under Thomas Ruane had confiscated some petrol from the railway station stock in the summer of 1920 and given it to people whom Ruane claimed had lent them a motorcar. As this was considered private benefit, he was ordered to return the petrol and apologize. When he refused, he was court-martialled by the brigade staff and dismissed, leaving some disgruntled men. At about the same time the brigade adjutant had been accused of cowardice by Éamon Corbett, an officer from Galway who had moved to the area for safety. The same visiting GHQ men held a court-martial on the adjutant and found him good at administration but incompetent as a fighting man and as having furthered private interests. They recommended his dismissal and ordered Corbett to return to Galway. The accusation had created bad blood, and when Corbett revisited the area on 20 November, he was attacked by a local man. This led to a shoot-out at the railway station in Kiltimagh and the wounding of a female bystander. The entire Kiltimagh company was subsequently suspended, causing anger all around.[29]

Besides preparing for renewed conflict, the IRA also attempted to extend the Dáil government structures, in particular the republican courts. In August men with republican police badges were for the first time observed taking over police tasks by controlling traffic at the Knock shrine. In north Mayo poteen-making was licenced and restricted by them to two people in each parish. If there were any complaints the license could be revoked. The RIC CI was unnerved by this increased activity: 'Ordinary police work is being done but we are hampered by the fact that there is a rival organization working in the same way.' The lenient attitude of the RIC towards republicans was challenged in December when they were taken to court by a local man. He was said to have been 'boiling with indignation' on seeing an RIC sergeant look on when a man was held up by the republican police: 'an illegal force'.[30]

The SF courts now operated as a full judicial system, including quarter sessions dealing with criminal cases, which up to then had been the almost exclusive domain of the established court system. On 14 October a notice was posted by the north Mayo IRA warning people not to take part in any 'enemy court' as plaintiff, defendant, witness or otherwise unless they had written permission of the minister of home affairs. Otherwise they were deemed 'guilty of assisting the enemy in time of war'. One unidentified woman, who had taken out a decree against another woman for burning down her house, was gently accosted and told: 'We have a court of our own ... why do you not come to us?'

Although generally SF court decisions were accepted, there were some grumblings, particularly in cases where it decided in favour of the interest of landlords. At one point two pro-SF tenants were evicted from their home by sixty Volunteers as the owner wanted to use the premises for starting a business.[31]

One of the first displays of SF popularity was at an aeridheacht held in Balla at the end of September at which all surrounding towns and villages were represented. The spectators, including a number of TDs, were treated to songs, dances and recitations, a drill display by the East Mayo Brigade, and an interbattalion tug-of-war contest. As the local TD William Sears put it: 'After all the alarms and the terrors of the past year or two the people were certainly entitled to any pleasure or amusement they could have.' In his speech he made no attempt to spare England which he held responsible for economic ruin, the death of the Irish language, the Famine and migration among other issues. The truce was called, he claimed, 'because men had rifles, and knew how to use them'. He then introduced Tom Maguire as the victor of Tourmakeady, who 'supported by two dozen men on the Partry Mountains, fought and put to flight 400 English troops, who left 50 of their comrades on the mountain side.' In reality only about twenty soldiers had engaged Maguire's column directly of which one was wounded. On stage, Maguire stepped forward in full uniform 'amidst salvos of cheers, repeated again and again, and it was several minutes before he could commence his speech, which he introduced in Irish.' A similar meeting the following week at the East Mayo Brigade training camp in Oldcastle drew an estimated 12,000 people. The local priests predicted renewed fighting as de Valera would not 'take the few crumbs Lloyd George was prepared to give'.[32]

The largest displays of republican power were witnessed at IRA funerals. In early October, Bangor saw what the police described as the largest turnout ever for a burial when Michael Healy, a local IRA officer who had died of natural causes, was brought to his grave. There was also a huge turnout for the reinterment of two ASU men from the West Mayo Brigade, Jim Duffy from Westport and Paddy Marley from Glenhest, Newport, who had been shot accidentally during the fighting.[33] Despite all this there was only one open confrontation between the IRA and the Crown forces before October. This occurred in Swinford when the IRA attempted to stop some young women emigrating to the US with the RIC interceding. With serious negotiations between the Dáil and the British government commencing in October the hold of the authorities on Mayo became increasingly tenuous, with the CI arguing that: 'Only its [the IRA's] murders are at an end'. Policemen observing the 'provocative displays of force' were frequently accused of spying and breaching the truce, making it difficult for them to function. The RIC actually accepted that they were on their way out and ceased drawing up full monthly reports and for the rest of the year simply tabulated the breaches of the peace.[34]

The uncertain conditions also began to affect the general population. A degree of lawlessness arose, with the number of robberies increasing. Disputes over land and labour were also again more prominent. Both authorities tried to deal with that through their court systems or by other means. Internal tensions in Kiltimagh meant decisions of the Dáil land courts that favoured the landlords were not enforced by the local IRA. Aggression against known loyalists also increased. Although armistice day was commemorated, it was reported that a local Catholic priest had publicly argued that Protestants should be dealt with like St Patrick had treated snakes. Relations were not aided by the first sittings of the official claims court at which victims from both sides testified about their sufferings during the previous years. The impression was that members of the Crown forces received more in compensation than republican-minded civilians. Charles Hughes, a local shopkeeper in Westport who had supplied the IRA, was awarded £3,257 for damages caused by the police to his shop, and £500 for personal damages, while Major Ibberson was granted £6,350 for injuries to his arm received during the Tourmakeady ambush. Sentiments were further inflamed in November when an inquiry into the death of Michael Tolan from Ballina, who had been killed by Auxiliaries in May and illegally buried in a bog, laid bare the extent of his mutilation after his disinterment. Tolan had been an intelligence officer of the IRA and summons server for the local SF court. He had been taken from his home and was probably murdered after being tortured on his way to Galway prison.[35]

The IRA also demanded much from the population. In a speech by Thomas Derrig on 21 November he urged older people and women to force shops to stock Irish and speak Irish, help organize SF, support Irish courts and the republican police, observe the Belfast and British boycott and prepare for war if negotiations fail. Observance of these demands did not happen without some pressure. A new republican tax on alcohol to pay for provisions for the IRA training camps met with some resistance. Some publicans simply raised their prices to cover it, whereas others refused to pay after it was stated in the British press that the tax was illegal. The proprietor of the Ballina Royal was subsequently visited by three armed men in uniform who asked him to pay the tax voluntarily. He agreed, but as the police justifiably observed, he had little option. Sometimes more than an implicit threat was needed. People wanting to emigrate, which was considered an act of treason by the IRA, were stopped and sometimes kidnapped. To facilitate this the IRA visited emigration agents in November to take the names of prospective migrants directly from their books.[36]

None of those affected seem to have gone to the RIC for protection. A man preparing to emigrate disappeared for a couple of days. On his return he was interviewed by the police but refused to give any information, only telling them that he was taken on a long journey and treated well. The same was true of a man taken by the IRA after he refused to drive them around in his motorcar, and of an employer who was intimidated by IRA members of the Motor Drivers' Union after he dismissed one of their members. When the IRA failed to punish the men responsible for the intimidation, the authorities saw an opportunity: 'If he does not get adequate satisfaction from the IRA he may be induced to give evidence.' This was a vain hope. Even a priest in Charlestown who was stabbed in October by Hugh Gregg, an IRA man whom he had denounced 'from the pulpit for having brought misfortune to a girl', was unwilling to make a complaint. Privately, he told them he was probably saved by wearing four layers of garments and the use of a clumsy knife. Three men were subsequently arrested by the IRA, but they refused to hand them over to the RIC, which accepted 'that this should be left alone for the present.'[37]

The IRA's growing assertiveness worried the CI: 'The non-interference with these "acts of Government" is tantamount to recognizing the Irish Republic.' Indeed, it became increasingly difficult for the authorities to fulfil their duties. When the Belmullet IRA started to patrol the streets, trying to control drunkenness and clear the streets of an RIC presence, this became too much for the local police. They were willing to close their eyes for 'whatever duty these so-called police might do out in the bogs', but 'we would not give them an opportunity nor allow them to do duty shoulder to shoulder with us in the streets of Belmullet.'[38] Some policemen took matters into their own hands. After a home-made bomb exploded on Sunday 10 December at midnight in Ballina, shattering a few windows, a policeman and a civilian were arrested by the local IRA. Only after direct instructions from their brigade commandant were they handed over to the RIC, who subsequently took disciplinary action. In the same week a prominent Volunteer returning home from being on the run was fired at in Ballina by unknown assailants.[39]

To make the new republican authority visible for all, buildings, including the abandoned workhouses in Westport, Ballina and Swinford, and some vacated police barracks, were occupied and used as IRA barracks, republican police stations and courthouses. According to the truce provisions, the IRA were not allowed to display arms, but the RIC in Westport reported that: 'It is stated machine-guns are posted on the upper windows' of the workhouse, which they considered 'a grave menace to the peace … intended to intimidate Crown Forces.' Attempts at enforcement of the truce regulations were not appreciated. When two RIC officers visited the occupied workhouse in Ballina they were treated with 'utmost disrespect'.[40]

The hesitancy both sides displayed during the months of treaty negotiations was directly related to the uncertainty of its outcome. This came sharply into focus when a Treaty was signed by Irish and British representatives on 6 December, which gave Ireland dominion status but not a republic. Reaction in the press was positive. Even the overtly pro-SF *Mayo News* declared that 'The Treaty of Peace is the crowning victory of the Sinn Féin movement.'[41] The local

TDs who had to vote on the Treaty in the Dáil were more divided. P.J. Ruttledge came out against it and stated that he stood for uncompromising principle, while Joseph MacBride argued that the Dáil should follow the country, 'the people to whom the members of the Dáil owed their position', in favour of the Treaty.[42]

Most elected representatives sided against the Treaty, but there was a concerted effort detectable by vested interests to sway them. Mayo newspapers reported that Bishop Michael Fogarty of Killaloe publicly announced that the Treaty was worthy of all the sacrifices. Michael Lavelle, the vice-chairman of the county council, called on TDs to heed the voice of the people through their representatives on the popularly elected bodies. Now the Dáil was divided 'it was for the people to use their own discretion and openly express their views'. Many established bodies also made their position known. The North Mayo Farmers' Association, for instance, unanimously called on Dáil Éireann to ratify the Treaty because 'rejection would be fraught with the gravest danger to the country' and local TDs should, 'act in accordance with the unanimous wishes of their constituents'. Public meetings were organized in every parish under direction of the bishops and presided over by local priests. Most of them backed the settlement. Towards the end of the debates in the Dáil in January tensions rose. At a meeting in Castlebar called by the Farmers' Union, tempers frayed. Bags of flour were thrown at Lavelle by a group of young men who objected to his pro-Treaty stance, while others shouted they would not be dictated to by ex-British soldiers. After order had been restored by local Volunteers, a resolution calling for a united stance was carried, regardless of what that stance would be.[43]

In the Dáil debates, Mayo TDs were relatively quiet. One of the most vocal in his support for the Treaty was William Sears. He warned if the Dáil rejected the settlement 'that assembly would be guilty of the greatest act of political folly that was recorded in history.' Commenting on those opposed to the Treaty, he claimed 'You have not the people behind you because it is madness sheer madness. They know a good thing when they see it. And they have a good thing in the Treaty.' John Crowley opposed the Treaty because of the threat of immediate and terrible war that Lloyd George had issued if it was rejected. All who elected him were 'in their hearts Republicans', and if given a free choice they would vote for a republic. Dr Francis Ferran, TD for Sligo–Mayo East, concurred, arguing that the Treaty brought discord to a people once united in their fight for liberty.[44]

Over Christmas most TDs returned home where they were further pressured to vote in favour, most of them finding that more than half of local SF members supported the Treaty. The clergy played an active role in this. Tom Maguire, who stayed in Dublin to convalesce, was approached by priests who were encouraged by Archbishop Gilmartin of Tuam to use their influence. The IRB was another vehicle used to drum up support for the Treaty. The organization, which had been largely dormant during the War of Independence, was revived after the truce. Seán Ó Murthuile had come from Dublin in the autumn to replace the pre-1916 generation with men who had come up during the struggle, appointing them as centres for the four brigade areas in Mayo. Maguire replaced Dick Walsh, who had collapsed from physical exhaustion, as centre for south Mayo. The IRB supreme council now pressured Maguire to vote in favour, but he refused. Five of the seven Mayo TDs eventually voted against the Treaty, with only MacBride and Sears supporting it. Daniel O'Rourke TD for South Mayo–South Roscommon admitted he opposed the Treaty on principle but had voted in favour because of popular opinion.[45]

Despite the passing of the Treaty in the Dáil by 64 votes to 57, the local press remained worried about the implications. The *Connaught Telegraph* argued that acceptance of the Treaty was the will of the majority and that rejection would be an 'act of madness'. Although showing understanding for those who had pledged to a Republic and voted against, it lamented the cleavage that had developed in the movement and called upon all to unite. It appeared a majority in Mayo wanted an end to fighting, but the greater majority of the IRA, both leaders and men, including the many newly joined 'Trucileers', were anti-Treaty. These anti-Treatyites also had a majority on most local bodies, including the county council. For the time being, their opposition was expressed in small ways such as refusing to put in effect the summer time introduced by the Provisional government. With the internal divisions extending to the political and military leadership in Dublin, confusion was rife. The British authorities nevertheless started to hand over control to the new Provisional government led by Michael Collins, which was not accepted as legitimate by those opposed to the Treaty in Mayo.[46]

This confusion created space for other interests to assert themselves and made it difficult for the anti-Treaty IRA, who were now effectively in control of the county, to maintain order. British intelligence reports were positive about Maguire, who was not regarded as 'an extremist; he rules his area justly, and stops profiteering by the shopkeepers.' Crime, in particular simple robberies, nevertheless increased. Labour disputes also seemed to be more prevalent and to some extent mixed with the new political conflict. The dismissal of an apprentice by the Davis Bros. firm in Crossmolina in February caused a strike by the ITGWU and serious violence by the workers. An egg shed belonging to the brothers was burned down and the tails of twenty-six cows owned by one of their supporters were cut off. The situation deteriorated to the extent that the IRA felt forced to declare martial law locally.[47] The fight over control of the land also escalated. Some saw their opportunity to regain farms they had been evicted from or to force the break-up and sale of remaining estates and grazier farms. Cattle driving became rife, farms were burned down, and people were intimidated. One farmer was 'compelled to go down on hands and knees and swear that he would give up lands he purchased many years ago'. In the most serious case, a girl was killed and her sister wounded when a group of armed men came to their farm near Straide to intimidate their father and brother into giving up the property. Father and son got away through the back door as the girl stalled the intruders before shots were fired. The republican police subsequently made seven arrests and the case was heard by 'the Republican Circuit Court in Swinford'.[48]

The response of the IRA was not always straightforward. In extreme cases, such as around Crossmolina, Castlebar and Newport, martial law was imposed to restore order. This compelled everyone to remain indoors between 11 p.m. and 6 a.m. Lands forcibly taken were to be vacated, and anyone responsible for trespassing, breaking fences, and commandeering was warned they would be severely dealt with. In other areas, the IRA took the opposite position. In May the IRA in Ballycastle district seized a Protestant-owned 500-acre farm, announcing that in future it was 'to be worked for the benefit of the Belfast Expelled Workers' Fund'.[49] In an effort to generate support among small farmers, it was seemingly decided that land rents were no longer to be paid. The chairman of a parish court in Castlebar, where tenants were charged with non-payment of rent by the local landlord, Mrs Pratt, dismissed the case after the chairman read out an instruction from the local IRA commander. The solicitor for the landlord objected vehemently: 'there will be an end to all courts, and an end to liberty, if military officers are entitled to send notices to our courts as to what cases they will or will not hear. I will now ask the Court to protest also against this dictation from an autocracy.' Although the IRA stated afterwards that the non-payment of rent only applied in this case, many took it to be a general order.[50]

This growing social unrest was partly due to deteriorating economic conditions. An anonymous nurse active in Lady Dudley's Scheme for Nurses, which did relief work in Mayo, described the deplorable conditions of the poor in a letter to the *Irish Times* in early February. She claimed there were hundreds of starving and insufficiently clothed people: 'I have seen families with nothing in the house but a few potatoes, which they boiled and ate during the day – no milk, tea, or flour, or any means of getting it. Others have nothing but flour which they got from the White Cross Fund.' A family of five with a pregnant mother and an epileptic husband she was helping 'had nothing but black tea and awful bread made of water. The mother lay on a heap of straw at the fireside and had only a piece of blanket and a shawl to cover her. These were the only bedclothes they had for the whole family.' The children could not go to school either for want of clothes. None of the neighbours were in a position to help and the absence of employment and a functioning market, where they could sell their animals for a decent price if they had any, made the suffering extreme.[51]

To alleviate the distress a combination of private and public initiatives developed. Charities, like the Society of St Vincent de Paul, organized a sale for the poor in Castlebar and the local cinema organized a fundraiser in March. In the same month the Provisional government made some money available for relief of unemployment in Achill, Erris and parts of Swinford district that were badly hit by the lack of migratory work in Britain. In the following months, the Dáil allocated a further £40,000 for relief of distress in the union areas of Ballina, Belmullet, Swinford and Westport: 'it was represented to them that the death-rate [in Erris] was steadily rising, and the cause was that the people were dying of malnutrition.' Local authorities had also started to mobilize. In April a rate for the destitute poor was proposed by the county council. A decision to give road contracts to landless men and the smallest farmers did not, however, receive approval from the local government department as it 'would restrict competition and tend to make [the work] more expensive and less efficient'. The political divisions affected the allocation of government funds. After the county council had declared its support for de Valera, Ruttledge complained that money stopped flowing 'because they entertained certain views'.[52]

Despite the rising political and social tensions, ordinary life did continue as much as possible. Local bodies occupied their time with mundane issues, and individuals tried to maintain social standards or shape a new future. It was proudly reported in March that the Imperial Hotel in Castlebar had installed an electric powerplant, in which a petrol-powered engine automatically charged batteries if they became depleted by the 100 bulbs lighting up the hotel, the strongest of which sported '100 candle power'. The many GAA, Gaelic League and Irish-language classes that were organized in various places showed the growing dominance of Irish nationalism. In March Westport UDC suggested the removal of the statue of George Glendinning, an agent for Lord Sligo, erected in 1845 and that it be replaced with one of Major John MacBride. This took some time as Glendinning was still used for target practice by the National army during the subsequent Civil War. In May a play was staged in Castlebar that recounted the ambushes of the ASUs in west and south Mayo during the War of Independence.[53]

A divisive issue that demonstrated the rising tensions between pro- and anti-Treaty supporters were the payments of debts incurred by the IRA during the War of Independence. Already in October 1921, Michael Kilroy had asked GHQ for funds to pay off shopkeepers and others to whom they had given their word of honour. He claimed the IRA owed £2,200 to grocers and £1,200 to drapers and needed £200 for travelling expenses. In March 1921 the issue came to a head when GHQ's suggestion to raise the money locally was taken up by the anti-Treaty dominated county council through the introduction of a special levy. The Dáil local government department then declared such a rate illegal but the majority on the council denounced the Provisional government and tried to force the issue. Following an exchange of insults about their opponents' commitment during the War of Independence, the minority pro-Treaty men, including the chairman, walked out, and the levy was accepted. The ministry of defence then offered to pay the arrears if the council recognized the Provisional government. The council would only accept the money if it came through the anti-Treaty IRA Executive now established in the Four Courts in Dublin. The levy was nevertheless withdrawn at the next council meeting and instead a sum of £2,000 was approved to be paid out from the council's accounts. With the advent of the Civil War, Kilroy eventually took the money from local banks, issuing them with receipts.[54]

The growing assertiveness of the anti-Treaty forces towards the RIC became more obvious during 1922. In December a series of murder attempts on RIC men was initiated. One of the first casualties was Constable Michael Slattery, who had come home to Ballyhaunis to spend Christmas with his wife and newborn baby. He was approached by an armed man with a red handkerchief across his face who asked him if he was Slattery and then shot him in the chest at point blank range. Early in 1922 two former RIC men were shot there, and another in nearby Crossard. Patrick Cassidy was shot four times but survived and was taken to Galway hospital where the IRA killed him in his bed. The evacuation of the RIC following the Treaty was also used as an opportunity to obtain their weapons. Officially, the police and military barracks were to be handed over to the local republican police, but a number of barracks were raided before the Crown forces left. In Swinford, the IRA simply walked into the barracks the night before it was abandoned and overpowered the police who were having a drink. In Charlestown a large group of IRA rushed the RIC contingent and beat them up. When they resisted, the sergeant was shot in the leg after he drew his baton. In both cases a large quantity of rifles and other items were taken. In other places the withdrawal was a more peaceful affair. The evacuation of Ballina RIC barracks in early February 'evoked loud cheers from a large crowd of spectators'.[55]

Some took advantage of the absence of law or law enforcement. A number of robberies took place in the spring of 1922, at least some by IRA men. Although it was claimed the money was for buying arms, occasionally it was used for other purposes. The most serious incident was a spree of robberies of nineteen houses, including two post offices, in one night by three drunken Volunteers, driven around by a hired chauffeur. During the trial in a SF court the men claimed not to remember any details, but one of them admitted that he had suggested they go out for a stunt after a night of drinking. They were very apologetic and promised to return the money. The IRA commander in charge of proceedings felt embarrassed and apologized 'for this regrettable and unfortunate occurrence ... They knew what the army stood for – it stood for principle, but the country was passing through a grave crisis, and, as in every army, some men were open to temptation.'[56]

To avoid negative impact from these cases, there was a tendency to censor the local press. A discussion had taken place about whether to allow the press into the proceedings in the case of the drunken spree. One reporter was asked not to publish anything pending an investigation, after six armed men had terrorized a family in Cornacool near Castlebar. In another case in January, the journalist Michael Tobin was arrested after reporting on a case in which a priest was criticized by Tom Heavey for releasing a Volunteer who had been chained to the church railings after failing to show up for sentry duty. The priest subsequently went to the bishop who spoke to Kilroy who publicly apologized. After the prelate stated at Mass that Heavey had been censored, the latter resigned from the IRA. An investigation by GHQ found that the arrest had been correct and that the newspaper headlines, which included the words 'Priest Threatened', were considered 'unnecessary, irritating and untrue'. The journalist was released and Kilroy asked Heavey to withdraw his resignation.[57]

The slowly developing split in the movement nationally was also evident in Mayo. Although the local IRA went almost entirely anti-Treaty, the newly developing military and police forces of the Provisional government made attempts to organize themselves locally in early 1922. This was led by the few prominent Volunteers who joined the National army or the new Civic Guards such as Joe Ring, who had replaced Staines as liaison officer in December, and Thomas Ruane, who had been expelled from the East Mayo Brigade. Ring actively used his IRA reputation to recruit an army battalion, locally known as 'Ring's Own'. To distinguish themselves he had special capes made for them. To stop this, anti-Treaty forces arrested Ring and two others in March. In a letter from prison published in the papers, Ring railed against this illegal act and announced that he was going on hunger strike until released. After a visit by Michael Collins, he was eventually released from Castlebar Jail on 13 April. On returning to his native Westport, he was received 'as a conquering hero', and told the crowd that he was 'happy with overwhelming majority registering their solemn protest against an act of despotic militarism'.[58]

The continuous recruiting efforts created further antagonisms. Young men who wanted to join the National army were actively prevented from doing so, some being arrested by the anti-Treaty IRA. Two brothers who had made their intention to join the National army clear were summoned to IRA headquarters in Ballinrobe in early June. When they did not turn up, a party of IRA dragged them from their beds and demanded an assurance that they would have nothing further to do with the army. When they refused they were kicked and beaten.[59]

On a number of occasions a military stand-off developed between the two sides. In early May, a crisis followed the attempted arrest of National army commander Symonds who had continued his recruiting efforts, despite having been previously arrested. The parochial house in Kilmaine where he stayed was besieged by the local IRA. He was eventually let go on order of Liam Lynch, the national anti-Treaty leader. Symonds was picked up by an armoured car, but on his way to Roscommon stopped in Ballinrobe where he demanded the release of six of his men and threatened force if necessary. This prompted a major mobilization of anti-Treaty forces, obliging the armoured car to withdraw. Similar near outbreaks of hostilities over comparable issues took place in Charlestown and Dromore West, but always led to the anti-Treaty IRA taking control. In this way the military presence of the Provisional government in Mayo was slowly marginalized.[60]

Wider efforts to avoid a conflict between the pro- and anti-Treaty sides also affected the IRA in Mayo. In March an exchange of weapons was agreed between the two sides so as to facilitate Provisional government support for action against the Ulster Special Constabulary in Northern Ireland. The government would provide the anti-Treaty IRA with British-supplied rifles and exchange them with those already in the hands of the IRA before the Treaty which would be sent north. The Mayo men drove a few lorries with rifles to a meeting point in Sligo, but the Provisional government side never showed up. This was possibly caused by a near outbreak of fighting in Limerick over control of the city. Anti-Treaty forces from all over the west and south, including about fifty Mayo men, rushed to Limerick, only to return after an agreement was reached.[61]

National politics also came to Mayo in early April when Collins visited Mayo as part of the campaign for the election of a new Dáil in June. In general, anti-Treatyites dominated the campaign and gave little space to those in favour of the Treaty. Given his popularity, it was not possible to prevent Collins from speaking in Castlebar. but on his journey there was told 'he would be torn to pieces if he entered Mayo'. On receiving a special address of welcome in Ballyhaunis signed by the parish priest and more than forty parishioners, he publicly claimed he would not be in any danger. Specials trains were organized from Athlone, Ballina, Ballinrobe, Tuam and Westport, but anti-Treaty forces made a concerted effort to prevent his supporters from attending by blocking the railway lines and the roads into Castlebar. As a result, only the train from Athlone arrived and just 2,000 people attended, which included a sizeable group of ardent republicans. The meeting itself ended in chaos. First, the podium, filled with about twenty 'priests and prominent gentleman from all parts of the county', had to be moved as young men inundated it with anti-Treaty pamphlets from the roof of the courthouse. When Collins stepped forward, he was cheered for some minutes but when he began to speak there was much interruption and the mention of the Provisional government was met with boos. Some sang 'The Soldier's Song' to prevent him from being heard. Collins reacted agitatedly, stating he would not 'support men who tried to murder people by tearing up railway lines' and calling anti-Treatyites, 'Green and Tans'.[62]

After a short time, a lorry forced its way through the crowd to the platform. On it stood Thomas Campbell, an anti-Treaty member of the county council from Swinford, who heckled Collins. This started a heated exchange during which some spectators were restrained by clergymen and women from attacking

Campbell. After a while, McCabe, one of Collins's bodyguards, pulled a gun after which a large number of local IRA men moved in to arrest McCabe. Charlie Byrne, another of Collins's men, then ran away pursued by the IRA. 'Panic ensued amongst a group of women and children, Some fainted and others screamed and became hysterical, but most of the crowd stood fast.' The commotion was not noticed on the periphery of the meeting where those engaged in playing three card trick and a shooting gallery simply continued. Eventually, Byrne was held up at a local hotel where he was found hiding under a bed, after accidently shooting the owner, Mrs Fogarty.[63]

The meeting was proclaimed by the IRA and Collins and his men retired to a local hotel. There they were besieged by the IRA who demanded they hand over McCabe to be court-martialled. This was refused. Collins's party was treated with a mix of admiration and aggression. The officer who had proclaimed the meeting came to explain to Collins that it was done in the interest of peace and no disrespect was meant, but added no one would be allowed to leave until McCabe gave himself up. After a while Collins, who seemed to have been incensed, asked for Kilroy. The latter ordered the guard to withdraw from the hotel but had a tiff with Collins over the arrest of Joe Ring for recruiting and over the payment of the debts the IRA had incurred locally. Collins asked for patience, but Kilroy told him: 'We can't forget that you hold the purse strings, and you're too close to them [the British].' Collins replied that it was the meanest thing a man ever said to another. Eventually, Byrne and McCabe were handed over, tried and acquitted, while Ring was released, formally on doctor's orders.[64]

The population in Mayo did not get a chance to make clear their stance on the Treaty. Under a pact signed on 22 May it was agreed that only sitting TDs would be proposed as candidates for the upcoming election, meaning there would effectively be no contests except if other parties fielded opponents. It was clear the local IRA wanted to prevent this from happening. Cases of intimidation of those intending to stand were reported in all Mayo constituencies (map 6). Some were visited by armed men and implored to withdraw. A local candidate in South Mayo–South Roscommon did so at the last moment 'in the interest of peace and harmony.' A man who took the train from Ballina to Westport to lodge nomination papers for the Farmers' nominee, Bernard Egan, was reported to have been kidnapped en route and his nominating papers burned. As a result, no alternative candidates were fielded and all sitting TDs, five pro-Treaty and eight anti-Treaty, were declared re-elected. Without a clear expression of opinion, uncertainty remained rife.[65]

The level of support for the anti-Treaty side in Mayo is thus hard to ascertain. It was clear the establishment including the churches and the press, which both accused anti-Treatyites of wanting to establish a Bolshevik republic in Mayo, were opposed to them as well as many local bodies. In a report on the political outlook of the people written by the liaison officer in the spring of 1922,

The anti-Treatyites take control, 1921–2

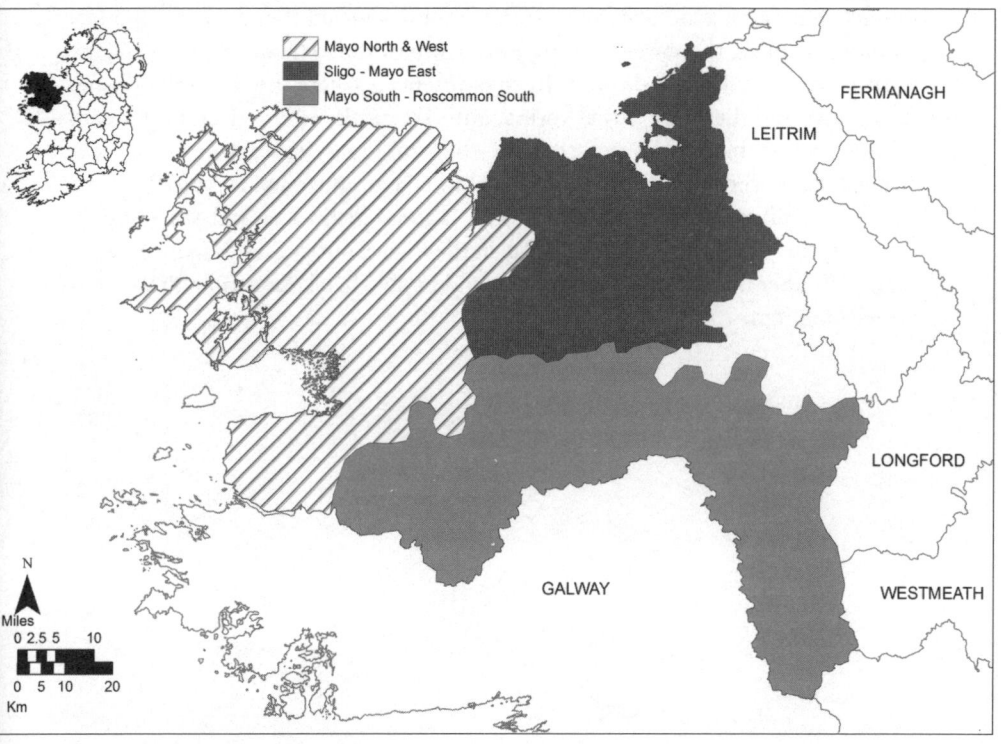

6 Parliamentary constituencies, 1922

it was argued that businesses and farmers were pro-Treaty, while young men were divided. It also suggested that anti-Treatyites were gaining ground with women in particular, who were said to believe that if they elected an outright republican party, the British would be afraid to invade. What was clear is that meetings with anti-Treaty speakers, including Constance Markievicz and de Valera, generally passed without interruptions in Mayo, while pro-Treaty meetings were often disrupted. In the run-up to the election, tensions rose. The most serious incident saw a woman shot near Charlestown after a political disagreement. To highlight the political nature of the attack, her coffin was escorted to the graveyard by National army troops. In a heated exchange in the Castlebar UDC, Joseph MacBride railed against the IRA becoming a law unto themselves. He stated that he had been fighting for a republic all his life but 'not the kind of a Republic that these creatures advocated, as it stinks in the nostrils of all thinking and patriotic people … There was no liberty or fraternity where a brat came out with a revolver and said: "You cannot have an opinion of your own".'[66]

After the June general election the anti-Treaty party was still supported by a majority of Mayo TDs and was militarily almost entirely in control of the county. The homogenous nature of Mayo politics meant that apart from a few prominent voices, there was little organized opposition to them. Nationwide, the anti-Treaty side did not do well. In constituencies where there were opposing candidates and therefore actual voting, anti-Treaty SF received 21.77 per cent of the vote against 38.48 per cent for the pro-Treaty side. As a result, the Provisional government was emboldened to take on the anti-Treaty IRA. The resulting civil war broke out when the National army attacked the national headquarters of the anti-Treatyite IRA in the Four Courts in Dublin on 28 June 1922. Whether the government forces would be able to take control of Mayo was widely doubted.

8 'Revolver government'?: a hotbed of republicanism, 1922–3

Initially the outbreak of hostilities in Dublin and elsewhere had little effect on Mayo. Some of the main Mayo officers who had been in Dublin returned home, most of them by simply taking the train. The National army did not interfere with them on their journey, neither did they attempt to take control of Mayo. In contrast to the fight in the southern counties that followed three phases, from an open fight, through a guerrilla phase to a type of mopping-up operation, the Civil War in Mayo after about a month of quiet, immediately settled into a continuous guerrilla struggle, the features of which hardly changed and even extended beyond the formal end of the war.

At the outset normal life more or less continued in Mayo. Parish courts were held, the new county home and hospitals committee was hiring new staff, and for the first time in years the annual Corpus Christi procession was held in Castlebar. The IRA formed a guard of honour, houses were decorated with flowers, evergreens and holy pictures, and large groups were taking communion. The newspapers reported on sports activities organized by the Pioneer Total Abstinence Association, the prices at the markets and a travelling theatre group providing a variety of entertainment. In the absence of the RIC, bonfire night at the end of June seemed to have been a bit more rowdy than usual with youngsters exploding fireworks, and dancing and singing patriotic songs until after 2 a.m.[1]

There was some discussion among anti-Treaty IRA leaders on how to respond to the outbreak of hostilities. Many seemed to favour an attack on Northern Ireland to force a reunification of nationalist forces, but Kilroy and Maguire wanted to oppose the Provisional government directly. The threat of an attack by the National army was looming and efforts focused on preparing for this. The two divisions commanded by Kilroy and Maguire had their headquarters in Castlebar and Ballinrobe, but all major towns had an IRA garrison, with thousands of men under arms. Kilroy worked on improving armaments. He had cars fitted with metal plates to function as armoured cars and set up a factory where grenades and mines were produced. The anti-Treaty IRA in Mayo seemed a formidable force.[2]

To prevent an attack, all the main roads into the county were trenched, railway lines were torn up and bridges destroyed. To the amusement of the national newspapers one party out to blow up a bridge near Foxford, found they had parked the car they came in on the wrong side, forcing them to walk the ten miles back to their base. From the other side, the Provisional government instituted a sea-blockade, suspended postal services after the anti-Treaty IRA took over many post offices, and forbade train travel to Mayo. The Midland line was put out of action, but the Great Southern and Western Railway line was still running into Mayo during July despite the attempts to block it from both sides. To add to the sense of isolation, telephone and telegraph connections were also cut.[3]

The blockade caused serious concerns about food scarcity and people began to stock up. It was reported in early July that shops were busier than at Christmas. To ensure a fair distribution, the IRA introduced food permits. The fact the anti-Treaty IRA had confiscated most cars and motorcycles made alleviating the scarcity difficult but a local man managed to break the government blockade in mid-July to bring in some supplies.[4] The ability of the anti-Treaty IRA to deal with the impact of the blockade defied the expectations of the government-supporting *Connaught Telegraph*: 'we admit candidly ... while acting politically contrary to the will of the majority of the people, [the anti-Treaty IRA] are worthy of admiration. There is no chaos: life and property are respected; food supplies are conserved and order prevails.' It continued by mentioning that a steady stream of cars and carts laden with provisions was observed moving from Westport to the remotest parts of the county.[5]

Despite this apparent continuation of civilian life, the first signs of the inevitable battle occurred on 29 June with the attempted arrest of Thomas Ruane, chairman of Swinford RDC, and his brother for recruiting for the National army. When the arresting party arrived at the Ruane home in Kiltimagh, the occupants opened fire and killed IRA captain William Moran. After a short exchange of fire, the Ruanes were wounded and captured. Thomas died a few days later in hospital. However, most of the action by Mayo men at this stage took place outside the county. The numerous new recruits and their long period in control of the county had made the anti-Treaty IRA eager for action. Many of them aided in the defence of places like Boyle and Castlerea in Roscommon. The main offensive action they participated in was an attack on Collooney barracks in Sligo held by the National army. Although successful in capturing a lot of equipment, the anti-Treaty IRA were eventually driven off by the superior firepower of the government forces. The same occurred in Roscommon and elsewhere, leading most Mayo men to return home. One anti-Treaty group ran into one of its own roadblocks at the bottom of a hill near Ballinrobe, leading to the third Civil War fatality in Mayo.[6]

These early encounters in neighbouring counties indicated that the National army was gradually closing in on Mayo after clearing resistance along the way. In newspaper reports in late July, it was stated that next to Dublin and the South, Mayo was the major stronghold of the anti-Treaty IRA. The last post outside the county held by about 300 Mayo Volunteers was Clonalis Castle near Castlerea, which only fell after it was bombarded by an 18-pounder artillery piece. Although the castle was surrendered, only two men were wounded, and most of the IRA escaped and returned to Mayo. This made clear to the anti-Treaty IRA that buildings were hard to defend against the superior firepower of the National army. In response they mined all the major buildings they occupied, including former workhouses and police barracks, so they could be destroyed if they were forced to leave them.

The advance of the National army caused many citizens to flee, often going to coastal towns they assumed were safe, while four or five presumably landlord families were reported to have moved to their homes in England taking some of their furniture. For the national newspapers the situation in Mayo was difficult to report on as there were no trains or other forms of communications. They were, however, in no doubt that at least part of the county was held by a strong force of anti-Treaty IRA, and the *Irish Independent* predicted that the 'fight in Mayo, when it begins, may be as thrilling as the operations now proceeding in Munster.'[7]

The National army prepared its approach to Mayo carefully. A large force moved in through Roscommon to east Mayo, which was relatively lightly defended by anti-Treaty IRA who had their strongholds in Castlebar and Ballinrobe and to a lesser extent in Ballina. For a while there were conflicting reports of who actually controlled the eastern part of the county.[8] Eventually, a concerted attack to take Claremorris was initiated on 23 July, followed by a naval landing in Westport on 24 July led by Joe Ring. With the strongest force of the anti-Treaty IRA in the West, the National army anticipated a tough battle. However, their heavy weaponry, in the shape of armoured cars and artillery, intimidated the anti-Treaty IRA in their lightly fortified bases which were abandoned without a fight. They thus ceded control of the towns after attempting to destroy all military infrastructure.[9]

The landing in Westport was unexpected. One of the officers stationed there, P.J. McDonnell, recorded the unorganized retreat of the anti-Treaty IRA in his diary. After hearing about the landing, he tried to borrow a car to get away. When this was refused, he took the car by force, promising to return it in 24 hours. On the outskirts of Westport he met five of his men, who told him 200 troops had landed. He subsequently drove to divisional headquarters in Castlebar where he found the garrison preparing to burn down their posts and retreat to the hills. Up to the last moment, the staff were collecting grenades, mines, batteries and electrical appliances, as well as jars of chemicals. The next morning the men paraded at Barrack Square for the last time and were addressed by Michael Kilroy:

> the situation was made clear to all present, away on our left we could see the sky red, and could hear explosions, which we knew were caused by the roofs of the various Departments of our old Div. HQ falling in and

unexploded bombs going off in the flames. M[ichael].K[ilroy]. remarked that he had hoped we had seen the darkest day in our country's history and the dawn would soon be there. All gave him a fine cheer.

Each brigade officer present was instructed to return with their men to their respective areas, while the main body moved off to Balla, abandoning their cars at a destroyed bridge on the way.[10]

By the end of July, all Mayo towns had been vacated by the anti-Treaty IRA even if no troops were observed moving in on them directly. Only in a few places, including Castlebar and Ballinrobe, were short skirmishes reported. The road blocks did make it difficult for the National army to advance quickly. When moving from Claremorris to Ballinrobe, a newspaper reporter was allowed to accompany them. The soldiers were apparently cheery, singing a lot of the way, even though they had to take many byroads through bogs. They also had a specialist party responsible for clearing the well-constructed barricades with hatchets. Coming to Ballinrobe, some anti-Treaty IRA were seen to observe them. After a short burst of machine-gun fire, which slightly wounded two, the men left on bicycles. Ballina was simply taken by an advance cycle patrol of just six soldiers. When the rest of the troops arrived they were welcomed by a cheering crowd, which dispersed in a panic when a man came out of a house and discharged two shots, probably in an attempt to warn any remaining anti-Treaty IRA.[11]

Destroying the fortified buildings proved difficult. The barracks in Castlebar adjoined a convent and the local priest objected. While a promise was made not to use bombs, the barracks were nevertheless set on fire. Together with a group of civilians the same priest prevented the burning of the local post office. An attempt by Tommy Heavey to use force was foiled as his men abandoned him when confronted by the clergyman. The *Connaught Telegraph* described the scenes in apocalyptic terms as 'a holocaust to the war god'. The town was 'like a sea of fire – a raging inferno that would have made the very devils jealous of its immensity and scope'. In Westport the hastily arranged burning of the barracks largely failed as the advancing troops extinguished the fire.[12]

Large sections of the local population were glad to see the National troops arriving after weeks in which contact with the outside world had been minimal. When National army troops entered Ballyhaunis on their way to Claremorris it was described by the *Mayo News* as the 'relief of Ballyhaunis'. The commander of the troops responsible for taking Mayo, Edward Cooney, wrote to Seán Mac Eoin that: 'The receptions we are getting in every town is something to write home about, and seems to be increasing as it goes on.' In Claremorris he stated that a 100 local girls made tea for the men, while the *Irish Independent* reported all night celebrations after the arrival of 'the rescuing troops'.[13] When General Mac Eoin came to Claremorris with the first train arriving there for a month

'Ladies, in the exuberance of their joy, rushed from their doors to embrace them.' Then a banquet and dance were held well into the night. This hospitality was quite welcome as Cooney also reported the army was short of sugar, baking powder and cigarettes.[14]

Civilian life had been severely disrupted during the month since the outbreak of the Civil War. Ordinary traffic between many areas was largely impossible and economic life and contact with the rest of the country was disrupted. As a result, farmers were stuck with large supplies of butter, milk and eggs as well as sheep and bullocks they could not sell. Workers were hit by the closing of companies, like the woollen mills in Foxford, which alone resulted in a loss of employment for 300 people. Many businesses also had been forced to supply the anti-Treaty IRA. Although they tried to pay or at least provide a promise of payment in the future, many goods and all motor vehicles were simply taken. One woman from Claremorris consequently called them 'the looters', while the troops termed them 'Bolshies'. This latter term was apparently strongly endorsed by the military and Catholic Church authorities. In January 1923 the archdeacon in Castlebar spoke to the Men's Sodality of the Sacred Heart about the 'hydra-headed threat of Bolshevism in Russia' that had now come to Ireland. 'The monster was at our throats' he argued, and recommended that the sodality should take matters in their own hands like the fascists had done in Italy and root it out themselves. People were also largely starved of information. The post had not been delivered for a month, and newspapers had only rarely reached Mayo. These had been replaced by a makeshift bulletin controlled by the anti-Treaty IRA, but this mainly detailed their successes elsewhere. Distress was so severe that the government immediately made £15,000 available from the funds allocated previously to relieve Mayo.[15]

The delivery of a backlog of post and a fresh supply of newspapers was, therefore, widely welcomed, although new mail for Mayo was still not accepted. Local markets slowly began to function. The arrival of troops in Foxford seemed to have been particularly welcome with bunting bedecking the town. The potential support for the IFS among locals was shown by successful recruiting for the army. It was reported that 200 young men joined up in Ballinrobe immediately after the arrival of the troops, and another eighty in Castlebar, and thirty in Crossmolina. The local priest claimed this was explained by the petty tyrannies of the anti-Treaty IRA, but this may also have been a result of economic hardship. Together with the Archbishop Gilmartin of Tuam, the priest recognized that there were also many ani-Treatyite supporters, but called on them to now support the majority instead of what he called 'Revolver Government'.[16]

Normality returned quickly. Castlebar UDC met early in September, but without most of its anti-Treaty members who formed the majority. Their absence was immediately made evident when the council formally expressed its sympathy for Arthur Griffith and Michael Collins, who had died the previous month. However, there was no expression of sympathy for the fallen local TD and leading anti-Treatyite, Harry Boland.[17] Most of the discussions concerned economic issues, such as the merits of a housing scheme funded largely by the government but needing an increase in the rates of 3*d*. in the pound. The business lobby argued there were no workers who could afford the rent so they should not build them. It was added there would have been plenty of housing 'if imitation Black & Tans would not have burned the barracks'. The workers' interest argued there were more than 100 people on the waiting list who should be cared for, and that building housing would create employment. It was also emphasized that funds were limited because few people had paid their taxes during the conflict while the expenses, particularly for maintaining the asylum, had continued to accrue. Eventually it was decided to initiate the build by at least acquiring the land necessary for it.[18]

A similar argument between conservative and more progressive voices ensued over the appointment of female instructors for commercial classes. The wisdom of it was challenged by some because it was 'doubtful if a lady is capable of exercising the discipline essential to success, though she might be the most competent teacher in the world'. As with housing, the more forward-thinking voices prevailed and the Mayo technical committee eventually appointed two female teachers. Other aspects of local administration, like the court system, were also revived. This was not always easy. In November the Swinford quarter sessions were held in Castlebar because their own courthouse has been burned, while many cases were problematic given the absence of postal services. All seventy-five criminal injury applications were, therefore, postponed to a later date.[19]

School exams also resumed with prizes and scholarships awarded. Markets and dances were staged, while sports competitions were revived. Although Mitchells GAA club had been active in Castlebar since 1895, the *Connaucht Telegraph* reporter claimed that an interest in Gaelic football developed for the first time in Castlebar in 1922, showing the lack of activity during the revolutionary years. The consequent lack of skill was overlooked by the referee in the first match held there for years to the satisfaction of the reporter: 'Of course, he closed his eyes to many minor fouls, but in future he must prevent deliberate tripping and the abominable practice of catching the ball when on the ground.' That the more mundane aspects of public life again became important was apparent in the discussion by Castlebar UDC about residents failing to keep the footpath in front of their houses clean after market days.[20]

Local people actively tried to restore civilian life. In the absence of a regular police force after the disbandment of the RIC, a volunteer Civilian Guard was set up in early August. Others took it on themselves to repair the many damaged roads and bridges. This was necessary to enable traffic as the anti-Treaty IRA were still engaged in a campaign against communication lines to make it difficult for the National army to operate. On 19 August the *Irish Times* reported that all roads were impassable and no car travel was possible. It was considered too dangerous for official parties to repair the roads, and the troops concentrated on keeping the railway lines open. The makeshift repairs to blown up bridges sometimes triggered further problems as they acted as dams causing fields to flood after heavy autumn rains. As a result, 'Potatoes are turning black, oats are lying and will be difficult to save, and wheat is not ripening.'[21]

The quick take-over of the towns, the positive welcome for the government troops and the swift return of a semblance of normality gave the impression that the Civil War in Mayo was as good as over by early August. The newspapers were particularly optimistic. On 25 July the stridently pro-government *Irish Independent* had already written that: 'The tyranny of the Irregulars in Co. Mayo has collapsed like a house of cards'.[22] The next day it went a step further, practically announcing the end of the anti-Treaty IRA as a military force: 'From a defeat it became a rout, and now it has resulted in a veritable debacle, in which the force that tyrannized over the county for so long has become a demoralized horde of fugitives, torn by mutiny and dissensions, and incapable of offering any serious resistance.' It claimed some anti-Treaty IRA had taken to the hills, but most had gone home, intent on surrendering or taking the boat to Glasgow. The paper also reported that one officer had been executed in Charlestown by his own forces, without providing evidence for this.[23]

Although a small number of mostly junior anti-Treaty IRA and their sympathizers were arrested and others had fallen away following the National army advance into Mayo, the reality was less dramatic for anti-Treatyites than the press claimed. On 5 August the *Connacht Tribune* noted there were still many anti-Treaty IRA in the hilly countryside of Mayo which, as it put it, favoured guerrilla. The National army may control the urban centres, but most of the countryside was still firmly in republican hands. The 2nd Western Division under Maguire had based its forces in sheltered areas in the Partry Mountains and around Ballaghaderreen, while the stronghold of the 4th Western under Kilroy was in the Ox Mountains, straddling the border with Sligo, with a secondary force north of Newport. The number of anti-Treaty men was significant. In July 1922 the West Mayo Brigade claimed to have 715 men, while in north Mayo the 1st Battalion alone comprised 646 with 190 having joined after the truce. Excluding the 2nd Battalion, the Brigade numbered 1,658 men, including 448 so-called trucileers, who had only joined after the truce. By comparison, in west Mayo the National army presence comprised only 200 soldiers in Westport and 300 in Castlebar.[24]

Some units, such as the newly formed 5th Northwest Mayo Brigade around Bangor and Belmullet, were seriously affected. At the end of August, the brigadier reported that all the battalions were again functioning with a small

ASU in each, after having been 'completely disorganized owing to depletion of columns and some arrests'. The brigade was also practically unarmed. For the time being it and many other local anti-Treaty units concentrated on the reorganization of various support services. Classes were provided on road blocking, scouting, engineering, signalling, medical services and, in particular, intelligence gathering. The inability to provide adequate training in medical services was keenly felt but it would take too much time. Mundane tasks such as bookkeeping and copying general orders were also still given attention. On 12 September the only instructions issued concerned keeping the divisional headquarters clean and organizing sanitation.[25]

The anti-Treaty IRA nevertheless soon made clear that they were not giving up the fight. Their ASUs made their presence known by nightly attacks on National army posts in the towns. The recently established Civic Guard was another favoured target. To make police attempts to enforce a curfew difficult, the anti-Treaty IRA disabled the electric street lights in places like Ballinrobe and Castlebar, and attacked Civic Guard patrols with grenades, which put a stop to such patrolling. The anti-Treaty IRA also engaged in various less dangerous operations such as raiding shops for supplies, and post offices and banks for money. The Northwest Mayo Brigade even levied a license fee on pubs in Belmullet and Bangor. Demonstrating their control over the countryside, 200 anti-Treaty IRA attended the funeral of one of their fallen comrades in early August without being disturbed.[26]

Individual supporters of the government also became a target. Big houses continued to be singled out due to their association with Britain and moneyed interests. A hunt was stopped by anti-Treaty IRA near Enniscrone. Family members of National army soldiers were also singled out. In at least one case the mother of an army officer was forced out of her home. A lack of civilian engagement with what was regarded as an existential struggle irritated the anti-Treaty IRA. A gramophone cabinet used at a dance held near Claremorris was destroyed because the raiders 'would not tolerate enjoyment of that kind while they were out "suffering for their country"'. The young dancers were then forced to cut a trench in a nearby road. A card playing party had been likewise forced to destroy a culvert a few days before.[27]

There were also positive efforts to show that the anti-Treatyites fought in the interest of the people. Poor areas, such as Erris district where the 'people live in an extremely unsanitary condition' in small, thatched cottages and where the worst typhus outbreak since the Famine was recorded, received special attention. In a spectacular move, the anti-Treaty IRA highjacked a ship close to Westport in October and forced it to unload its cargo of 400 tons of flour in Newport for distribution among the people.[28] They also tried to alleviate individual hardship, but such support was very difficult for them to provide, when even their own dependants were often suffering, as indicated by a list of needy relatives of men on active service. Despite the frequent robberies, the anti-Treaty IRA were largely dependent on locals for food. Numerous requests from divisional commanders for money from the Western Command to pay for this went unheeded.[29]

To limit the impact on civilians the opposing sides initially sought a set of rules of engagement. In particular the presence of family members of the anti-Treaty IRA became a pressing issue. On 31 August the 4th Western Division discussed the difficulties of an attack on the town of Newport with 'Grady's, Kilroy's and others marked as victims if we tried it.' Michael Kilroy's mother had previously written a letter to the local National army commandant to complain that she was constantly followed by troops 'with rifles at the ready', even to church. Although some advised him against it, P.J. McDonnell, the local IRA commander, subsequently wrote to the commandant about his apparent refusal to let anti-Treaty IRA supporters out of the town in the knowledge that it was going to be attacked: 'This is not the action of a gentlemen or soldier and it speaks very badly for you and your men when you have to take shelter behind defenceless women and babies of a few weeks old.' He also referred to the shooting into the home of John Kilroy and warned that if the soldiers would not let their 'supporters full liberty of movement', he would interfere with the family members of National army soldiers. In response, the commandant expressed his 'regret that the ugly incident happened'. The man who fired the shots had been 'severely dealt with' and he gave assurances that anti-Treaty supporters were 'not in any danger from my troops' and that the surveillance on Mrs Kilroy was as light as possible. Moving from a defensive to an aggressive tone, the commandant stated: 'we are merely out to protect our own defenceless Irish people from as gross and outrageous a military tyranny as ever disgraced Prussia in its worst militarist days.' He intended to carry out his orders and hold Newport 'until the last shot is fired and the last national soldier killed.' Afterwards McDonnell issued an order to Mrs Chambers, whose son had joined the National army, that the IRA would not allow her out of town because 'their women were prevented also'.[30]

This initial attempt to shield civilians from the fighting became difficult to maintain, and a hardening of attitudes gradually set in on both sides. One example of this related to the ability of Red Cross workers to deal with the wounded without interference. This became controversial following a case in which a local man associated with the anti-Treaty IRA was shot in the stomach in Kilmeena in early November 1922. The Red Cross ambulance that came for him from Castlebar was stopped by anti-Treaty IRA to be destroyed but they let it through when they heard it was for one of their own. Such reticence was no longer shown in February 1923 when the military reported that one of their lieutenants 'was deliberately shot while dressing a wounded soldier and the Red Cross was prominently displayed on his arms.'[31]

Although the anti-Treaty IRA lacked a coherent strategy, they still had some advantages. The National army felt it was generally too dangerous to engage the still numerous and relatively well-armed anti-Treaty IRA in the countryside directly. National army recruits were not always willing to risk their lives, particularly as they were often poorly supplied. In mid-August reports reached the commandant of the anti-Treaty 4th Western Division that the National army garrison in Newport was rebellious because they had not received their pay. He described their soldiers as a 'weary infusion type', untrained and undisciplined, three-quarters of whom would not fight. If a more active campaign against them would be waged, he argued, their morale would be smashed in a month.[32]

Such a campaign was hard to develop without heavy weaponry. Most of the anti-Treaty IRA actions consisted of nightly attacks on army posts in the main towns, ranging from simple sniping to more sustained assaults. Occasionally small diversions were organized in the countryside intended to draw out the army garrisons and engage them in the open where their superior firepower did not count as much. Kilroy ordered his men to 'erect road blockages to draw enemy out and cut him off from his base', but this rarely bore results. In August one army patrol was, however, attacked three times during a 6-mile march. Besides sniping and some ambushing, the most serious engagements developed when the two sides met accidently and some long-range firefights took place between large forces. On a few occasions the anti-Treaty IRA were surprised in their billets and subsequently often forced to surrender after a machine-gun or artillery was trained on them. Some of the smaller garrisons of the National army were similarly vulnerable, a number of them were overrun and patrols were forced to surrender, including a 50-strong detachment from Ballina in September. However, the number of casualties in these skirmishes remained small.[33]

The minor successes and the hesitancy of the National army soon restored the confidence of anti-Treatyites after their retreat from the towns. Already in late July they started to reoccupy some of the minor towns such as Kiltimagh and Newport that were weakly garrisoned by government forces. In early August the National army garrison in Swinford surrendered after their post was set on fire. Their commander refused to do so and died in the flames. In September Balla was given up by the National army. Attacks of varying degrees of seriousness were made in the following months on various other garrisons. The biggest coup was the taking of Ballina on 12 September. Although an attack on the town was expected, the anti-Treaty IRA did not strike until most of the garrison of about 50 men were at the funeral of Lieutenant Moran, who had been killed in an internal row. Ballina was captured with the aid of the 'Ballinalee', an armoured car seized from the National army in Sligo. In the exchange of fire, a girl and a cattle dealer were killed, but neither of the fighting sides suffered fatalities. However, Private Thomas Lackey eventually died on 22

July 1924 from a wound sustained during the attack, making him the last fatality of the conflict in Mayo. After celebrating their success with tea and drinks in the local bars, the anti-Treaty IRA released the captive government soldiers and left with a large amount of weapons, money from the local bank, and two prominent local government supporters seized as hostages.[34]

The victorious anti-Treaty IRA retreated to their headquarters in Bonniconlon at the foot of the Ox Mountains, where they were quickly engaged by a strong National army force which approached from four sides, seeking retaliation for the Ballina attack. This led to what was probably the largest extended military confrontation of the entire Civil War in Mayo, which included diversion attacks by anti-Treatyite forces elsewhere. A number of running battles took place during the chase in which leading officers on both sides were captured and then escaped. Brigadier Neary of the National army was captured and taken away by two anti-Treaty IRA men who had failed to search him. When out of sight of the main force, he drew a hidden pistol and shot his two guards. In a similar manner, Kilroy escaped when he was found hiding in a house which the National army was unwilling to machine-gun due to the presence of women. A number of casualties were sustained by both sides in the days that followed, Joe Ring being the most prominent Mayo man to die. As a senior officer from the War of Independence, he was widely mourned in the county and his funeral drew thousands, including a pipe band from Athlone.[35]

Whereas anti-Treatyites were buoyed up by these apparent successes, the National army grew increasingly worried, particularly after Clifden, County Galway, was taken on 18 October by a force that included many Mayo men. In a letter to General Richard Mulcahy, the minister of defence, the strength of Kilroy's forces was estimated at between 600 and 700 with 8 machine-guns, 3 armoured cars and 7 or 8 lorries, as well as a factory for mines and grenades. It was pointed out that with such a force he could take over towns one by one, picking up about 100 rifles each time. At this stage the anti-Treaty IRA had already captured and released 330 government soldiers.[36]

Although the anti-Treaty IRA continued their campaign, which still included sniping, ambushing, destroying railway lines, raiding post offices and even large-scale attacks on towns, the continuous fighting and lack of support from outside eventually began to take their toll. A shortage of ammunition and reliable grenades and mines were already limiting their ability to stage sustained attacks on army posts. Losses, some through accidents but particularly the growing number of arrests, depleted their forces. The drives organized by the National army in the autumn rounded up hundreds of anti-Treaty IRA often with their weapons. The first substantial group was arrested in mid-August when thirty-seven anti-Treaty IRA were overcome by a large National army detachment from Ballina. The losses included 37 rifles, 14 revolvers, 32 bombs as well as bomb-making equipment. During the following months such events became a regular feature: 45 ASU men were captured at Millford house in south Mayo when surprised in their encampment, and another 30 in the Ballaghaderreen area in mid-September. The National army became increasingly adept at locating the ASUs. Sometimes this took weeks of intelligence gathering but in one case they simply followed the tracks of a stolen car. On one occasion they pretended to stage a dance in a school building, subsequently arresting a group of anti-Treaty IRA that intended to attack the dance.[37]

During the months before New Year, several hundred anti-Treaty IRA were interned and a lot of their weaponry was captured. One of the last armoured cars they had fabricated themselves by mounting a boiler on a Ford truck nicknamed 'The Queen of the West' had to be abandoned when it got stuck in the mud during a retreat in late December. The losses also included some of the prominent leaders. In late October, Tom Maguire was captured with 100 men near Shrule by a party led by the same man who had carried him to safety after the Tourmakeady ambush in 1921. A month later, Michael Kilroy was captured after a fight near Newport during which he was wounded in the shoulder; in the same fight five National army soldiers, including two officers, were killed. Such a large number of casualties in one incident was an exception despite the frequent clashes. Exceptionally, the fallen soldiers were given an official funeral.[38]

The anti-Treaty IRA was increasingly under pressure in other ways. There were numerous accounts of the poor state of their clothing and health. As early as August 1922, a report described about 50 anti-Treaty IRA coming into a village 'drenched, unkempt and weary, suffering from coughs and colds.' They were given milk and hot bread, but slept in wet clothes and left in the morning, sick and tired. During a later round-up near Achill, some of the men arrested 'were actually in rags and had scarcely any boots on their feet'. In January one man died from pneumonia.[39] Although in certain places they were well received, they also encountered opposition. An anonymous letter was sent to Richard Mulcahy from someone in Louisburgh asking for a National army garrison to be based there because 'the shopkeepers are being robbed and looted every other night'. The IRA commander of the area around Belmullet wanted to know from his divisional officer what he was to do with civilians helping government troops because information on the anti-Treatyite movements was apparently passed on.[40]

It was also difficult for the anti-Treaty IRA to put its case across to the wider population as most of the larger institutions, including all newspapers, were explicitly pro-Treaty. A journalist for the *Freeman's Journal* was arrested by them on suspicion of being a government spy in August, and the destruction of all hostile newspapers was later ordered by the 4th Western Division. The Catholic Church also generally supported the Free State in word and deed. This could be simply by priests blessing the troops before going out on patrol. The hierarchy issued a pastoral letter on 10 October which was published in the press the following day and read at all Masses on 22 October. It stated that confession and Holy Communion would be withheld from anyone engaged in armed actions against the legitimate forces of the government as these acts were deemed 'grievous sins'. Some anti-Treatyites, like Joe Baker, a ASU leader with War of Independence experience, could be satisfied with the observation that 'the Bishops were not always right'. Others were more assertive. One divisional officer sent a letter to Bishop Naughton of Killala in early September warning him of the consequences of allowing government troops to use church grounds. In light of the possibility of imminent death many of the men wanted to observe their religion irrespective of the position of the church. Reports indicated that the men regularly went to Mass and made their confession to sympathetic priests throughout the Civil War.[41] The anti-Treaty IRA tended to put a positive spin on its potential support. The success of the attack on Ballina was attributed to the good intelligence they had locally, while they were not given away on their subsequent retreat. A claim that the public were indignant and fed up with the Free State was backed up by referring to fifteen local women who were arrested for refusing to swear allegiance to it.[42]

The National army only slowly gained ground in Mayo while the anti-Treaty IRA remained relatively strong. In this sense they stood out together with other remote mountainous regions like south Kerry where they had strongholds. Elsewhere, the forces were more scattered and often ineffective.[43] In early November anti-Treaty forces still controlled Newport, while it was not until the end of December that a National army post was established in Achill. Part of the explanation for this lay with the army itself. In a report to the chief of staff in December 1922, National army officers argued that their men were 'very badly disciplined, frequently mutinous and very inefficient (militarily) sometimes treacherous and except in certain barracks, dirty and slovenly.' Officers, it was claimed, knew nothing of tactics and were frequently drunk, while soldiers were dirty and fraternized with anti-Treaty IRA, sometimes selling ammunition to them.[44]

These problems were also evident in Mayo, where a lack of supplies and discipline, mostly drunkenness, was noted in an internal army report in January 1923. One deserter allegedly complained that men were forced at gunpoint to fight and they had received no uniforms, underwear or pay for four months. Canon D'Alton of Ballinrobe wrote to William Sears TD about a case in which a soldier who had sold his rifle in Ballinrobe was simply brought to Claremorris, set free and given a new rifle. The priest wondered 'How can we expect discipline or efficiency in an army where there is no drilling, no practice in arms, no marching?' He also described how a 100-strong column had come to Ballinrobe from Ballina, having had little sleep and a breakfast of bread and porter. As soon as they came under fire, they retreated without firing a shot and sustained four casualties. They arrived back in Ballinrobe 'in scattered bands not a few without shoes or stockings.' Such reports became so numerous that headquarters intervened and in January 1923 General Lawlor was replaced by Michael Hogan. He brought in new military practices and established extra military posts in Ballyhaunis, Foxford, Lahardane, Mulranny and Swinford. He also supplemented the existing garrisons in Ballina, Ballinrobe, Castlebar, Claremorris, Newport and Westport and better medical care was provided to tackle an outbreak of scabies among the soldiers based in Claremorris.[45]

Despite the continuous losses, the strength of the anti-Treaty IRA forces in Mayo remained substantial. The National army estimated that in January there were still six active columns as well as a strong force in the Ox Mountains under the Sligo commander Frank Carty. The largest of these units operated around Castlebar. It comprised seventy men under Dr Madden, while the other five in the Westport, Newport/Shramore, Castlerea, Ballyhaunis/Kilkelly and Cross/Cong areas together fielded another 150 men. Many other Mayo men had retreated to the Tuam area after a round-up in the Mayo mountains. They were believed to have been well armed, with each man possessing a rifle and ample ammunition. Madden's unit also possessed two Lewis guns and three Thompson machine-guns, with another three Thompsons in the possession of two other units, most of them captured from National forces. Each unit also possessed some bombs and mines, a few motorcycles, a good supply of bikes, and had some armoured cars at their disposal. Later reports on insurgent strength indicated that these units moved around continuously in different groupings.[46]

To undercut the remaining opposition, the government had introduced an amnesty scheme for IRA men in October, while at the same time introducing the death penalty for those found carrying arms. Anyone who surrendered, gave up their arms and signed an undertaking not to oppose the government would not be prosecuted. Although newspapers were increasingly optimistic about this, it seemed to have had little effect in Mayo. In February a total of four men surrendered, in March two unarmed man reported at Castlebar barracks, while in April just one ASU member with a revolver knocked at the door of a barracks: 'He signed the usual undertaking and was released.' The *Freeman's Journal* claimed in February that many men just went home without surrendering, suggesting 'a good deal of quiet and effective work is being done to persuade the others to lay down arms and turn to regular civic life.' However, on 7 March Tom Derrig, now a member of the anti-Treaty IRA army council and the new local divisional commander, proudly reported that 'there have been no desertions from the IRA in this area since the 1st of January, nor of any arms being handed up to the enemy'. He added that 'All Volunteers in this area who have been released from enemy prisons were not asked to sign any undertaking whatever.' In fact, the number of National army defections to the IRA was almost as great, despite the much greater risks involved.[47] In some cases switching allegiance also appears to have been a ploy to infiltrate the anti-Treaty IRA. In January the 4th

Western Division warned its brigades that a scheme had been developed whereby specially selected soldiers were given a course of training and then may 'appear in any area in the county asking admission to our army ... [and] may be supplied with recommendations and transfers purporting to be from one or other of our Commands or well-known officers.'[48]

Although the death penalty was in practice rarely implemented, surrendering during a fight had become risky for the anti-Treaty IRA. Joe Baker and Tom Maguire were sentenced to death, despite the fact Maguire was captured unarmed, having apparently thrown away his weapons just before being apprehended. Probably due to the men's standing in the movement, these sentences were not implemented. Although quite a few more death sentences were handed down, only a handful of Mayo men were actually executed; among them was John Maguire, a younger brother of Tom. He had been arrested in February in possession of a rifle and ammunition but faced the firing squad on 11 April 1923 in Tuam as punishment for an attack by another anti-Treaty IRA unit on an army base in Headford. Apart from the risk of execution, there were various reports of the maltreatment of anti-Treaty IRA prisoners and the shootings of men in custody. The torture of Joe Baker led to an official inquiry. Early in March a prisoner who was forced to clear mines laid by his comrades was allegedly shot accidently by his guards. As a consequence of these risks, many prisoners tried to escape, quite frequently with success, while others were rescued by their comrades. In Baker's case this failed because the travel times of the train on which he was carried were miscalculated by his would-be rescuers.[49]

Despite the new National army tactics, the conflict in Mayo retained its established features during the first months of 1923 with sniping incidents, the burning of former RIC barracks and a post office raid. There were also about six major engagements, often resulting from an attack by a large force of anti-Treaty IRA on one of the towns. The most successful operation in February was the capture of a supply train between Castlebar and Newport. The anti-Treaty IRA forced the train to stop, overpowered the twelve-strong guard, and took their equipment, which according to the commander included 22 rifles and 15,000 rounds of much-needed ammunition.[50]

Although there was clearly a stream of information coming the army's way, they rarely utilized it successfully. In February they failed to locate the anti-Treaty IRA on thirty-nine occasions despite receiving details on their whereabouts. They had some successes, however. When searching an arms dump near Shramore, a 22-strong column was surprised and overcome with the help of army reinforcements from Newport. There was one fatality, five were wounded and eight anti-Treaty men were arrested. Over the course of February and March there were 10 dumps located and 160 anti-Treaty IRA, including 6 women, arrested.[51]

Detailed reports from both sides show a professional approach was often lacking. The anti-Treaty IRA commander complained about a lack of preparedness of his men. National army officers complained about the poor marching ability of their soldiers, while a search of Achill had to be called off because the tide was out. Many planned operations failed and most engagements did not lead to any casualties or a clear victor. A five-hour attack on Ballyhaunis in February did not cause any casualties, while a swoop by 100 anti-Treaty IRA on Charlestown, meant to draw troops from Swinford into an ambush site, resulted in protracted fighting with just one fatality on each side. In March all the fighting led to just two casualties among the anti-Treaty IRA and three among the army.[52]

The army assessment of anti-Treaty IRA strength in late March provides an illuminating and diverse picture. In south Mayo the regular searches seemed to have had a significant impact. The ASUs had been broken up and the estimated eighty or so remaining activists were reported as going around in small groups and receiving support from the local population. In east Mayo the estimated forty remaining anti-Treatyites on the run needed to use compulsion against the local population to sustain themselves, while their 150 comrades in north Mayo, particularly around Bonniconlon, still seemed in complete control. A strong force in the north-west of the county seems to have been successful in tying the local population to them by distributing food supplies confiscated from boats and local farmers. In the view of the National army, this kept 'a certain class on their side', while 'those who are not sympathetic with the anti-Treaty IRA must submit to their "Laws" and Edicts.' The local IRA commander was less sanguine about the losses around Newport: 'It looks as if this area will be completely mopped up before I shall be free to attend to it.'

The continued ability of the anti-Treaty IRA forces to function was in part due to the support given by women. Although no formal Cumann na mBan activity is recorded, many women were involved in keeping communication lines open and providing other essential support services, but some clearly perceived their role as military, indicated by the steady number of women arrested in uniform.[53] It is clear this assertiveness by anti-Treaty women was challenging the perceptions of government soldiers. Although violence against women in Mayo was rarely referred to during the entire Irish Revolution, there is irrefutable evidence that Margaret Doherty, a Cumann na mBan member from Foxford, was gang-raped by National army soldiers at the end of the Civil War. The case was covered up, and she never fully recovered from the ordeal, dying in a psychiatric hospital in 1928.[54]

In April there was a certain tapering off of violence. Although the anti-Treaty IRA in the Ox Mountains were still able to stage attacks on Bonniconlon and Enniscrone barracks in late April, larger confrontations did not take place.[55] Minor incidents like sniping, sometimes with deadly consequences, stripping of

Civic Guards, and seizing the mail were, however, even more prevalent than in the previous months. On one occasion two Guards who were serving summonses for poteen-making were stopped by about sixty 'armed men' who took their money, bicycles and civil clothing, except for their trousers and shirts. They were then brought to a house where they were asked several times 'where were they two years ago when there was fighting to be done' and challenged to a fight with fists or revolvers. When they declined they were beaten and let go. A concerted effort to trench roads, break bridges and disrupt train traffic followed an order to that effect in late February. All this resulted in only one National army casualty in April. Despite numerous searches, arrests also declined to about fifty, including three women of which one was in uniform, and six civilians for aiding the anti-Treaty IRA.[56]

Civilians had been increasingly affected by the conflict. The nightly sniping attacks were unsettling, while the executions caused anti-Treaty IRA to threaten reprisals on Free State supporters. No one was actually killed but the gentry and prominent pro-Treatyites remained favoured targets. Downhill House near Ballina went up in flames as a random reprisal for the execution of anti-Treaty IRA prisoners while Moore Hall, situated between Ballinrobe and Claremorris and owned by the writer George Moore, Colonel Maurice Moore's estranged brother, was burned. Officially, this was to prevent soldiers being billeted there, but locally the motive was believed to be agrarian related rather than political. The homes of some government soldiers and that of William Sears were also burned. Joseph MacBride was kidnapped as were some people travelling from Foxford to the quarter sessions in Ballina.[57] Business people were largely assumed to support the government, and their shops and workshops became targets. The ulterior motive of raiding businesses was to obtain supplies such as foodstuff, clothes, boots and whiskey for the anti-Treaty IRA.

The need for supplies and money to support the families of those on active service was extremely pressing for the anti-Treaty IRA. The local population was the main source of basic supplies. Although some gave support willingly, others were found to hide their food when the anti-Treaty IRA visited their area. GHQ and the republican dependant funds did contribute something on top of this, but this was not enough. The most regular way to supplement funds was by collecting taxes, such as dog licenses and land annuities, in the name of the Republican government. More irregular forms included the frequent raiding of post offices and banks, but the actual return on this was limited. Glenhest post office in the Nephin Mountains was robbed for the twenty-fifth time by early May. A dangerous, but more rewarding option, was holding up the assistant paymaster-general who brought in army pay. In a second attempt to do this in late April the paymaster was killed.[58]

Providing support for the anti-Treaty IRA was also fraught with danger. Although the army was confident that most people, except in what they called backward places, only supported the anti-Treaty IRA out of fear, there was clearly a lot of spontaneous backing. Events like the execution of John Maguire generated a lot of concern even among pro-Treatyites. The Westport UDC passed a resolution calling on the government to stop the executions as they were 'calculated to increase and perpetuate the present chaos'. Various people from Westport were arrested in early 1923 for selling the anti-Treaty newspaper *Éire*. The special emphasis the National army accorded to raiding dances also showed the extent to which the anti-Treaty IRA remained part of local communities. This could have fatal consequences. In March Michael Henry, a farmer from Cloonroe, was killed after he refused to let the army into his house, while a local driver who refused to take on what he termed 'Free Staters' was also shot.[59]

All the regular newspapers continued to be published weekly throughout the Civil War period, although the *Mayo News* missed an odd issue. Their reports showed that many features of ordinary life, such as dances, fairs and markets, continued as much as possible. It was especially difficult for local government to function. Many of the county council's members were on the run, which meant a quorum was difficult to reach. The councils were all suffering financially from unpaid taxes. To remedy this a system was introduced in which they could be paid through the post office by way of money orders. This was successful with about eighty per cent of taxes coming in that way. Expenses also came down. The amalgamation of workhouses had reduced running costs from £40,000 to £30,000 annually. This allowed rates to be reduced in 1923 to pre-war levels.[60] However, the conflict created new financial burdens. Pensions needed to be paid to workers laid off during the fighting, but most problematic were the large claims for compensation from local landowners and railway companies. In March the marquis of Sligo demanded £25,807 from the county council and Westport UDC for four destroyed properties, while George Moore claimed £25,000 from Ballinrobe RDC for the burning of Moore Hall.[61]

The lay-offs and economic dislocation caused hardship. The local pro-Treaty TDs Sears and MacBride asked the government in January to aid the Mayo town tenants and to restart land sales. Although Kevin O'Higgins, the minister for home affairs, supported the idea 'to make every tenant in Ireland the owner of his holding', he claimed there was no money to make it possible. Mayo farmers then again took matters into their own hands. In May the minister admitted that what he called land grabbing was 'carried on to such an extent in Mayo ... that he had been compelled to inform the military authorities that it constituted a problem incapable of being adequately dealt with by an unarmed police force, or by legal processes.'[62] To alleviate some of the hardship the government co-funded the building of two trunk roads in Mayo: one from Westport to Dublin via Castlebar and Claremorris, and another from Galway to Sligo via Castlebar, Ballinrobe and Ballina. These had the added advantage of facilitating military movements (see map 1).[63]

All the military activity of the National army notwithstanding, the *Irish Times* had to acknowledge on 24 April that Mayo was one of the few counties still not completely in the hands of government forces. To clear out remaining anti-Treaty IRA strongholds, the army then initiated major sweeps of north-west Mayo and the Ox Mountains. They estimated a total of 500 anti-Treaty IRA were still based in fortified positions in Glenree Valley, north of Bonniconlon, and occupied all villages at the base of the mountains northwards to Dromore West and along the main Ballina to Dromore West road to Enniscrone. The manoeuvres exposed the relative weakness of the National army in Mayo: 'Although only two Irregulars were captured the moral effect of the operations was very great. National troops had never previously been seen within the area and were welcomed sincerely by the people.' To maintain a presence, the army established some manned posts in the area.[64]

This continued strength of the anti-Treaty IRA forces made Mayo one of only a handful of counties where they could still control rural areas in late spring 1923. Nationally, the situation had become increasingly desperate for the anti-Treaty IRA, leading to a growing number of peace moves. In February the 4th Western divisional commandant had still made short shrift of an attempt by Maurice Sweeney, a recently released IRA officer, to broker a peace: 'You are to inform him that his actions in this direction are <u>absolutely contrary to G.H.Q. Orders</u> and that he must desist from conducting this business any further.'[65] Gradually pressure mounted. A large public meeting was held in Crossboyne in early April, which decided to send a deputation to the 'Republican Army in Mayo' to ask them to stop fighting and negotiate 'a permanent and lasting peace.' Although that did not materialize, some weeks later the IRA army council ordered all its units to cease fire from 30 April onward, ostensibly putting an end to the Civil War and the fighting.[66]

In reality, the situation was more complicated. As the ceasefire was a one-sided affair, the immediate effects were limited. Although the National army had noted that a few anti-Treaty IRA were 'arranging a surrender' and some new prisoners had 'stated that arms were dumped according to orders', the Free State government continued to round-up anti-Treaty IRA, including eighty-three men and one woman in May alone. One of these prisoners, Thomas McNicholas, was shot after being captured on 10 May, while Joseph Healy was killed on 6 June trying to escape a round-up.[67] This put the anti-Treaty IRA in a challenging position. Returning home was difficult for fear of being arrested. The only way to get out safely was to surrender and sign an undertaking not to oppose the government. For most this was unacceptable, and they therefore simply continued to evade arrest. A substantial number of Mayo men even refused to accept the ceasefire order and the subsequent instruction from de Valera on 24 May to dump arms; they continued to fight. The army reported on an anti-Treaty IRA meeting in Connemara where after some debate it was decided to ignore de Valera. Confusion was widespread in the months that followed. On one hand, the National army continued its drives and arrested large numbers of anti-Treaty IRA, including, on the day of de Valera's order, the entire 4th Western divisional staff. In the process a large amount of arms and equipment was captured. On the other hand, the anti-Treaty IRA remained active. In May alone five sniping incidents, one ambush and some attacks on government supporters, including the burning of a soldier's family home, were recorded.[68]

Both sides kept the possibility of an official renewal of hostilities open. On 10 May the Western Command of the anti-Treaty IRA asked all divisions for a telegraphic covering address 'which we could use to transport Renewal of Hostilities Order, immediately it arrives here, from GHQ'. In June a higher officer sent to reorganize local units in case of future action was killed.[69] At the end of July the army in Mayo still maintained 'that Irregulars are preparing for another campaign of destruction' in the winter months and were just 'resting on their oars' until then. As a result, small-scale attacks, arrests and even killings continued on both sides in the following months. Near Kiltimagh, an anti-Treaty IRA man in National army uniform went up to two soldiers, had a friendly chat, took out his gun and shot one of them, before being killed himself. The feelings of anger among National army forces resulting from such attacks were not dissipated by the numerous deaths among comrades, including by drowning, some unintended discharge of arms, two outright murders by fellow soldiers and on one occasion at the end of June a fight between two National army units that mistakenly believed the other was anti-Treaty IRA. Possibly as a consequence, anti-Treaty IRA in custody or running away were still 'accidently' shot. It is striking that during the later months of the Civil War, National army deaths as a result of accidents and even murder by comrades outstripped the number of those killed in action. In total, forty-nine dependants of soldiers killed in the Civil War sought a service pension as against fifteen anti-treaty IRA men.[70]

By mid-July IRA units were still recorded as operating around Westport, the Ox Mountains, Aughagower, Louisburgh and Tourmakeady, while individuals evading arrest were observed everywhere. Many anti-Treaty IRA simply hid out in dugouts: '[they] only show themselves to commandeer food and clothing and then back to their haunts in the ground'.[71] Clearly there was still a lot of support among the population as they were not given away. Over the summer, the actions of the remaining activists became focused on the general election planned for August: 'They are making every effort to win over the sympathy of the people who were opposed to them for the past 12 months, and to a certain extent they are succeeding.' The army acknowledged that the anti-Treaty IRA were still popular in places: 'In remote districts the people are more or less friendly, due mainly to their being unaffected by our Propaganda, and being led on to impossible expectations by the stories of the Irregulars.'[72]

The main IRA and SF leaders of previous elections were again candidates in the newly created North and South Mayo constituencies. On the anti-Treaty side this included men on the run like Tom Maguire, who had escaped from Athlone prison in June, Michael Kilroy and Tom Derrig in South Mayo, and P.J. Ruttledge and Henry Coyle in North Mayo. The pro-Treaty party fielded sitting TDs William Sears and Joseph MacBride in South Mayo, and the lesser known Joseph McGrath in North Mayo. Their new party, Cumann na nGaedheal, was constituted in Mayo on 26 June at a large rally in Castlebar. Despite the difficult circumstances, in which the state, church and media all took the side of Cumann na nGaedheal, Sinn Féin campaigned openly, and on election day were reported to be singing republican songs such as 'Shramore' in public. Of the nine Mayo TDs, five were elected for Cumann na nGaedheal and four for Sinn Féin, notwithstanding the presence of Labour, Farmer and independent candidates. SF actually did better than during the 1922 election, receiving 37.43 per cent of the vote against 54.65 per cent for Cumann na nGaedheal. Support in North Mayo, where Ruttledge topped the polls, was marginally higher than in South Mayo where Maguire came second after Sears, outvoting Kilroy who took the fourth seat and Derrig who was not elected.[73]

The relatively successful elections did buoy anti-Treatyites' spirits. During the remainder of 1923 a number of well-armed ASUs, all led by veterans of the War of Independence, still operated with local support in all the more mountainous parts of Mayo. They still staged occasional attacks on army outposts, in which a final National army soldier was killed on 31 August 1923, but mainly engaged in drilling and organizing. The Civic Guards, who extended their presence rapidly in the late summer, remained a favoured target. The low intensity of this conflict allowed the National army to withdraw from the more remote areas, but this allowed the anti-Treaty IRA to reassert control. As soon as the 26th Infantry Battalion evacuated the countryside around Belmullet, eleven anti-Treaty IRA immediately marched into Geesalagh district.[74] Consequently, a more innocuous tactic to deal with the men on the run was introduced in August: 'going out in small groups at night and waiting quietly at crossroads and by-roads frequented by anti-Treaty IRA seems to be a very good one and is making anti-Treaty IRA in all districts feel very insecure and consequently to a great extent breaking up the Irregular Morale.'[75]

In many ways the Civil War thus did not end in April or May 1923. The stand-off between the two side in the more remote rural areas of Mayo continued for quite some time. The anti-Treatyites in Mayo had shown remarkable strength and resilience compared to most other counties, but eventually growing numbers of them returned home. Many of them continuing to refuse to participate in the new state, often feeling compelled to emigrate, while the political divisions engendered by the Civil War remained the dominant feature of the county for a long time to come, influencing people's lives, individually and collectively.

9 Revolution?

The conflict as fought out in Mayo deviated somewhat from the pattern and characteristics of other areas in the Irish Revolution. In Mayo, actual fighting came late and never developed the extreme viciousness it did in many other counties. There had always been a radical political streak in Mayo, as witnessed in the founding of the Land League and United Irish League in the county. This continued in the twentieth century, particularly in Westport, but this did not translate into much violence. Even agrarian agitation remained relatively restrained for a western county. This was associated with a tendency to homogeneity in political allegiance at a local level. So although political opinions differed somewhat in the eastern and western districts of Mayo over time, internal opponents remained small in number and were unable to resist the dominant grouping. Politically, the unionist voice in Mayo was irrelevant and as soon as SF replaced the IPP, there was little need to enforce control over the population by the movement in charge. This also explained the relative strength of the anti-Treaty IRA which gained virtually total control over the county after the split over the Treaty and could depend on large-scale support even until well after the end of the Civil War.

As a result, the Irish Revolution did not cause fundamental changes, although the political face of Mayo had been transformed by 1923. At social, economic and cultural levels certain developments can be identified but whether these were entirely a result of the political conflict is less obvious. Politically, power had, however, clearly moved into new hands. Nationally, there was now a largely independent Irish government with which people in Mayo and local institutions had to interact. The old organizations that fought for the rights of tenants and were associated with the IPP had lost control over the population. SF and its offshoots, Cumann na nGaedheal and Sinn Féin later Fianna Fáil, became the dominant political parties. In this way the divisions caused by the Civil War determined the face of politics up until the present century, and fundamentally altered the tendency towards political uniformity and homogeneity.

From the 1923 election to the present day, the two parties have been more or less equally strong in Mayo. For decades the names of IRA and SF men active in the revolutionary period dominated the candidates and representatives elected for the Dáil in Mayo, particularly Fianna Fáil TDs such as Michael Kilroy, Edward Moane, Dick Walsh and Patrick J. Ruttledge, and for a while also Joseph MacBride and William Sears for Cumann na nGaedheal. Others were side-lined or moved elsewhere. Tom Maguire and John Madden refused to accept the Free State and stayed with SF but were soon politically marginalized. Maguire was particularly principled in this, not even accepting the use of official postal stamps. By the end of his long life in 1993, he was the only surviving member of the second Dáil elected in 1921. Thus, he formed by himself the only legitimate authority for hard-line republicans, although this authority had been formally signed over by him and other survivors to the IRA army council in 1938. Thomas Derrig was also forced to move away from Mayo as a result of his initial refusal to sign a declaration of allegiance to the Free State as a requirement for his job as teacher in Westport. He found a position in Dublin and became a founding member and leading Fianna Fáiler at national level, representing Carlow–Kilkenny as a TD. The names of these men also aided some of their family members in their political careers later on, such as the Ring family.

Certain underlying long-term developments were continued during the conflict and some were accelerated. The economic and social power of landlords and that of Protestants in general almost completely vanished. Land sales had begun after the land acts of the late nineteenth century but really only became substantial in the pre-war period, leaving the greater majority of tenants in control of their land by 1923. This also explained the dominance of the two parties who both had a rural base, Fianna Fáil among small farmers and Cumann na nGaedheal among the larger farmers and business interests. Nevertheless, the rise of labour that began in the years before the revolution was certainly accelerated. Labour candidates did quite well in the 1923 election and had their first and only TD elected in June 1927 when Tom O'Connell topped the polls in South Mayo. Afterwards labour interests seemed to have been submerged in the struggle between the two major parties. However, both these developments can be viewed as revolutionary, with wide social and even cultural implications.

Although the power of the landlords in almost all areas of life had basically been broken and some new powerful families had come to the fore, mostly through their involvement in the republican movement, the lives of the greater majority of Mayo citizens were not fundamentally altered in an economic or even social sense. The economic conditions only slowly improved, although the change in government certainly had some influence on this. The impact of the change was felt more acutely in a cultural sense, with a much stronger emphasis on expressions of Irish culture in schools and also local politics. The rise of Gaelic games in the county was perhaps the most obvious aspect of this, with these games now becoming a major feature of county life.

Traditionally, developments in Ireland between 1912 and 1923 were never seen as a 'revolution', as this was defined as a cataclysmic event that fundamentally altered social-economic relations. However, this definition was based on the successful great revolutions of the twentieth century, beginning with the Russian and ending perhaps with the Cuban one. Since then a re-evaluation has taken place and great political changes such as in the Irish Revolution are now also seen as genuine revolutions. This was the case in Mayo where the Irish Revolution caused major cultural change and at least accelerated a fundamental alteration in social and economic relations.

Notes

CHAPTER ONE *County Mayo before the Revolution*

1 *Freeman's Journal* (hereafter *FJ*), 30 Mar. 1914; John Burke, *Roscommon: the Irish Revolution, 1912–23* (Dublin, 2021), pp 4–7.
2 *Census of Ireland 1911, Area, houses, and population: also the ages, civil or conjugal condition, occupations, birthplaces, religion, and education of the people; Province of Connaught, County of Mayo, HC, 1912–13* (Cd. 6052).
3 *Census of Ireland 1911, Area, houses, and population*; Breandán Mac Giolla Choille (ed.), *Intelligence notes, 1913–16* (Dublin, 1966), pp 119, 181, 194–5.
4 *Census of Ireland 1911, Area, houses, and population.*
5 CI Mayo, July 1912 (TNA, CO 904/87).
6 *Census of Ireland 1911, Area, houses, and population*; Burke, *Roscommon*, p. 4.
7 *Census of Ireland 1911, Area, houses, and population.*
8 Reg Hindley, *The death of the Irish language: a qualified obituary* (London, 1990), p. 27; Timothy G. MacMahon, *Grand opportunity: the Gaelic revival and Irish society, 1893–1910* (Syracuse, 2008), pp 14–16, 122–3; CI Mayo, Jan.–Dec. 1914 (TNA, CO 904/92–95).
9 Owen McGee, 'William Doris', *DIB*; CI Mayo, Jan. 1912 (TNA, CO 904/86); Ned Maughan (UCDA, O'Malley notebooks, P17b/109).
10 Sinn Féin movement. Possession of and carrying of arms, 1907–1912 (The National Archives (TNA), CO 904/23/1).
11 Kilroy, 'The awakening', Clew Bay Heritage Centre, Westport (CBHC). See also Richard Walsh (BMH WS 400).
12 James Chambers, 'Statement' (private possession).
13 Richard Walsh (BMH WS 400, p. 2).
14 Chambers, 'Statement'; Edward Moane, 'Statement' (private possession).
15 Moane, 'Statement'. See also Chambers, 'Statement'.
16 Moane, 'Statement'; Thomas Heavey, 'Statement' (private possession).
17 Patrick Cassidy (BMH WS 1,017); Patrick Joseph Cannon (BMH WS 830); Martin Mooney (BMH WS 1,602); John Timony (BMH WS 1,629); Patrick Lyons (BMH WS 1,645); Michael Henry (BMH WS 1,732); Richard Walsh (BMH WS 400); Seán T. Ruane (BMH WS 1,588); Michael McHugh (BMH WS 1,632); P.J. (Paddy) Kelly (BMH WS 1,735).
18 IG, Apr.–May 1912 (TNA, CO 904/86–87); CI, Mayo, Sept. 1912 (TNA, CO 904/88).
19 CI Mayo, Mar. 1914 (TNA, CO 904/92); Jack Feehan (UCDA, O'Malley notebooks, P17b/113); Michael Moran, 'With Michael Kilroy during Easter Week 1916 and the years before', CBHC; Ned Maughan (this is the same man as Edward (Ned) Moane) (UCDA, O'Malley notebooks, P17b/10); Chambers, 'Statement'; P.J. (Paddy) Kelly (BMH WS 1,735); Kilroy, 'The awakening'; Jack Feehan (UCDA, O'Malley notebooks, P17b/113); Charles Hughes, Interview, Dec. 1989.
20 CI Mayo, Feb., Mar. 1912 (TNA, CO 904/86); Marnie Hay, *Na Fianna Éireann and the Irish Revolution, 1909–23: scouting for rebels* (Manchester, 2019), chapter 3.
21 CI Mayo, Dec. 1912 (TNA, CO 904/88); Ned Maughan (UCDA, O'Malley notebooks, P17b/109); Vincent Keane, 'Westport Sluagh', *Cathair na Mart*, 26 (2006/7), 38; Thomas Kettrick (BMH WS 872); Seán Gibbons (BMH WS 927).
22 Seán Gibbons (BMH WS 927, p. 2).
23 CI Mayo, Jan. 1912 (TNA, CO 904/86).

24 'Narrative of Edward O'Connor' (National Library of Ireland (hereafter NLI), MS 17,506).
25 Tom Maguire, Interview, Dec. 1989.
26 *Connaught Telegraph* (hereafter *CT*), 16 Mar., 7 Dec. 1912, 8 Feb., 1, 8, 15 Mar. 1913.
27 *CT*, and *Mayo News* (hereafter *MN*), 17 Aug. 1912.
28 Ibid.
29 *CT*, 1 Mar. 1913.
30 Ibid., 11 July 1914. See also ibid., 1, 22 Feb., 1 Mar., 12 July 1913, 4 July 1914.
31 Ibid., 20 July 1912.
32 *MN*, 18 July 1914.
33 *CT*, 23 Aug. 1913.
34 *Connacht Tribune* (hereafter *CTr*), 20 June 1914.
35 *CT*, 16 Aug. 1913.
36 Ibid., 9 Aug., 18 Oct. 1913.
37 IG, Oct. 1913 (TNA, CO 904/91); R.F. Foster, *Vivid faces: the revolutionary generation in Ireland, 1890–1923* (London, 2014), p. 212.
38 *CT*, 10 Jan. 1914.
39 *Irish Independent* (hereafter *II*), 25 Sept. 1911.

CHAPTER TWO *'A state of great unrest and agitation': the home rule crisis in Mayo, 1912–14*

1 Patrick Maume, *The long gestation: Irish nationalist life, 1891–1918* (New York, 1999), pp 105–6.
2 *Irish Times* (hereafter *IT*), 7 Feb. 1910.
3 Ibid., 2, 5, 10 Dec. 1910; *CT*, 10 Dec. 1910; *Weekly Irish Times* (hereafter *WIT*), 10 Oct. 1910; Maume, *Long gestation*, p. 116; Burke, *Roscommon*, p. 9.
4 Maume, *Long gestation*, pp 116–17.
5 *WIT*, 10 Oct. 1910.
6 *CT*, 1 Jan. 1910; Maume, *Long gestation*, p. 106.
7 *CT*, 22 Oct. 1910, 1 Jan. 1920, 19 Jan. 1910, 3 Dec. 1910; Brian Walker, *Parliamentary election results in Ireland, 1801–1922* (Dublin, 1978), pp 365–7; Maume, *Long gestation*, pp 116–17.
8 *CT*, 13 Aug. 1910.
9 Ibid., 10 Dec. 1910.
10 *IT*, 26 Jan. 1910.
11 *CT*, 3 Dec. 1910. See also *IT*, 26 Jan. 1910.
12 *CT*, 3 Sept. 1910. See also Maume, *Long gestation*, p. 116.
13 *CT*, 17 Sept. 1910. See also *CT*, 17, 24 Dec. 1910.
14 *IT*, 26 Jan. 1910; Walker, *Parliamentary election results*, p. 366; Maume, *Long gestation*, pp 116–17.
15 Daniel E. Jordan, *Land and popular politics in Ireland: County Mayo from the Plantations to the Land War* (Cambridge, 2011), pp 191, 222, 252; Maume, *Long gestation*, p. 117.
16 Maume, *Long gestation*, p. 117; *FJ*, 19 Dec. 1910.
17 *IT*, 24 Dec. 1910.
18 Maume, *Long gestation*, p. 117.
19 *FJ*, 21 Jan. 1910.
20 *CT*, 17 Sept. 1910; *FJ*, 1 Jan. 1910.
21 *IT*, 20 Dec. 1910.
22 *FJ*, 15 June, 7 July 1911; *CT*, 4 Feb., 29 July 1911.
23 *FJ*, 15 May, 16 June 1911.
24 Ibid., 8 Mar. 1912; *II*, 28 Dec. 1911; *CT*, 16 Mar. 1912.
25 *II*, 28 Dec. 1911.
26 *IT*, 28 May 1910.

27 *II*, 19, 28 Dec. 1911; Burke, *Roscommon*, pp 4–7; Michael Farry, *Sligo: the Irish Revolution, 1912–23* (Dublin, 2012), p. 5.
28 CI Mayo, Jan., Feb. 1912 (TNA, CO 904/86).
29 RIC Inspector–General (IG), CI Mayo, Feb. 1912 (TNA, CO 904/86).
30 CI Mayo, Mar.–Dec. 1912 (TNA, CO 904/86–88).
31 *FJ*, 20 Apr. 1912; *CT*, 8 June 1912.
32 *CT*, 8 June 1912.
33 *MN*, 20 Apr. 1912.
34 *FJ*, 19, 20 Apr. 1912.
35 Ibid., 15 Aug. 1913.
36 *CT*, 22 Mar. 1913, 13 June 1914; *FJ*, 8 Apr., 1 May 1913.
37 *FJ*, 18 Sept. 1913.
38 *II*, 5 Dec. 1913.
39 *CT*, 31 Jan. 1914.
40 *II*, 20 Jan. 1914.
41 *CT*, 13 June 1914.
42 Ibid., 10 Oct. 1914.
43 *II*, 20 May 1914.
44 Ibid.; IG, June–Nov. 1913 (TNA, CO 904/90–91).
45 *IT*, 4 June 1912.
46 IG Feb. 1913, CI Mayo, Jan.–Feb. 1913 (TNA, CO 904/89).
47 *IT*, 11 Mar. 1913; CI Mayo, Apr., July, Aug., Dec. 1913 (TNA, CO 904/90–91); *MN*, 26 July 1913.
48 CI Mayo, Feb. 1914 (TNA, CO 904/92).
49 *CT*, 25 July 1914.
50 *II*, 22 July 1914.
51 CI Mayo, Apr. 1914 (TNA, CO 904/93).
52 CI Mayo, Feb. 1914 (TNA, CO 904/92).
53 CI Mayo, May 1914 (TNA, CO 904/93).
54 Mac Giolla Choille, *Intelligence notes*, p. 66; Burke, *Roscommon*, p. 5.
55 *CT*, 28 Sept. 1912.
56 *FJ*, 30 Mar. 1914.
57 Mac Giolla Choille, *Intelligence notes*, p. 89; CI Mayo, Apr. 1914 (TNA, CO 904/93).
58 CI Mayo, Feb. 1914 (TNA, CO 904/92).
59 IG, Jan. 1912 (TNA, CO 904/86).
60 IG, Jan.–July 1913 (TNA, CO 904/89–90).
61 IG, Aug. 1913 (TNA, CO 904/90).
62 IG, Mar., June 1913 (TNA, CO 904/89–90).
63 IG, Sept.–Nov. 1913 (TNA, CO 904/91).
64 IG, CI Mayo, Apr., July 1912 (TNA, CO 904/86–7).
65 *FJ*, 18 Sept. 1913.
66 *II*, 20 Jan. 1914.
67 *CT*, 31 Jan. 1914.
68 IG, CI Mayo, Aug. 1912 (TNA, CO 904/87).
69 IG, Oct.–Nov. 1912 (TNA, CO 904/88).
70 Richard Walsh (BMH WS 400, p. 3).
71 IG, July, Nov.–Dec. 1912 (TNA, CO 904/88).
72 IG, Nov.–Dec. 1913 (TNA, CO 904/91).
73 *MN*, 6 Dec. 1913.
74 *FJ*, 15 Dec. 1913.
75 Ned Maughan (UCDA, O'Malley notebooks, P17b/109); Jack Feehan (UCDA, O'Malley notebooks, P17b/113); Moran, 'With Michael Kilroy'.

76 CI Mayo, Jan. 1914 (TNA, CO 904/92); Victor Keane, 'Westport and the Irish Volunteers', *Cathair na Mart*, 22 (2002), 5; Kilroy, 'The awakening'.
77 *MN*, 16 May 1914; William King (BMH WS 1,381); Kilroy, 'The awakening'; Moane, 'Statement'; John Moran (BMH WS 1,549); Richard Walsh (BMH WS 400).
78 Peter McDonnell (BMH WS 1,612); John Haran (BMH WS 1,458); *MN*, 21 Mar. 1914.
79 Kilroy, 'The awakening'; IG, July 1913 (TNA, CO 904/90).
80 *CT*, 13 June 1914; *II*, 6 June 1914.
81 *FJ*, 31 Dec. 1913.
82 *MN*, 1 Mar. 1913.
83 Ibid., 14 Feb. 1914. See also CI Mayo, 1914 (TNA, CO 904/92–95).
84 Keane, 'Westport and the Irish Volunteers', 5.
85 CI, Apr. 1914 (TNA, CO 904/93).
86 *CT*, 16 May 1914.
87 Seán Walsh (BMH WS 1,733); Peter McDonnell (BMH WS 1,612).
88 *CT*, 16 May 1914; CI Mayo, May 1914 (TNA, CO 904/93).
89 IG, Apr. 1914 (TNA, CO 904/93).
90 Liam S. Gogan (BMH, WS 799); F.X. Martin, *The Irish Volunteers, 1913–1915: recollections and documents* (Dublin, 1963), p. 166; Charles Townshend, *Easter 1916: the Irish rebellion* (London, 2005), pp 52–4.
91 Keane, 'Westport and the Irish Volunteers', 5; Mac Giolla Choille, *Intelligence notes*, pp 90, 109.
92 Richard Walsh (BMH WS 400, p. 4); Sligo to Moore, 13, 15 Aug. 1914, Moore to Sligo, 17 Aug. 1914 (NLI, Maurice Moore papers, MS 10,561/37).
93 Richard Walsh (BMH WS 400); Michael McHugh (BMH WS 1,632).
94 George Hewson (BMH WS 1,569); William J. O'Hora (BMH WS 1,554); Stephen Donnelly (BMH WS 1,548); Michael Henry (BMH WS 1,732); John Timony (BMH WS 1,629); Patrick Coleman (BMH WS 1,683); John Moran (BMH WS 1,549); Patrick Hegarty (BMH WS 1,606); Seán T. Ruane (BMH WS 1,588); Martin Mooney (BMH WS 1,602); Patrick Lyons (BMH WS 1,645); Richard Walsh (BMH WS 400); Seán Gibbons (BMH WS 927); Michael McHugh (BMH WS 1,632); P.J. (Paddy) Kelly (BMH WS 1,735); John Haran (BMH WS 1,458).
95 Michael McHugh (BMH WS 1,632).
96 Seán Gibbons (BMH WS 927, p. 1).
97 Patrick Moylett (BMH WS 767, p. 1).

CHAPTER THREE '*Sham feiners and sham physical force men*': *war and protest, 1914–16*

1 CI Mayo, Aug.–Sept. 1914 (TNA, CO 904/94); *CT*, 8 Aug. 1914; *Western People* (hereafter *WP*), 8 Aug. 1914.
2 CI Mayo, Sept. 1914 (TNA, CO 904/94).
3 IG, Aug. 1914 (ibid.).
4 IG, Sept. 1914 (TNA, CO 904/94); Maume, *Long gestation*, p. 117.
5 CI Mayo, Sept. 1914 (TNA, CO 904/94).
6 *CT*, 12 Sept. 1914.
7 IG, Sept. 1914 (TNA, CO 904/94).
8 *CT*, 2 Sept. 1914; *CTr*. 8, 15 Aug. 1914; *WP*, 15 Aug. 1914.
9 *II*, 27 Mar. 1915. See also *CT*, 10 Oct. 1914.
10 *CT*, 31 Oct. 1914.
11 IG, Sept. 1914 (TNA, CO 904/94).
12 CI, Sept.–Dec. 1914 (TNA, CO 904/94–95).
13 IG, Oct.–Nov. 1914 (TNA, CO 904/95); Dillon to Moore, 25 Nov. 1914 (NLI, Moore papers, MS 10,561/9).

14 Seán Gibbons (BMH WS 927, p. 2). See also Moane, 'Statement'.
15 *CT*, 10 Oct. 1914; Michael McHugh (BMH WS 1,632).
16 Moane, 'Statement'; Kilroy, 'The awakening'.
17 *CT*, 31 Oct., 14 Nov. 1914; *WP*, 19 Dec., 6 Feb. 1915.
18 *MN*, 8 Aug. 1914.
19 *CT*, 19 Dec. 1914.
20 Ibid., 6 Feb. 1915.
21 Ibid.
22 Ibid., 15 Apr. 1916.
23 Ibid., 27 Feb. 1915.
24 Ibid., 3 Apr. 1915. See also ibid., 6 Nov. 1915.
25 Ibid., 26 Feb., 18 Mar. 1916.
26 Ibid., 11 Sept. 1915. See also *CT*, 29 May 1915; *WP*, 21 Nov. 1914.
27 *CT*, 15 Apr., 6 Nov. 1915.
28 Ibid., 3 Apr. 1915.
29 Ibid., 4 Sept. 1915; CI Mayo, May 1916 (TNA, CO 904/100).
30 Patrick Hegarty (BMH WS 1,606); Police reports (TNA, CO 904/122/2); Mac Giolla Choille, *Intelligence notes*, p. 153; IG, Mar. 1915; CI Mayo, Feb., Apr.–June, Aug., Oct., Dec. 1915, Aug. 1916 (TNA, CO 904/96–98, 100); Burke, *Roscommon*, p. 30.
31 CI Mayo, Aug. 1915 (TNA, CO 904/97); *CT*, 26 Feb. 1916.
32 *CT*, 4 Mar. 1916.
33 Ibid., 8 Jan. 1916.
34 Ibid., 4 Mar. 1916.
35 *II*, 27 Mar. 1915. See also ibid., 6 Mar. 1915.
36 *CT*, 10 Oct., 7, 29 Nov. 1914; *WP*, 7 Nov. 1914, 23 Jan. 1915; *MN*, 30 Jan. 1915; CI Mayo, Feb. 1915 (TNA, CO 904/96).
37 *II*, 9 Apr. 1915; *CT*, 20 Mar. 1915; Burke, *Roscommon*, p. 29; Farry, *Sligo*, p. 26.
38 *CT*, 31 Oct. 1914; *WP*, 31 Oct. 1914.
39 Patrick Hegarty (BMH WS 1,606).
40 *IT*, 20 Sept. 1915; *CT*, 18 Sept. 1915; Burke, *Roscommon*, p. 30.
41 *CT*, 30 Jan., 22 May, 23 Oct., 27 Nov., 4 Dec. 1915; *IT*, 20 Mar. 1916; *CTr*, 28 Aug. 1915; George Hewson (BMH WS 1,569); William King (BMH WS 1,381).
42 *WP*, 24 Apr. 1915; CI Mayo, Apr. 1915 (TNA, CO 904/96).
43 CI Mayo, June, Oct. 1915 (TNA, CO 904/97–98); *CT*, 20 Mar., 18 Sept. 1915; *WP*, 22 May 1915.
44 IG, May 1915 (TNA, CO 904/97); Mac Giolla Choille, *Intelligence notes*, p. 181; *CT*, 18, 25 Mar. 1916; *IT*, 20 Mar. 1916.
45 IG, Oct. 1914, Nov. 1915; CI Mayo, Sept.–Oct. 1915 (TNA, CO 904/95, 98); Patrick Cassidy (BMH WS 1,017).
46 Patrick Hegarty (BMH WS 1,606, p. 5).
47 *CT*, 26 June 1915; *WP*, 13 Nov. 1915; Seán Gibbons (BMH WS 927); Diarmuid Lynch (BMH WS 4).
48 Charles Wyse-Power (BMH WS 420); Moane, 'Statement'.
49 *CT*, 2 Jan., 6 Feb., 13, 27 Mar., 17 Apr., 4 Sept., 13 Nov. 1915; *WP*, 20 Feb., 27 Mar., 8 May 1915; Chambers, 'Statement'.
50 *CT*, 17 Oct. 1914.
51 IG, Dec. 1914, Jan. 1915 (TNA, CO 904/95–96).
52 Kilroy, 'The awakening'.
53 Diarmuid Lynch (BMH WS 4).

54 Richard Walsh (BMH WS 400); P.J. (Paddy) Kelly (BMH WS 1,735); Brodie Malone (UCDA, O'Malley notebooks, P17b/109); Brigadier Éamonn Moane and Vice-Commandant Brodie Malone, 'Transcript of tape recordings' (private possession).
55 Moane, 'Statement'; Chambers, 'Statement'; Moane and Malone, 'Transcript'; Kilroy, 'The awakening'.
56 CI Mayo, Dec. 1915, Jan. 1916 (TNA, CO 904/98–99); Mac Giolla Choille, *Intelligence notes*, p. 178.
57 Patrick Moylett (BMH WS 767).
58 CI Mayo, Sept. 1914 (TNA, CO 904/94); Heavey, 'Statement'.
59 Seán T. Ruane (BMH WS 1,588); Martin Mooney (BMH WS 1,602); Seán Walsh (BMH WS 1,733); Martin Conneely (BMH WS 1,611); William J. O'Hora (BMH WS 1,554); Patrick Cassidy (BMH WS 1,017); Patrick Lyons (BMH WS 1,645); Richard Walsh (BMH WS 400); Thomas Hawley (BMH WS 1,122); Michael McHugh (BMH WS 1,632); Chambers, 'Statement'; John Haran (BMH WS 1,458); Peter McDonnell (BMH WS 1,612); Mac Giolla Choille, *Intelligence notes*, p. 153.
60 Membership of Volunteers, CI Mayo, 1914–16 (TNA, CO 904/92–101).
61 'Statement of Michael Kilroy's wife' (CBHC); Kilroy, 'The awakening'.
62 Brodie Malone (UCDA, O'Malley notebooks, P17b/109); Moane and Malone, 'Transcript'.
63 Patrick Moylett (BMH WS 767).
64 *CT*, 3 Apr. 1915; Mac Giolla Choille, *Intelligence notes*, p. 178; CI Mayo, Apr. 1915 (TNA, CO 904/96); Chambers, 'Statement'.
65 John Feehan (BMH WS 1,692).
66 Brodie Malone (UCDA, O'Malley notebooks, P17b/109); Moane, 'Statement'.
67 Martin Conneely (BMH WS 1,611); P.J. (Paddy) Kelly (BMH WS 1,735).
68 Mac Giolla Choille, *Intelligence notes*, pp 119, 171; CI Mayo, Dec. 1914, June, Aug. 1915, Feb. 1916 (TNA, CO 904/95, 97, 99); Patrick Lyons (BMH WS 1,645).
69 'Statement of Michael Kilroy's wife'.
70 Seán Gibbons (BMH WS 927, p. 5). See also William King (BMH WS 1,381); Patrick Hegarty (BMH WS 1,606).
71 CI Mayo, Aug. 1915 (TNA, CO 904/97).
72 Richard Walsh (BMH WS 400).
73 Peter McDonnell (BMH WS 1,612); Tadhg Crowley (BMH WS 435).
74 John Feehan (BMH WS 1,692).
75 Richard Walsh (BMH WS 400, p. 10).
76 Martin Conneely (BMH WS 1,611); P.J. (Paddy) Kelly (BMH WS 1,735); Patrick J. Kelly, 'One of the men of the West' (CBHC); John Feehan (BMH WS 1,692); Mac Giolla Choille, *Intelligence notes*, p. 220.
77 Moane, 'Statement'.
78 'Statement of Michael Kilroy's wife'; Michael McHugh (BMH WS 1,632); Patrick Hegarty (BMH WS 1,606); Patrick Moylett (BMH WS 767).
79 Chambers, 'Statement'.
80 CI Mayo, Apr.–May 1916 (TNA, CO 904/99–100); Patrick Cassidy (BMH WS 1,017); Stephen Donnelly (BMH WS 1,548); Richard Walsh (BMH WS 400); Michael McHugh (BMH WS 1,632); Seán Glancy (BMH WS 946); Thomas Kettrick (BMH WS 872); Liam S. Ó Rioghbhardain (BMH WS 888); Moane, 'Statement'; Thomas Hawley (BMH WS 1,122); Seán T. Ruane (BMH WS 1,588).
81 John Feehan (BMH WS 1,692, p. 3). See also Jack Feehan (UCDA, O'Malley notebooks, P17b/113).
82 CI Mayo, Apr. 1916 (TNA, CO 904/99); *CT*, 6, 13 May 1916; Thomas Kettrick (BMH WS 872); Seán Gibbons (BMH WS 927); P.J. (Paddy) Kelly (BMH WS 1,735).

83 CT, 6 May 1916; WP, 13 May 1916.
84 Thomas Hawley (BMH WS 1,122); Richard Walsh (BMH WS 400); Seán T. Ruane (BMH WS 1,588); Seán Gibbons (BMH WS 927); Thomas Kettrick, 'Statement' (private possession); CI Mayo, May 1916 (TNA, CO 904/100); CT, 13 May 1916.
85 CI Mayo, Apr.–May 1916 (TNA, CO 904/99–100); Patrick Cassidy (BMH WS 1,017); Thomas Kettrick (BMH WS 872); Michael McHugh (BMH WS 1,632); P.J. (Paddy) Kelly (BMH WS 1,735); Richard Walsh (BMH WS 400).
86 Seán T. Ruane (BMH WS 1,588).
87 CI Mayo, May 1916 (TNA, CO 904/100); Prison records, Castlebar prison (NAI MFGS/51/004); Sean O'Mahony, *Frongoch: university of revolution* (Killiney, 1987), pp 208–9; Michael McHugh (BMH WS 1,632); Seán Gibbons (BMH WS 927); CT, 13 May 1916; Richard Walsh (BMH WS 400); Mac Giolla Choille, *Intelligence notes*, pp 220, 240; 'Statement of Michael Kilroy's wife'.
88 CT, 13 May 1916; CI Mayo, May 1916 (TNA, CO 904/100).
89 CT, 6 May 1916; CI Mayo, Apr.–May 1916 (TNA, CO 904/99–100); CT, 26 Feb. 1916.
90 MN, CT, 13 May 1916.
91 CTr, 13 May 1916; WP, MN, CT, 20 May 1916.
92 CI Mayo, May 1916 (TNA, CO 904/100); Mac Giolla Choille, *Intelligence notes*, p. 220.
93 CT, 13 May 1916.

CHAPTER FOUR *'Up the Rebels': republicans take over local politics, 1916–18*

1 Stephen Donnelly (BMH WS 1,548, p. 3). See also Moane, 'Statement'; Kilroy, 'The awakening'; Seán Gibbons (BMH WS 927).
2 CI Mayo, May–Dec. 1916 (TNA, CO 904/100–101); WP, 21 Oct. 1916.
3 Tom Maguire, in Uinseann Mac Eoin (ed.), *Survivors* (Dublin, 1980), p. 278.
4 IG, July 1916 (TNA, CO 904/100); WP, 23 June 1917.
5 IG, Sept. 1916 (TNA, CO 904/101).
6 CI Mayo, June–Aug 1916 (TNA, CO 904/100).
7 IG, June–July 1916, CI Mayo, June–July 1916 (TNA, CO 904/100); Burke, *Roscommon*, pp 34–5; Farry, *Sligo*, p. 33.
8 CI Mayo, June–Nov. 1916, Feb. 1917 (TNA, CO 904/100–102). See also Moane, 'Statement'; Martin Mooney (BMH WS 1,602); Caoimhe Nic Dháibhéid, 'The Irish National Aid association and the radicalization of public opinion in Ireland', *Historical Journal*, 55:3 (2012), 705–29.
9 CI Mayo, Aug.–Dec. 1916, Jan. 1917 (TNA, CO 904/101); Thomas Hawley (BMH WS 1,122); Thomas Kettrick (BMH WS 872); CT, 6 Jan. 1917.
10 Richard Walsh (BMH WS 400); Seán T. Ruane (BMH WS 1,588); Thomas Hawley (BMH WS 1,122); Stephen Donnelly (BMH WS 1,548); Michael Henry (BMH WS 1,732); Moane, 'Statement'; Seán Walsh (BMH WS 1,733); CI Mayo, Feb. 1917 (TNA, CO 904/102); Michael Laffan, *The resurrection of Ireland: the Sinn Féin party, 1916–1923* (Cambridge, 1999), pp 76–106.
11 Jim O'Donnell, 'Recollections based on the diary of an Irish Volunteer 1898 to 1924' (CBHC). See also Patrick Owen Mugan, Interview; CI Mayo, Dec. 1916 (TNA, CO 904/101).
12 Johnny Duffy (UCDA, O'Malley notebooks, P17b/109); Philbin, 'Statement'; Joost Augusteijn, *From public defiance to guerrilla warfare* (Dublin, 1996), Chapter 2.
13 Moane, 'Statement'. See also Moane and Malone, 'Transcript'. Moane's arrest, Moane, 'Statement'; Kettrick, 'Statement'; Tom Maguire, in Mac Eoin (ed.), *Survivors*, p. 278.
14 Patrick Lyons (BMH WS 1,645); Seán Walsh (BMH WS 1,733); John Timony (BMH WS 1,629); Tommy Heavey, Interview 24 Jan. 1990; Thomas Conroy, Interview 1 Dec. 1990/.
15 John Timony (BMH WS 1,629).

16 Michael Henry (BMH WS 1,732); Tom Maguire, Interviews; Moane, 'Statement'; Seán Walsh (BMH WS 1,733); Paddy Duffy (UCDA, O'Malley notebooks, P17b/128); John Joe Philbin, 'Statement' (private possession); Patrick Fallon (UCDA, O'Malley notebooks, P17b/109); Edward O'Malley, *Memories of a Mayoman* (Dublin, 1981), p. 20; John Feehan (BMH WS 1,692); Seán Gibbons (BMH WS 927).

17 CI Mayo, Feb.–May 1917 (TNA, CO 904/102–103); Michael McHugh (BMH WS 1,632); Kilroy, 'The awakening': Seán Walsh (BMH WS 1,733); Patrick Hegarty (BMH WS 1,606).

18 NLI, Collins papers, P 921/66; UCDA, Mulcahy papers, P7A19/101, 116.

19 Richard Walsh (BMH WS 400); Patrick Cassidy (BMH WS 1,017); William King (BMH WS 1,381); Martin Conneely (BMH WS 1,611); Jack Feehan (UCDA, O'Malley notebooks, P17b/113); Petie Joe MacDonald (UCDA, O'Malley notebooks, P17b/113).

20 CI Mayo, Jan.–May 1917 (TNA, CO 904/102–103).

21 *CT*, 9 Sept. 1916. See also ibid., 16, 23 Sept., 11 Nov. 1916; *WP*, 3 Mar. 1917.

22 CI Mayo, Jan.–May 1917 (TNA, CO 904/102–103); Patrick Moylett (BMH WS 767).

23 Patrick Moylett (BMH WS 767).

24 Kilroy, 'The awakening'; CI Mayo, June–Dec. 1917 (TNA, CO 904/103–104); Liam S. Ó Rioghbhardain (BMH WS 888); Thomas Kettrick (BMH WS 872).

25 *CT*, 28 July 1917; *MN*, 9, 30 June 1917; *WP*, 23 June 1917; Patrick Moylett (BMH WS 767).

26 CI Mayo, Oct. 1917 (TNA, CO 904/104). See also CI Mayo, June–Dec. 1917 (TNA, CO 904/103–104); Thomas Kettrick (BMH WS 872); Kilroy, 'The awakening'; Stephen Donnelly (BMH WS 1,548); *MN*, 7 July 1917; Burke, *Roscommon*, p. 59; Farry, *Sligo*, pp 32–3, 37.

27 CI Mayo, Sept.–Nov. 1917 (TNA, CO 904/104); Seán Walsh (BMH WS 1,733).

28 Moane, 'Statement'. See also Moane and Malone, 'Transcript'. Moane's arrest, Moane, 'Statement'; Kettrick, 'Statement'; Tom Maguire, in Mac Eoin (ed.), *Survivors*, p. 278.

29 Patrick Coleman (BMH WS 1,683); Richard Walsh (BMH WS 400); Stephen Donnelly (BMH WS 1,548); Michael Henry (BMH WS 1,732); Thomas Hawley (BMH WS 1,122); John Feehan (BMH WS 1,692); Seán Gibbons (BMH WS 927); CI Mayo, Jan.–May 1917 (TNA, CO 904/102–103).

30 Battie Cryan (UCDA, O'Malley notebooks, P17b/120); Prison records, Castlebar prison (NAI MFGS/51/004).

31 Richard Walsh (BMH WS 400, p. 84).

32 Patrick Coleman (BMH WS 1,683, pp 2–3); Seán Gibbons (BMH WS 927); Michael Henry (BMH WS 1,732); Richard Walsh (BMH WS 400).

33 Patrick Joseph Cannon (BMH WS 830); Michael Henry (BMH WS 1,732); P.J. (Paddy) Kelly (BMH WS 1,735); Patrick Cassidy (BMH WS 1,017); Seán Walsh (BMH WS 1,733); John Timony (BMH WS 1,629); George Hewson (BMH WS 1,569); Michael Staines (BMH WS 944); Stephen Donnelly (BMH WS 1,548); O'Malley, *Memories*, p. 20; John Feehan (BMH WS 1,692); CI Mayo, Apr. 1917 (TNA, CO 904/102); Nic Dháibhéid, 'The Irish National Aid Association'.

34 Kettrick, 'Statement', *CT*, 8 Dec. 1917. See also *CTr*, 15 Dec. 1917; Tom Maguire (UCDA, O'Malley notebooks, P17b/100); Johnny Duffy (UCDA, O'Malley notebooks, P17b/109); Thomas Kettrick (BMH WS 872); Kelly, 'One of the men of the West'; Brodie Malone (UCDA, O'Malley notebooks, P17b/109); Michael McHugh (BMH WS 1,632); Seán Gibbons (BMH WS 927); CI Mayo, 1916–18 (TNA, CO 904/99–107); IG, Jan. 1918 (TNA, CO 904/105).

35 'Arms and ammunition. Returns of arms in possession of Irish, National and Ulster Volunteers, 1917' (TNA, CO 904/29/2).

36 Óglaigh na hÉireann. GHQ, Dublin: Orders, dispatches, etc. to Cork, 1917–1921 (NLI, Florence O'Donoghue papers, MS 31,190). See also IG, 1918 (TNA, CO 904/105–107).

37 Ned Maughan (UCDA, O'Malley notebooks, P17b/109); Michael Kilroy (UCDA O'Malley notebooks, P17b/101); Patrick Cassidy (BMH WS 1,017); Seán Gibbons (BMH WS 927); Richard Walsh (BMH WS 400); Thomas Kettrick (BMH WS 872).
38 Charles Townshend, *The British campaign in Ireland, 1919–1921* (Oxford, 1975), p. 5. See also IG, Feb. 1917 (TNA, CO 904/102).
39 Police reports (TNA, CO 904/122/2). See also CI Mayo, Nov.–Dec. 1917 (TNA, CO 904/104); Moane, 'Statement'; Ned Maughan (UCDA, O'Malley notebooks, P17b/109); Chambers, 'Statement', 4; Thomas Hawley (BMH WS 1,122); Seán T. Ruane (BMH WS 1,588); Burke, *Roscommon*, pp 57, 61–2; Farry, *Sligo*, pp 32–3, 37–8
40 Police reports (TNA, CO 904/122/2). See also CI Mayo, Nov.–Dec. 1917 (TNA, CO 904/104).
41 Chambers, 'Statement': 4; CI Mayo, Jan. 1918 (TNA, CO 904/105).
42 Chambers, 'Statement'.
43 Seán T. Ruane (BMH WS 1,588, p. 12). See also CI Mayo, Dec. 1917, Feb. 1918 (TNA, CO 904/104–105); Stephen Donnelly (BMH WS 1,548); Martin Mooney (BMH WS 1,602); Moane, 'Statement'; Ned Maughan (UCDA, O'Malley notebooks, P17b/109); John Feehan (BMH WS 1,692); Thomas Kettrick (BMH WS 872); Martin Mooney (BMH WS 1,602); Patrick Hegarty (BMH WS1,606); Seán Walsh (BMH WS 1,733).
44 CI Mayo, Jan.–Mar. 1918 (TNA, CO 904/105); Kilroy, 'The awakening'.
45 Patrick Coleman (BMH WS 1,683, p. 3). See also CI Mayo, Oct. 1918 (TNA, CO 904/107).
46 IG, Sept. 1917–Jan. 1918 (TNA, CO 904/104–105); Police reports (TNA, CO 904/122/2); Kilroy, 'The awakening'; Tom Maguire, in Mac Eoin, *Survivors*, p. 278; John Timony (BMH WS 1,629); Patrick Coleman (BMH WS 1,683).
47 Brodie Malone (UCDA, O'Malley notebooks, P17b/109). See also Kettrick, 'Statement'.
48 Patrick Hegarty (BMH WS1,606); Seán Walsh (BMH WS 1,733).
49 Kilroy, 'The awakening'.
50 Johnny Duffy (UCDA, O'Malley notebooks, P17b/109).
51 Kilroy, 'The awakening'; CI Mayo, Mar. 1918 (TNA, CO 904/105).
52 *WP*, 9, 16, 30 Mar. 1918; *MN*, 9, 16 Mar. 1918, *CT*, 9, 16 Mar. 1918.
53 *CT*, 14 Apr. 1917.
54 Desmond Greaves, *The Irish Transport and General Workers' Union* (Dublin, 1982), pp 203–4; CI Mayo, Jan.–Mar. 1918 (TNA, CO 904/105); *MN*, 5 May 1917.
55 Burke, *Roscommon*, pp 10, 69; Farry, *Sligo*, pp 16–17, 43.
56 Seán T. Ruane (BMH WS 1,588); Martin Mooney (BMH WS 1,602); Kevin R. O'Shiel (BMH WS 1,770); Patrick Lyons (BMH WS 1,645); *WP*, 5 May 1917, 16 Feb. 1918; CI Mayo, June–Dec. 1919 (TNA, CO 904/109–110).
57 CI Mayo, May 1916–Dec. 1918 (TNA, CO 904/100–107); *MN*, 2 Feb. 1918; Burke, *Roscommon*, passim.
58 CI Mayo, Jan. 1918 (TNA, CO 904/105).
59 CI Mayo, Jan.–June 1918 (TNA, CO 904/105–106).
60 O'Donnell. 'Recollections'. See also Patrick Coleman (BMH WS 1,683); Burke, *Roscommon*, p. 56; Farry, *Sligo*, pp 42–3.
61 Pat Fallon (UCDA, O'Malley notebooks, P17b/109). See also CI Mayo, Feb.–Mar. 1918 (TNA, CO 904/105); Police reports (TNA, CO 904/122/2); Stephen Donnelly (BMH WS 1,548).
62 *WP*, 30 Mar. 1918. See also CI Mayo, Apr.–Dec. 1918 (TNA, CO 904/105–107); Seán Gibbons (BMH WS 927); Patrick Cassidy (BMH WS 1,017); *WP*, 27 Apr. 1918; *CT*, 4 May 1918; Farry, *Sligo*, p. 41; Burke, *Roscommon*, p. 64.
63 *WP*, 20 Apr. 1918; *CT*, 20 Apr. 1918; Seán Walsh (BMH WS 1,733). See also John Shouldice (BMH WS 679); Patrick Cassidy (BMH WS 1,017).
64 John Feehan (BMH WS 1,692); O'Malley, *Memories*, 23.

65 Michael McHugh (BMH WS 1,632); Chambers, 'Statement'; P.J. (Paddy) Kelly (BMH WS 1,735); Philbin, 'Statement'; Patrick Coleman (BMH WS 1,683); Martin Mooney (BMH WS 1,602); Patrick Cassidy (BMH WS 1,017); O'Donnell, 'Recollections'; CI Mayo, May 1918 (TNA, CO 904/106); Kilroy, 'The awakening'; Seán Walsh (BMH WS 1,733); Michael Henry (BMH WS 1,732); Kelly, 'One of the men of the West'; John Feehan (BMH WS 1,692).
66 Seán Walsh (BMH WS 1,733, p. 4). See also William J. O'Hora (BMH WS 1,554); Seán Gibbons (BMH WS 927); Tom Maguire, in Mac Eoin (ed.), *Survivors*, p. 278; Tom Maguire, Interview; Philbin, 'Statement'; Patrick Coleman (BMH WS 1,683); Patrick Cassidy (BMH WS 1,017).
67 Richard Walsh (BMH WS 400); Michael Henry (BMH WS 1,732); Seán Walsh (BMH WS 1,733); Seán T. Ruane (BMH WS 1,588); Chambers, 'Statement'; Martin Mooney (BMH WS 1,602); Moane, 'Statement'; Chambers, 'Statement'.
68 Jack Connolly (UCDA, O'Malley notebooks, P17b/120). See also Chambers, 'Statement'; Patrick Joseph Gannon (BMH WS 830); Patrick Cassidy (BMH WS 1,017); 'Statement of Michael Kilroy's wife'.
69 O'Donnell, 'Recollections'. See also Chambers, 'Statement', 6; Michael Henry (BMH WS 1,732); UCDA, Mulcahy papers, P7b172/27.
70 CI Mayo, Apr. 1918 (TNA, CO 904/105).
71 Michael McHugh (BMH WS 1,632, p. 4). See also Seán Gibbons (BMH WS 927); Martin Mooney (BMH WS 1,602); Patrick Lyons (BMH WS 1,645).
72 Seán T. Ruane (BMH WS 1,588).
73 Liam S. Ó Rioghbhardain (BMH WS 888); Richard Walsh (BMH WS 400); John Moran (BMH WS 1,549); Michael Kilroy (UCDA, O'Malley notebooks, P17b/101, P17b/136); Edward Moane (UCDA, O'Malley notebooks, P17b/136); Michael Henry (BMH WS 1,732); Dominick Molloy (BMH WS 1,570); John Madden (UCDA, O'Malley notebooks, P17b/113); Robert Brennan (BMH WS 779 (Section1); John Feehan (BMH WS 1,692).
74 CI Mayo, Apr. 1918 (TNA, CO 904/105).
75 Moane, 'Statement'; Seán Gibbons (BMH WS 927).
76 CI Mayo, Apr.–May 1918 (TNA, CO 904/105–106).
77 CI Mayo, May–Dec. 1918 (TNA, CO 904/106–107).
78 CI Mayo, Sept.–Nov. 1918 (TNA, CO 904/107); Stephen Donnelly (BMH WS 1,548); Brodie Malone (UCDA, O'Malley notebooks, P17b/109); Peadar McMahon (BMH WS 1,730); Joseph Good (BMH WS 388); Philbin, 'Statement'; Patrick Coleman (BMH WS 1,683); Patrick Cassidy (BMH WS 1,017); Seán Walsh (BMH WS 1,733); John Feehan (BMH WS 1,692).
79 *WP*, 9, 16 Nov. 1918. See also *CT*, 9 Nov. 1918; *WP*, 9 Nov. 1918; CI Mayo, Nov. 1918 (TNA, CO 904/107).
80 William J. O'Hora (BMH WS 1,554, p. 3). See also Patrick Hegarty (BMH WS 1,606); CI Mayo, Oct. 1918 (TNA, CO 904/107).
81 Richard Walsh (BMH WS 400); Seán Gibbons (BMH WS 927).
82 Patrick Lyons (BMH WS 1,645); Patrick Joseph Cannon (BMH WS 830).
83 William J. O'Hora (BMH WS 1,554).
84 On distributing food in Mayo, Patrick Owen Mugan, Interview. Violence and campaigns for election, CI Mayo, Oct.–Dec. 1918 (TNA, CO 904/107). P.J. (Paddy) Kelly (BMH WS 1,735); Kelly, 'One of the men of the West'.
85 Seán Walsh (BMH WS 1,733); Richard Walsh (BMH WS 400); William J. O'Hora (BMH WS 1,554).
86 Patrick Cassidy (BMH WS 1,017); Charles Gildea (BMH WS 1,313); Seán Gibbons (BMH WS 927).

87 Seán McNamara (BMH WS 1,047, p. 17). See also Hugh Hehir (BMH WS 683); Seamus Connelly (BMH WS 976); Patrick Kerin (BMH WS 977); Peter O'Loughlin (BMH WS 985); Anthony Malone (BMH WS 1,076); Charles Gildea (BMH WS 1,313); Thomas Hawley (BMH WS 1,122); Patrick Lyons (BMH WS 1,645); Seán Walsh (BMH WS 1,733); John Shouldice (BMH WS 679); Óglaigh Na hÉireann. G.H.Q., Dublin: Orders dispatches, etc. to Cork, 1917–1921 (NLI, O'Donoghue papers, MS 31,191); Ida Milne, *Stacking the coffins: influenza, war and revolution in Ireland, 1918–19* (Manchester, 2020), pp 60–7.
88 Seán Gibbons (BMH WS 927); Seán Walsh (BMH WS 1,733).
89 Seán Walsh (BMH WS 1,733, p. 11). See also Patrick Joseph Cannon (BMH WS 830); William J. O'Hora (BMH WS 1,554); Patrick Coleman (BMH WS 1,683); Martin Mooney (BMH WS 1,602); Seán Walsh (BMH WS 1,733); Patrick Lyons (BMH WS 1,645).
90 CI Mayo, Nov. 1918 (TNA, CO 904/107).
91 Patrick Lyons (BMH WS 1,645).
92 Johnny Duffy (UCDA, O'Malley notebooks, P17b/109).
93 Patrick Cassidy (BMH WS 1,017, p. 3).
94 Walker, *Parliamentary election results*, p. 394; John Shouldice (BMH WS 679); Martin Mooney (BMH WS 1,602); William J. O'Hora (BMH WS 1,554).
95 CI Mayo, Dec. 1918 (TNA, CO 904/107).

CHAPTER FIVE *'If the police with their local knowledge go, farewell to civil government': the struggle for dominance, 1919–20*

1 Richard Walsh (BMH WS 400); Joseph Good (BMH WS 388); Seán Gibbons (BMH WS 927); Patrick Dunlevy (BMH WS 1,489); CI Mayo, May 1919 (TNA, CO 904/109).
2 CI Mayo, Jan. 1919 (TNA, CO 904/108).
3 CI Mayo, Jan.–Dec. 1919 (TNA, CO 904/108–110); *CT*, 15 Feb., 29 Mar. 1919; *WP*, 15 Mar. 1919.
4 CI Mayo, July–Dec. 1919 (TNA, CO 904/109–110); *WP*, 13 Dec. 1919.
5 CI Mayo, Jan. 1919 (TNA, CO 904/108).
6 CI Mayo, June–Dec. 1919 (TNA, CO 904/109–110); Patrick Lyons (BMH WS 1,645).
7 *WP*, 25 Jan. 1919; *CT*, 25 Jan. 1919; *MN*, 25 Jan., 1 Feb. 1919; CI Mayo, Jan. 1919 (TNA, CO 904/108).
8 Patrick Hegarty (BMH WS 1,606, p. 10).
9 *CT*, 18 Jan. 1919.
10 Stephen Donnelly (BMH WS 1,548, p. 9). See also Patrick Coleman (BMH WS 1,683).
11 P.J. (Paddy) Kelly (BMH WS 1,735).
12 F.S. Bourke collection (NLI, MS 10,723/2); David Fitzpatrick, *Politics and Irish life, 1913–1921: provincial experience of war and revolution* (Dublin, 1977), pp 200–1; Patrick Owen Mugan, Interview; Seán Gibbons (BMH WS 927).
13 UCDA, Mulcahy papers, P7a158.
14 Lt. John Joe Philben, 'Statement'; O'Donnell, 'Recollections'; Paddy Duffy (UCDA, O'Malley notebooks, P17b/138); Patrick Cassidy (BMH WS 1,017).
15 Stephen Donnelly (BMH WS 1,548, p. 9).
16 P.J. (Paddy) Kelly (BMH WS 1,735); Thomas Hawley (BMH WS 1,122); Michael Henry (BMH WS 1,732); Patrick Hegarty (BMH WS 1,606); Patrick Dunlevy (BMH WS 1,489); Richard Walsh (BMH WS 400).
17 Patrick Owen Mugan, Interview.
18 CI Mayo, Jan.–July 1919 (TNA, CO 904/108–109); Michael Henry (BMH WS 1,732). Attention to organizing: Thomas Kettrick (BMH WS 872). Patrick Cassidy (BMH WS 1,017); P.J. (Paddy) Kelly (BMH WS 1,735); William J. O'Hora (BMH WS 1,554).

19 Brian Heffernan, *Freedom and the Fifth Commandment* (Manchester, 2014), pp 24, 46; Burke, *Roscommon*, p. 74; Farry, *Sligo*, p. 46.
20 K. Griffith & T. O'Grady, *Curious journey: an oral history of Ireland's unfinished revolution* (London, 1982), p. 187.
21 *CT*, 25 Jan. 1919; CI Mayo, Jan., Mar. 1919 (TNA, CO 904/108); *WP*, 28 June 1919; Heavey, 'Statement'. GHQ order to ask permission for serious operations (NLI, P 919/AO525).
22 CI Mayo, Jan.–Dec. 1919 (TNA, CO 904/108–110).
23 Gus Connolly (UCDA, O'Malley notebooks, P17b/91). See also Stephen Donnelly (BMH WS 1,548).
24 O'Donnell, 'Recollections'; John Timony (BMH WS 1,629); Patrick Joseph Cannon (BMH WS 830); Michael Henry (BMH WS 1,732).
25 Patrick Coleman (BMH WS 1,683); Patrick Joseph Cannon (BMH WS 830); Stephen Donnelly (BMH WS 1,548); Patrick Cassidy (BMH WS 1,017); Patrick Hegarty (BMH WS 1,606); Martin Mooney (BMH WS 1,602); William J. O'Hora (BMH WS 1,554); Michael Henry (BMH WS 1,732); John Timony (BMH WS 1,629).
26 Seán Gibbons (BMH WS 927); P.J. (Paddy) Kelly (BMH WS 1,735); Patrick Lyons (BMH WS 1,645).
27 William J. O'Hora (BMH WS 1,554, p. 6).
28 Patrick Coleman (BMH WS 1,683); Patrick Joseph Cannon (BMH WS 830); John Feehan (BMH WS 1,692); Seán Gibbons (BMH WS 927); Paddy Cannon (UCDA, O'Malley notebooks, P17b/136); Thomas Kettrick (BMH WS 872); Kettrick, 'Statement'; Moane, 'Statement'; Seán Gibbons (BMH WS 927); James J. Slattery (BMH WS 445).
29 Arthur Mitchell, *Revolutionary government in Ireland: Dáil Éireann, 1919–1922* (Dublin, 1995), p. 134.
30 Patrick Cassidy (BMH WS 1,017); Ned Maughan (UCDA, O'Malley notebooks, P17b/109); Conor A. Maguire (BMH WS 708); CI Mayo, Nov.–Dec. 1919 (TNA, CO 904/110).
31 Moane, 'Statement'; Kettrick, 'Statement'; Thomas Hawley (BMH WS 1,122); Michael Henry (BMH WS 1,732); John Timony (BMH WS 1,629).
32 Patrick Cassidy (BMH WS 1,017, p. 5).
33 Statement by J.R.W. Goulden (TCD, MS 7377); Patrick Cassidy (BMH WS 1,017).
34 William J. O'Hora (BMH WS 1,554, p. 7).
35 Mitchell, *Revolutionary government*, pp 57–60.
36 Burke, *Roscommon*, pp 87–8; Farry, *Sligo*, pp 50–1.
37 CI Mayo, Nov.–Dec. 1919 (TNA, CO 904/110).
38 Patrick Cassidy (BMH WS 1,017, p. 4).
39 Thomas Hawley (BMH WS 1,122, p. 5). See also Patrick Hegarty (BMH WS 1,606); Thomas Hawley (BMH WS 1,122); Thomas Kettrick (BMH WS 872); CI Mayo, Nov. 1919 (TNA, CO 904/110).
40 CI Mayo, 1919 (TNA, CO 904/108–110); *CT*, 1 Nov. 1919; Linda Connolly, 'Towards a further understanding of the violence experienced by women in the Irish Revolution' in Linda Connolly (ed.), *Women and the Irish Revolution: feminism, activism, violence* (Dublin, 2020), pp 103–28.
41 CI Mayo, 1919 (TNA, CO 904/108–110); Michael Laffan, *The resurrection of Ireland: the Sinn Féin party, 1916–1923* (Cambridge, 1999), p. 186.
42 CI Mayo, Jan. 1920 (TNA, CO 904/111); *WP*, 17 Jan. 1920. See also *CT*, 17, 24 Jan. 1920.
43 *WP*, 17 Jan. 1920; *CT*, 17, 24 Jan. 1920.
44 William J. O'Hora (BMH WS 1,554).
45 Conor A. Maguire (BMH WS 708, p. 2). See also Patrick Hegarty (BMH WS 1,606); Burke, *Roscommon*, p. 90; Farry, *Sligo*, p. 53.
46 Seán Walsh (BMH WS 1,733).

47 Kevin R. O'Shiel (BMH WS 1,770, p. 955). See also Mitchell, *Revolutionary government*, pp 134–5; Conor A. Maguire (BMH WS 708); *CT*, 10 Apr. 1920.
48 Conor A. Maguire (BMH WS 708, p. 4). See also Mitchell, *Revolutionary government*, pp 134–5; Kevin R. O'Shiel (BMH WS 1,770).
49 *WP*, 22 May 1920; Kevin R. O'Shiel (BMH WS 1,770, p. 955). See also Conor A. Maguire (BMH WS 708).
50 Burke, *Roscommon*, p. 81. See also Mitchell, *Revolutionary government*, pp 134–5; Kevin R. O'Shiel (BMH WS 1,770); Conor A. Maguire (BMH WS 708).
51 John Feehan (BMH WS 1,692); Seán Walsh (BMH WS 1,733).
52 Patrick Cassidy (BMH WS 1,017, p. 6). See also William J. O'Hora (BMH WS 1,554); Patrick Coleman (BMH WS 1,683); Patrick Joseph Cannon (BMH WS 830); Seán Gibbons (BMH WS 927); Thomas Kettrick (BMH WS 872); Michael McHugh (BMH WS 1,632); Seán Walsh (BMH WS 1,733); Stephen Donnelly (BMH WS 1,548); Patrick Lyons (BMH WS 1,645).
53 Cahir Davitt (BMH WS 993, pp 26–7). See also Conor A. Maguire (BMH WS 708); Michael Henry (BMH WS 1,732).
54 Peter Hart, *The IRA at war, 1916–1923* (Oxford 2003), p. 63; IG, Feb. 1920 (TNA, CO 904/111); IRA orders (UCDA, O'Malley notebooks, P17b/127).
55 CI Mayo, Jan.–Feb. 1920 (TNA, CO 904/111).
56 Patrick Lyons (BMH WS 1,645, p. 4); Patrick Hegarty (BMH WS 1,606, p. 13). See also Martin Mooney (BMH WS 1,602); P.J. (Paddy) Kelly (BMH WS 1,735); Patrick Hegarty (BMH WS 1,606).
57 Martin Mooney (BMH WS 1,602); Patrick Coleman (BMH WS 1,683); Patrick Cassidy (BMH WS 1,017); Patrick Hegarty (BMH WS 1,606); Martin Mooney (BMH WS 1,602).
58 Patrick Joseph Cannon (BMH WS 830, p. 2). See also Patrick Hegarty (BMH WS 1,606); Patrick Cassidy (BMH WS 1,017); Thomas Hawley (BMH WS 1,122).
59 Townshend, *British campaign*, p. 65, Appendix V; CI Mayo, 1920 (TNA, CO 904/111–113).
60 William King (BMH WS 1,381, p. 6).
61 Martin Mooney (BMH WS 1,602, p. 3). See also Charles Hughes, Interview; Chambers, 'Statement'; Seán Walsh (BMH WS 1,733); Patrick Cassidy (BMH WS 1,017); Patrick Lyons (BMH WS 1,645).
62 Martin Mooney (BMH WS 1,602); Patrick Lyons (BMH WS 1,645); Seán Walsh (BMH WS 1,733); Seán T. Ruane (BMH WS 1,588); Richard Walsh (BMH WS 400); Patrick Joseph Cannon (BMH WS 830); Thomas Kettrick (BMH WS 872); Patrick Hegarty (BMH WS 1,606); John Feehan (BMH WS 1,692); Stephen Donnelly (BMH WS 1,548); Patrick Dunlevy (BMH WS 1,489); Patrick Coleman (BMH WS 1,683); Patrick Cassidy (BMH WS 1,017); John Timony (BMH WS 1,629); Pension application of John Joe Keleghan (IMA, MSPC, 1D300); CI Mayo, July–Aug. 1920 (TNA, CO 904/112).
63 CI Mayo, June 1920 (TNA, CO 904/112).
64 CI Mayo, June–July 1920 (TNA, CO 904/112); Letter to J.C. Garvey (NLI, MS 11,122); *CT*, 5 June 1920.
65 CI Mayo, June–July 1920 (ibid.).
66 CI Mayo, Jan.–July 1920 (TNA, CO 904/111–112).
67 CI Mayo, July 1920 (TNA, CO 904/112).
68 Election results, H. van der Wusten, *Iers verzet de staatkundige eenheid der Britse eilanden, 1800–1921* (Amsterdam, 1977), pp 193, 209–11. Patrick Hegarty (BMH WS 1,606); Conor A. Maguire (BMH WS 708); Richard Walsh (BMH WS 400).

CHAPTER SIX *'Sinn Féin agents were reported visiting the county to foment trouble': violence comes to Mayo, 1920–1*

1 Richard Walsh (BMH WS 400, p. 66).

2 Jack Feehan (UCDA, O'Malley notebooks, P17b/113); Kelly, 'One of the men of the West'; P.J. (Paddy) Kelly (BMH WS 1,735).
3 CI Mayo, July–Aug. 1920 (TNA, CO 904/112); Farry, *Sligo*, pp 55–7; 92–105.
4 Patrick Coleman (BMH WS 1,683, p. 10). See also CI Mayo, July 1920 (TNA, CO 904/112); Michael McHugh (BMH WS 1,632); Stephen Donnelly (BMH WS 1,548).
5 Patrick Dunlevy (BMH WS 1,489); John Feehan (BMH WS 1,692); P.J. (Paddy) Kelly (BMH WS 1,735); Tom Maguire, in U. Mac Eoin, *Survivors*, pp 279–81.
6 Seán Walsh (BMH WS 1,733); Patrick Lyons (BMH WS 1,645); Michael McHugh (BMH WS 1,632); Seán T. Ruane (BMH WS 1,588); Martin Mooney (BMH WS 1,602); *CT*, 28 Aug. 1920.
7 *CT*, 4 Sept. 1920; Stephen Donnelly (BMH WS 1,548); Patrick Coleman (BMH WS 1,683); Cormac K.H. O'Malley & Vincent Keane (eds), *The men will talk to me: Mayo interviews by Ernie O'Malley* (Cork, 2014), pp 230–4.
8 CI Mayo, Oct. 1920 (TNA, CO 904/113).
9 CI Mayo, Oct. 1920–Feb. 1921 (TNA, CO 904/113–114).
10 Townshend, *British campaign*, Appendix X.
11 CI Mayo, Oct. 1920 (TNA, CO 904/113).
12 CI Mayo, Nov. 1920–June 1921 (TNA, CO 904/113–115).
13 Mark Killilea (UCDA, O'Malley notebooks, P17b/109). See also Dr John Madden (UCDA, O'Malley notebooks, P17b/113); Chambers, 'Statement'; Michael Hughes, 'Statement'; Jimmy Swift (UCDA, O'Malley notebooks, P17b/136); Liam Langley (UCDA, O'Malley notebooks, P17b/101); Pat Fallon (UCDA, O'Malley notebooks, P17b/109); Tom Maguire (UCDA, O'Malley notebooks, P17b/100); Maguire in Mac Eoin (ed.), *Survivors*, p. 279.
14 Tom Kettrick (UCDA, O'Malley notebooks, P17b/136). See also Mark Killilea (UCDA, O'Malley notebooks, P17b/109); Michael Hughes, 'Statement'; Joe Baker, *My stand for freedom: autobiography of an Irish republican soldier* (Westport, 1988), p. 29; Patrick Owen Mugan, Interview.
15 Richard Walsh (BMH WS 400); Seán Gibbons (BMH WS 927); Michael Henry (BMH WS 1,732); Michael Henry (BMH WS 1,732); Michael McHugh (BMH WS 1,632); Charles Gildea (BMH WS 1,313).
16 Patrick Hegarty (BMH WS 1,606), p. 22. See also *CT*, 21 Aug. 1920; Jack Feehan (UCDA, O'Malley notebooks, P17b/113); Kelly, 'One of the men of the West'; P.J. (Paddy) Kelly (BMH WS 1,735).
17 Seán T. Ruane (BMH WS 1,588, p. 23).
18 Seán Gibbons (BMH WS 927).
19 Stephen Donnelly (BMH WS 1,548, p. 15).
20 Tommy Heavey (UCDA, O'Malley notebooks, P17b/120). See also Seán Gibbons (BMH WS 927); Charlie Hughes, Interview; CI Mayo, Nov. 1920 (TNA, CO 904/113).
21 Stephen Donnelly (BMH WS 1,548).
22 CI Mayo, Nov. 1920 (TNA, CO 904/113). See also Patrick Coleman (BMH WS 1,683); P.J. (Paddy) Kelly (BMH WS 1,735); Seán Broderick (BMH WS 1,677); John Feehan (BMH WS 1,692).
23 UCDA, O'Malley notebooks, P17b/127.
24 Seán Gibbons (BMH WS 927, p. 19).
25 West Mayo Brigade report, Mar. 1921 (UCDA, Mulcahy papers, P7A/38).
26 O'Donnell, 'Recollections'.
27 List of Flying Column members, CBHC; Dan Sammin, Interview 12 Dec. 1989; Moane and Malone, 'Transcript'; Michael Hughes, 'Statement'; Mark Killilea (UCDA, O'Malley notebooks, P17b/109); Paddy Cannon (UCDA, O'Malley notebooks, P17b/136); Patrick Joseph Cannon (BMH WS 830); Michael McHugh (BMH WS 1,632).
28 Patrick Cassidy (BMH WS 1,017).

29 Seán Gibbons (BMH WS 927); Thomas Kettrick (BMH WS 872); Brodie Malone and Ned Moane (UCDA, O'Malley notebooks, P17b/120); Heavey, 'Statement', Tommy Heavey (UCDA, O'Malley notebooks, P17b/120).
30 P.J. (Paddy) Kelly (BMH WS 1,735, p. 15). See also Seán Gibbons (BMH WS 927).
31 CI Mayo, Feb. 1921 (TNA, CO 904/114).
32 Patrick Cassidy (BMH WS 1,017, p. 15). See also Stephen Donnelly (BMH WS 1,548); Thomas Kettrick (BMH WS 872); Patrick Joseph Cannon (BMH WS 830).
33 CI Mayo, Feb. 1921 (TNA, CO 904/114).
34 UCD AD, P7A23/215; West Mayo Battalion rolls, CBHC; UCDA, P7a18; Augusteijn, *From public defiance*, Appendices.
35 Peter Hegarty (UCDA, O'Malley notebooks, P17b/109); Patrick Owen Mugan, Interview; Moane, 'Statement'; Kettrick, 'Statement'; O'Donnell, 'Recollections'; Thomas Conroy, Interview 1 Dec. 1990; O'Malley, *Memories*, 25–7; William J. O'Hora (BMH WS 1,554).
36 Kettrick, 'Statement'; Patrick Cassidy (BMH WS 1,017, p. 17). See also CI Mayo, 1921 (TNA, CO 904/114–116); UCDA, P7A38; UCDA, P7A19/88; Thomas Conroy, Interview 1 Dec. 1990; Patrick Owen Mugan, Interview; Thomas Hawley (BMH WS 1,122); Thomas Kettrick (BMH WS 872); Seán Gibbons (BMH WS 927); Michael McHugh (BMH WS 1,632); 'Activities list Owenwee Company', CBHC.
37 William J. O'Hora (BMH WS 1,554, p. 8).
38 CI Mayo, 1920–21 (TNA, CO 904/111–116); Patrick Cassidy (BMH WS 1,017).
39 Seán Gibbons (BMH WS 927, p. 62); Michael Henry (BMH WS 1,732, p. 8). See also Patrick Lyons (BMH WS 1,645); Michael McHugh (BMH WS 1,632).
40 Patrick Cassidy (BMH WS 1,017, pp 16–17).
41 Patrick Cassidy (BMH WS 1,017); Patrick Joseph Cannon (BMH WS 830); John Timony (BMH WS 1,629); Thomas Kettrick (BMH WS 872); Michael McHugh (BMH WS 1,632); Eunan O'Halpin & Daithí Ó Corráin, *The dead of the Irish Revolution* (New Haven and London, 1920); Brian Hughes, *Defying the IRA? Intimidation, coercion and communities during the Irish Revolution* (Liverpool, 2016).
42 Seán Gibbons (BMH WS 927, p. 63); *WP*, 23 Apr. 1921. See also *WP*, 28 May 1921.
43 William J. O'Hora (BMH WS 1,554).
44 William J. O'Hora (BMH WS 1,554, pp 10–11).
45 CI Mayo, Nov. 1920 (TNA, CO 904/113); P.J. (Paddy) Kelly (BMH WS 1,735).
46 William J. O'Hora (BMH WS 1,554); Seán Gibbons (BMH WS 927); P.J. (Paddy) Kelly (BMH WS 1,735); Patrick Cassidy (BMH WS 1,017); Seán Walsh (BMH WS 1,733).
47 NLI, MS 11,122.
48 CI Mayo, Dec. 1920 (TNA, CO 904/113).
49 CI Mayo, Jan.–Apr. 1921 (TNA, CO 904/114–115).
50 Stephen Donnelly (BMH WS 1,548, p. 20).
51 Seán Gibbons (BMH WS 927, p. 26).
52 Ibid., p. 43.
53 John Feehan (BMH WS 1,692, p. 70). See also Stephen Donnelly (BMH WS 1,548); Seán T. Ruane (BMH WS 1,588).
54 Patrick Hegarty (BMH WS1,606); Seán T. Ruane (BMH WS 1,588); Patrick Cassidy (BMH WS 1,017); Thomas Kettrick (BMH WS 872); John Moran (BMH WS 1,549); P.J. (Paddy) Kelly (BMH WS 1,735); Stephen Donnelly (BMH WS 1,548); Martin Mooney (BMH WS 1,602).
55 Heffernan, *Freedom*, Appendices 1–7; *CT*, 30 Oct. 1920.
56 Seán T. Ruane (BMH WS 1,588); Michael Henry (BMH WS 1,732); Heffernan, *Freedom*, p. 68.
57 John Feehan (BMH WS 1,692, p. 32).
58 Stephen Donnelly (BMH WS 1,548, p. 13).

59 Thomas Heavey (BMH WS 1,668).
60 Heffernan. *Freedom*, p. 32.
61 Ibid., p. 220.
62 Patrick Hegarty (BMH WS 1,606, p. 18). See also Martin Mooney (BMH WS 1,602).
63 John Moran (BMH WS 1,549); Patrick Lyons (BMH WS 1,645).
64 Stephen Donnelly (BMH WS 1,548, p. 14).
65 Heffernan, *Freedom*, pp 135, 156–7, 163–4, 182.
66 P.J. (Paddy) Kelly (BMH WS 1,735); Patrick Coleman (BMH WS 1,683).
67 Heffernan. *Freedom*, pp 105, 135, 156–7, 163–4, 182, 184, 200.
68 Seán T. Ruane (BMH WS 1,588, p. 23).
69 Patrick Cassidy (BMH WS 1,017).
70 Heffernan. *Freedom*, pp 135, 156–7, 163–4, 182; CI Mayo, Jan. 1921 (TNA, CO 904/114); *CT*, 19 Feb., 12 Mar. 1921.
71 *CT*, 14 May 1921. See also *CT*, 21 May 1921; *MN*, 14, 21 May 1921; *WP*, 14, 21 May 1921.
72 CI Mayo, Jan.–Feb. 1921 (TNA, CO 904/114).
73 South Mayo Report, 28 Apr. 1921 (UCDA, P7A38). See also West Mayo Brigade report, 4 Apr. 1921 (UCDA, Mulcahy papers, P7A38); Tom Kettrick (UCDA, O'Malley notebooks, P17b/136); Seán Gibbons (BMH WS 927); Patrick Cassidy (BMH WS 1,017); Michael Henry (BMH WS 1,732); Dan Sammin, Interview 12 Dec. 1989.
74 Thomas Hawley (BMH WS 1,122); Patrick Cassidy (BMH WS 1,017); William J. O'Hora (BMH WS 1,554).
75 William J. O'Hora (BMH WS 1,554, p. 9).
76 P.J. (Paddy) Kelly (BMH WS 1,735, p. 16).
77 Patrick Cassidy (BMH WS 1,017, p. 8); William J. O'Hora (BMH WS 1,554, p. 9).
78 Thomas Kettrick (BMH WS 872); Seán Gibbons (BMH WS 927); Séamus Reader (BMH WS 933); Michael Henry (BMH WS 1,732); Stephen Donnelly (BMH WS 1,548); William J. O'Hora (BMH WS 1,554); Michael McHugh (BMH WS 1,632); Kettrick, 'Statement'; John Madden (UCDA, O'Malley notebooks, P17b/113); Richard Walsh (BMH WS 400); Joseph Good (BMH WS 388); P.J. (Paddy) Kelly (BMH WS 1,735); William J. O'Hora (BMH WS 1,554).
79 Patrick Cassidy (BMH WS 1,017, pp 15–16); Thomas Kettrick (BMH WS 872, p. 52).
80 Statement by J.R.W. Goulden (TCD, MS 7377).
81 Stephen Donnelly (BMH WS 1,548, p. 11). See also Patrick Cassidy (BMH WS 1,017); Patrick Hegarty (BMH WS 1,606); Martin Mooney (BMH WS 1,602); William J. O'Hora (BMH WS 1,554); Michael Henry (BMH WS 1,732); Patrick Coleman (BMH WS 1,683); John Timony (BMH WS 1,629).
82 Patrick Cassidy (BMH WS 1,017); Jim Hunt (BMH WS 905); Thady McGowan and Tom Brehony (BMH WS 918).
83 Tom Maguire (UCDA, O'Malley notebooks, P7b/100). See also Pat Fallon (UCDA, O'Malley notebooks, P17b/109); Jimmy Swift (UCDA, O'Malley notebooks, P17b/136).
84 Moane and Malone, 'Transcript'. See also Patrick Owen Mugan, Interview; John Madden (UCDA, O'Malley notebooks, P17b/113); Johnny Duffy (UCDA, O'Malley notebooks, P17b/109); Moane, 'Statement'; Paddy Duffy (UCDA, O'Malley notebooks, P17b/138); Mossy McGrath (UCDA, O'Malley notebooks, P17b/127); Heavey, 'Statement'; Moane, 'Statement'; Michael Kilroy, 'ASU Operations', CBHC; Seán Gibbons (BMH WS 927); Patrick Cassidy (BMH WS 1,017); Michael Henry (BMH WS 1,732).
85 Brodie Malone (UCDA, O'Malley notebooks, P17b/109), CI Mayo, June 1921 (TNA, CO 904/115). See also Johnny Duffy (UCDA, O'Malley notebooks, P17b/109); Moane, 'Statement'; Edward Maughan (UCDA, O'Malley notebooks, P17b/109); Thomas Kettrick (BMH WS 872).

86 Stephen Donnelly (BMH WS 1,548, p. 18). See also Patrick Cassidy (BMH WS 1,017); Thomas Kettrick (BMH WS 872).
87 P.J. (Paddy) Kelly (BMH WS 1,735, p. 18). See also Michael McHugh (BMH WS 1,632); Baker, *My stand for freedom*, p. 24; Heavey, 'Statement'; Jack Connolly (UCDA, O'Malley notebooks, P17b/120); West Mayo monthly report May 1921 (UCDA, Mulcahy papers, P7A19/84); Mark Killilea (UCDA, O'Malley notebooks, P17b/109); Michael Hughes, 'Statement'.
88 Tom Maguire, in Mac Eoin, *Survivors*, p. 284. See also Ned O'Reilly (UCDA, O'Malley notebooks, P17b/126); Edward Moane and Brodie Malone (UCDA, O'Malley notebooks, P17b/120); Paddy Duffy (UCDA, O'Malley notebooks, P17b/113); Johnny Duffy (UCDA, O'Malley notebooks, P17b/109).
89 Michael Hughes, 'Statement' (private possession), Heavey, 'Statement'. See also Kilroy, 'ASU Operations'.
90 Heavey, 'Statement'. See also Tommy Heavey (UCDA, O'Malley notebooks, P17b/120); Seán Gibbons (BMH WS 927).
91 CI Mayo, Nov. 1920–Mar. 1921 (TNA, CO 904/113–114); Reports on Partry ambush (UCDA, Mulcahy papers, P7A38); Thomas Hawley (BMH WS 1,122).
92 Kilroy, 'ASU Operations', Kettrick, 'Statement'. See also Baker, *My stand for freedom*, p. 21; Moane and Malone, 'Transcript'; Heavey, 'Statement'.
93 Patrick Cassidy (BMH WS 1,017).
94 Michael Henry (BMH WS 1,732, p. 8).
95 Reports on Partry and Tourmakeady ambushes (UCDA, Mulcahy papers, P7A38); Tom Maguire (UCDA, O'Malley notebooks, P17b/100); Mac Eoin, *Survivors*, pp 283–8; Pat Fallon (UCDA, O'Malley notebooks, P17b/109); Major Geoffrey Iberson's account of an action at Tourmakeady, Co. Mayo, 3 May 1921 (TCD, MS 3491/10); CI Mayo, May 1921 (TNA, CO 904/115); Martin Ryan (BMH WS 1,417); Thomas Kettrick (BMH WS 872); William J. O'Hora (BMH WS 1,554); Statement by J.R.W. Goulden (TCD, MS 7377); Thomas Hawley (BMH WS 1,122).
96 Patrick Owen Mugan, Interview; Kettrick, 'Statement'; Seán Gibbons (BMH WS 927); Patrick Joseph Cannon (BMH WS 830).
97 Thomas Kettrick (BMH WS 872, pp 27–8). See also Moane and Malone, 'Transcript'; Seán Gibbons (BMH WS 927); Thomas Kettrick (BMH WS 872); Patrick Joseph Cannon (BMH WS 830); CI Mayo, May 1921 (TNA, CO 904/115).
98 Thomas Kettrick (BMH WS 872, p. 32). See also *CT*, 28 May 1921; Peter McDonnell (BMH WS 1,612); CI Mayo, May 1921 (TNA, CO 904/115); John Feehan (BMH WS 1,692); Thomas Kettrick (BMH WS 872); Seán Gibbons (BMH WS 927); Jimmy Swift (UCDA, O'Malley notebooks, P17b/136); Kilroy, 'ASU Operations'; Thomas Kettrick (BMH WS 872); Patrick Joseph Cannon (BMH WS 830); Seán Gibbons (BMH WS 927).
99 Tom Kettrick (UCDA, O'Malley notebooks, P17b/136); Baker, *My stand for freedom*, p. 23. Patrick Joseph Cannon (BMH WS 830); CI Mayo, May–June 1921 (TNA, CO 904/115); John Feehan (BMH WS 1,692); Thomas Kettrick (BMH WS 872); Seán Gibbons (BMH WS 927); John Feehan (BMH WS 1,692).
100 Stephen Donnelly (BMH WS 1,548, p. 20). See also *WP*, 28 May 1921; William J. O'Hora (BMH WS 1,554); John Timony (BMH WS 1,629); John Brennan (BMH WS 1,278).
101 Seán Walsh (BMH WS 1,733); Andrew Keaveney (BMH WS 1,178); Martin Mooney (BMH WS 1,602); Seán T. Ruane (BMH WS 1,588).
102 Patrick Cassidy (BMH WS 1,017); CI Mayo, May–June 1921 (TNA, CO 904/115).
103 Seán Gibbons (BMH WS 927); Seán Walsh (BMH WS 1,733); P.J. (Paddy) Kelly (BMH WS 1,735).

104 Thomas Hawley (BMH WS 1,122); Moane, 'Statement'; Tom Maguire, in Mac Eoin, *Survivors*, pp 185–9, 288; Pat Fallon (UCDA, O'Malley notebooks, P17b/109). West Mayo Column, Baker, *My stand for freedom*, p. 37; Michael Kilroy (UCDA, O'Malley notebooks, P17b/101) and 'ASU Operations'; CI Mayo, Mar.–July 1921 (TNA, CO 904/114–115).
105 William J. O'Hora (BMH WS 1,554, p. 20).
106 Patrick Cassidy (BMH WS 1,017, p. 15); Thomas Kettrick (BMH WS 872, p. 52). See also Patrick Joseph Cannon (BMH WS 830); Stephen Donnelly (BMH WS 1,548); Seán Gibbons (BMH WS 927); Peter McDonnell (BMH WS 1,612); John Feehan (BMH WS 1,692).
107 Hart, *I.R.A. at war*, Chapter 2–3; Townshend, *British campaign*, Appendix V; CI Mayo, 1920–1921 (TNA, CO 904/111–116); O'Halpin & Ó Corráin, *The dead*, p. 543; Augusteijn, *From public defiance*, p. 180.

CHAPTER SEVEN *'Glad for the respite – glad to get home to see our people and to get proper rest and regular meals': the anti-Treatyites take control, 1921–2*

1 *CT*, 16 July 1921.
2 *FJ*, 12 July 1921.
3 *CT*, 16, 30 July, 31 Aug., 1 Oct. 1921.
4 *CT*, 31 Aug. 1921. See also *CT*, 16 July, 1 Oct. 1921.
5 Seán Gibbons (BMH WS 927, p. 60).
6 Dominic Price, *The flame and the candle: war in Mayo, 1919–1924* (Cork, 2012), p. 197; Burke, *Roscommon*, pp 78–80; Farry, *Sligo*, pp 75–7; Patrick McGarty, *Leitrim: the Irish Revolution, 1912–23* (Dublin, 2020), pp 70, 103–4.
7 *MN*, 24 Sept. 1922 quoted in Price, *Flame and the candle*, 196–7. See also *Census of Ireland 1911, Area, houses, and population*; *CT*, 30 July, 1 Oct. 1921; *II*, 16 Aug. 1921.
8 Price, *Flame and the candle*, p. 197.
9 *CT*, 16 July 1921.
10 Ibid.
11 *FJ*, 20 July 1921; *WP*, 16 July 1921, quoted in Price, *Flame and the candle*, p. 169.
12 Thomas Kettrick (BMH WS 872, p. 52); Peter McDonnell (BMH WS 1,612, p. 82).
13 Seán Gibbons (BMH WS 927, p. 51).
14 Thomas Kettrick (BMH WS 872, p. 52). See also Patrick Joseph Cannon (BMH WS 830).
15 Ibid., p. 51.
16 Patrick Cassidy (BMH WS 1,017, p. 15).
17 CI Mayo, July 1921 (TNA, CO 904/116).
18 *CT*, 16 July 1921. See also Seán Gibbons (BMH WS 927); *FJ*, 5 Dec. 1921.
19 *FJ*, 9 Aug. 1921; *II*, 9 Aug. 1921.
20 *II*, 13 Sept. 1921.
21 *CT*, 8 Oct. 1921.
22 *CT*, 8 Oct. 1921; *FJ*, 21 Oct. 1921; Price, *Flame and the candle*, p. 197.
23 *WP*, 6 Aug. 1921. See also *CTr*, 3 Sept. 1921.
24 *WP*, 20 Aug., 24 Sept. 1921; *CTr*, 10 Sept., 5 Nov. 1921; *WP*, 10 Sept., 12 Nov. 1921.
25 *CT*, 22 Oct., 19 Nov. 1921.
26 CI Mayo, Aug.–Sept. 1921 (TNA, CO 904/116). See also Seán Gibbons (BMH WS 927).
27 John Feehan (BMH WS 1,692); Seán Gibbons (BMH WS 927); O'Malley & Keane (eds), *The men will talk*, p. 61.
28 Price, *Flame and the candle*, pp 175–6, 179–80; Richard Walsh (BMH WS 400); Seán Gibbons (BMH WS 927); O'Malley & Keane (eds), *The men will talk*, pp 265, 291.
29 Price, *Flame and the candle*, pp 181–3; Seán Walsh (BMH WS 1,733); O'Malley & Keane (eds), *The men will talk*, pp 198, 291.

30 CI Mayo, Aug.–Sept. 1921 (TNA, CO 904/116); *CT*, 17 Dec. 1921. See also O'Malley & Keane (eds), *The men will talk*, p. 254; *WP*, 19 Nov. 1921.
31 Breaches of the Truce, Oct. 1921 (TNA, CO 904/154).
32 *CT*, 1 Oct. 1921. See also CI Mayo, Aug.–Sept. 1921 (TNA, CO 904/116); *CT*, 16 July 1921; 'Major Geoffrey Iberson's account of an action at Tourmakeady, Co. Mayo, 3rd May 1921' (TCD, MS 3491/10); Breaches of the Truce (TNA, CO 904/154).
33 Breaches of the Truce, Oct. 1921 (TNA, CO 904/154); Seán Gibbons (BMH WS 927).
34 CI Mayo, Aug.–Sept. 1921 (TNA, CO 904/116); *CT*, 16 July 1921.
35 Dermot Keogh, *The Vatican, the bishops and Irish politics, 1919–1939* (Cambridge, 1986), p. 78, quoted in Heffernan, *Freedom*, p. 85; O'Malley & Keane (eds), *The men will talk*, p. 290; Price, *Flame and the candle*, pp 182, 184–5, 199; *FJ*, 9 Sept. 1921; *CT*, 1 Oct., 12 Nov. 1921; *IT*, 13 Mar. 1922; O'Halpin & Ó Corráin, *The dead*, p. 383.
36 Breaches of the truce, Oct. 1921 (TNA, CO 904/154).
37 Breaches of the truce, Oct., Nov. 1921 (TNA, CO 904/154).
38 Breaches of the truce, Oct. 1921 (ibid.).
39 *CT*, 17 Dec. 1921; *IT*, 7 Oct. 1921; Breaches of the truce, Oct. 1921 (TNA, CO 904/154).
40 Breaches of the truce, Oct. 1921 (TNA, CO 904/154). *CT*, 17 Dec. 1921; John Timony (BMH WS 1,629); O'Malley & Keane (eds), *The men will talk*, p. 255.
41 *MN*, 12 Dec. 1921.
42 *CT*, 24 Dec. 1921. See also *FJ*, 22 Dec. 1921; *CT*, 24 Dec. 1921; *II*, 12 Dec. 1921; Price, *Flame and the candle*, pp 191–5.
43 *FJ*, 2 Jan. 1922. See also *FJ*, 27 Dec. 1921, 4 Jan. 1922; *II*, 27, 31 Dec. 1921, 2 Jan. 1922; *CT*, 7 Jan. 1922; *IT*, 7 Jan. 1922.
44 *IT*, 5 Jan. 1922. See also *IT*, 7, 14 Jan. 1922; *CTr*, 7 Jan. 1922 *FJ*, 5, 9, 31 Jan. 1922; Dáil Éireann debate on Treaty, 4 Jan. 1922, www.oireachtas.ie/en/debates/debate/dail/1922-01-04/.
45 Richard Walsh (BMH WS 400); Thomas Hawley (BMH WS 1,122); Thomas Kettrick (BMH WS 872); Patrick Cassidy (BMH WS 1,017); O'Malley & Keane (eds), *The men will talk*, pp 62, 111, 218–19, 265, 271, 290, 314–15; Seán Gibbons (BMH WS 927); *IT*, 14 Jan., 3 Feb. 1922.
46 *CT*, 14 Jan., 25 Mar., 27 May 1922; *CTr*, 14 Jan. 1922.
47 Price, *Flame and the candle*, p. 219. See also *IT*, 13 Feb. 1922; *FJ*, 11, 13 Feb., 9, 22 May 1922.
48 *FJ*, 22 May 1922. See also *IT*, 11 Feb., 1 Mar. 1922; *FJ*, 11 Feb., 19 May 1922.
49 *FJ*, 22, 29 May 1922; *CT*, 27 May 1922; *IT*, 13 May 1922.
50 *CT*, 3 June 1922. See also *IT*, 3, 6 June 1922; *II*, 15 June 1922; *CT*, 17 June 1922.
51 *IT*, 15 Feb. 1922.
52 *CTr*, 27 May 1922; *CT*, 27 May 1922. See also *CT*, 25 Feb., 25 Mar., 29 Apr. 27 May, 3 June 1922; *FJ*, 19 May 1922; *IT*, 28 June 1922; Price, *Flame and the candle*, p. 213.
53 *CT*, 25 Mar., 27 May 1922. See also *CTr*, 25 Feb., 15 Apr. 1922; *IT*, 13 Mar. 1922; *CT*, 20, 27 May 1922.
54 *IT*, 25 Mar., 28 Apr. 1922; *FJ*, 26 Apr., 25 May 1922; *II*, 26 Apr. 1922; *CT*, 29 Apr. 1922; Price, *Flame and the candle*, pp 201, 210–12; Richard Walsh (BMH WS 400); O'Malley & Keane (eds), *The men will talk*, p. 63.
55 *FJ*, 16 Feb. 1922. See also *FJ*, 24 Dec. 1921, 19 Jan. 1922; *IT*, 24 Dec. 1921, 18, 19 Jan. 1922; *FJ*, 18 Jan. 1922; *II*, 19 Jan., 14 Feb. 1922; Price, *Flame and the candle*, pp 198, 201–3; O'Malley & Keane (eds), *The men will talk*, pp 291, 317–18; Kieran Waldron, 'The Civil War in Ballyhaunis', *Annagh*, 44th edition (2021), p. 33.
56 *IT*, 22 Apr. 1922. See also *II*, 3 Feb. 1922; *FJ*, 25 Feb. 1922; *CTr*, 22 Apr. 1922; *CT*, 8 Apr. 1922; *FJ*, 6 Feb. 1922.
57 *FJ*, 10 Feb. 1922. See also *CTr*, 22 Apr. 1922; *CT*, 8 Apr. 1922; *IT*, 22 Apr. 1922; *FJ*, 30 Jan., 6 Feb., 14 June 1922; O'Malley & Keane (eds), *The men will talk*, pp 140, 315–16.

58 *MN*, 22 Apr. 1922 quoted in Price, *Flame and the candle*, pp 196, 213, 207–9. See also O'Malley & Keane (eds), *The men will talk*, pp 63, 194–5, 221; *II*, 6 Apr. 1922; *CT*, 8 Apr. 1922; *FJ*, 25 Mar. 1922; Patrick Coy (BMH WS 1,203); Price, *Flame and the candle*, pp 196, 213.
59 *FJ*, 7 June 1922; *CT*, 27 May, 12 Nov., 10 Dec. 1921; O'Malley & Keane (eds), *The men will talk*, pp 139, 316; John Timony (BMH WS 1,629).
60 *FJ*, 16, 17 May, 3 June 1922; *II*, 16 May, 3, 5, 15 June 1922; *IT*, 19 May 1922; *CT*, 17 June 1922; O'Malley & Keane (eds), *The men will talk*, pp 196, 224, 255; Price, *Flame and the candle*, p. 213.
61 *CTr*, 29 Apr. 1922; Richard Walsh (BMH WS 400); O'Malley & Keane (eds), *The men will talk*, pp 64, 110–11, 141, 196–7, 219–20, 255; Richard Walsh (BMH WS 400); *FJ*, 11 Mar. 1922.
62 *CT*, 8 Apr. 1922. See also *CT*, 25 Mar. 1922; O'Malley & Keane (eds), *The men will talk*, p. 63; Price, *Flame and the candle*, pp 207–9.
63 *II*, 4 Apr. 1922.
64 O'Malley & Keane (eds), *The men will talk*, p. 63. See also *II*, 4, 8 Apr. 1922; *CT*, 8 Apr. 1922; *Irish Examiner*, 8 Apr. 1922; O'Malley & Keane (eds), *The men will talk*, pp 63, 141, 195–6; Price, *Flame and the candle*, pp 207–9.
65 *CT*, 20 May, 3 June 1922; *IT*, 4, 5, 17 June 1922; *FJ*, 7 June 1922; *II*, 7 June 1922.
66 *IT*, 6 June 1922. See also Price, *Flame and the candle*, pp 202, 212; *FJ*, 30 May, 3 June 1922; *II*, 6 Mar. 1922; *CT*, 25 Mar. 1922 *CT*, 6 May 1922; *FJ*, 11 Mar. 1922.

CHAPTER EIGHT *'Revolver government'?: a hotbed of republicanism, 1922–3*

1 *CT*, 1, 15 July 1922; O'Malley & Keane (eds), *The men will talk*, p. 293.
2 Price, *Flame and the candle*, p. 219; O'Malley & Keane (eds), *The men will talk*, pp 65–6, 142.
3 O'Malley and Keane (eds), *The men will talk*, pp 320–1; *CT*, 1 July 1922; *CTr*, 1 July 1922; *II*, 7, 20 July 1922; *IT*, 19 July 1922.
4 Price, *Flame and the candle*, p. 219; *CT*, 8 July 1922; *II*, 15 July 1922; *IT*, 15 July 1922.
5 *CT*, 15 July 1922.
6 Pension claim of Bridget Ruane (IMA, MSPC, 2D227); Pension claim of Ann Moran (IMA, MSPC, DP7558); Price, *Flame and the candle*, p. 220; *CTr*, 8, 22 July 1922; *CT*, 15 July 1922; O'Malley & Keane (eds), *The men will talk*, pp 198, 321.
7 *II*, 22 July 1922. See also *II*, 8, 15 July 1922; *CT*, 15 July 1922; *IT*, 15, 17 July 1922.
8 *CTr*, 15 July 1922. See also *IT*, 7 July 1922; *CT*, 15 July 1922.
9 O'Malley & Keane (eds), *The men will talk*, p. 142; *IT*, 24, 25, 27 July, 3 Aug. 1922; *II*, 25, 27, 28 July 1922; *CT*, 5 Aug. 1922.
10 Captured documents (IMA, CW/CAPT, Lot 19).
11 Captured documents (IMA, CW/CAPT, Lot 19); *II*, 26 July 1922; *IT*, 2, 5 Aug. 1922; *CT*, 5 Aug. 1922.
12 *CT*, 29 July 1922. See also O'Malley & Keane (eds), *The men will talk*, p. 142; Price, *Flame and the candle*, pp 216–21; *CTr*, 29 July 1922.
13 Price, *Flame and the candle*, pp 216–17; *II*, 25 July 1922; Waldron, 'The Civil War in Ballyhaunis', 34.
14 *II*, 28 July 1922. See also *IT*, 31 July 1922; *CT*, 5 Aug. 1922; Price, *Flame and the candle*, pp 216–17, 225–6.
15 *CT*, 13 Jan. 1923. See also *II*, 27 July 1922; *IT*, 26 July 1922; *CT*, 5 Aug. 1922; Operation reports, Feb. 1923 (IMA, CW/OPS/03/01).
16 *CTr*, 29 July, 5 Aug. 1922; *II*, 28, 29, 31 July 1922; *IT*, 1 Aug. 1922; *CT*, 12 Aug. 1922.
17 Price, *Flame and the candle*, p. 223.
18 *CT*, 2 Sept. 1922. See also ibid., 14, 28 Oct., 18 Nov. 1922.
19 Ibid., 14 Oct. 1922. See also ibid., 28 Oct., 4 Nov. 1922.

20 Ibid., 4 Nov. 1922. See also ibid., 5 Aug., 14, 28 Oct., 25 Nov. 1922; Seán Rice (ed.), *Castlebar Mitchels, 1885–1985* (Castlebar, 1985), pp 58–62, 233, 243.
21 *IT*, 22 Sept. 1922. See also *CTr*, 5 Aug. 1922; *CT*, 5, 19 Aug. 1922; *IT*, 8, 19 Sept., 24 Oct. 1922.
22 *II*, 25 July 1922.
23 Ibid., 26 July 1922. See also ibid., 27, 28 July 1922.
24 Captured papers, 25 Sept. 1922 (IMA, CAPT/Lot20/3); *II*, 28, 31 July 1922; *CT*, 5 Aug. 1922; *CTr*, 5 Aug. 1922; Captured documents, 18, 29 Aug., 22 Sept., 4 Oct. 1922 (IMA, CW/CAPT Lot 20/2); Captured documents, 2 Sept. 1922 (IMA, CW/OPS/03/07); 2 Oct. 1922 (IMA, CW/CAPT Lot20/3); O'Malley & Keane (eds), *The men will talk*, pp 256, 317.
25 Captured documents, 29 Aug., 22 Sept. 1922 (IMA CW/CAPT Lot 20/2). See also *II*, 28, 31 July 1922; *CTr*, 5 Aug. 1922; *CT*, 5 Aug. 1922; Captured documents, 2 Sept. 1922 (IMA, CW/OPS/03/07); Captured documents, 2 Oct. 1922 (IMA CW/CAPT Lot 20/3); Captured documents, 18 Aug., 4 Oct. 1922 (IMA CW/CAPT Lot 20/2).
26 *CT*, 5, 19 Aug., 14 Oct. 1922; *IT*, 8, 9, 19 Sept., 6, 20 Oct. 1922.
27 *II*, 1913 Dec. 1922. See also *CT*, 5, 19 Aug., 16 Dec. 1922; *IT*, 8, 9, 19 Sept., 6, 20 Oct., 25–27 Nov., 13, 14 Dec. 1922; *II*, 27 Nov. 1922.
28 *CT*, 14 Oct., 16 Dec. 1922; *IT*, 13, 14 Dec. 1922.
29 Captured documents, 15 Aug., 24 Oct. 1922 (IMA, OPS/03/07); Captured documents, 7 Feb. 1923 (IMA, CW/CAPT Lot 17).
30 Captured documents, 24 Aug. to 11 Sept. 1922 (IMA, CW/CAPT Lot 20/3); Captured documents, letter 1 Sept. 1922 and answer (IMA, CW/CAPT Lot 20/1).
31 Radio reports, 27 Feb. 1923 (IMA, CW/OPS/03/08). See also O'Malley & Keane (eds), *The men will talk*, p. 200; Divisional papers 4th Western Division, 4 Oct. 1922 (IMA, CAPT Lot 20/2); *CT*, 4 Nov. 1922; *II*, 4 Aug. 1922.
32 Captured documents, 24 Aug.–25 Sept. 1922 (IMA, CW/CAPT Lot20/3); Captured documents, 28 Aug. 1922 (IMA CW/CAPT Lot 20/4); Captured documents, 15, 26 Aug., 2 Sept. 1922 (IMA, OPS/03/07).
33 Captured documents, 26 Aug., 14 Sept. 1922 (IMA, CW/CAPT Lot 20/3). See also *II*, 4 Aug. 1922; *CT*, 5, 12, 19 Aug., 2 Sept. 1922; *IT*, 30 Aug., 3 Oct. 1922; *CTr*, 2 Sept. 1922; *II*, 4, 7 Sept., 14 Oct. 1922; Captured documents, 24 Aug. to 26 Sept. 1922 (IMA, CW/CAPT Lot 20/3).
34 *CT*, 5 Aug., 16 Sept., 4 Nov. 1922; *II*, 19 Sept., 3, 5 Oct. 1922; *IT*, 14, 15; Captured documents, 13, 19 Sept. 1922 (IMA, CW/CAPT Lot 20/3); Pension claim of Thomas Lackey (IMA, MSPC, 3P512); Price, *Flame and the candle*, pp 225–6.
35 *II*, 19 Sept. 1922; *IT*, 19, 22 Sept. 1922; *CTr*, 23 Sept. 1922; *CT*, 23 Sept. 1922; Captured documents, 16, 21 Sept. 1922 (IMA, CW/CAPT Lot 20/3); Price, *Flame and the candle*, p. 227; Captured documents, 24 Aug. to 18 Sept. 1922 (IMA, CW/CAPT Lot 20/4).
36 Price, *Flame and the candle*, pp 232–3; *CT*, 12 Aug. 1922.
37 Captured documents, 2 Sept. 1922 (IMA, CW/OPS/03/07); *IT*, 15 Aug., 14, 15, 19 Sept. 1922; *II*, 15 Sept., 23 Dec. 1922; Pension claim of Ellen Hynes (IMA, MSPC, DP3086); Pension claim of Patrick McNulty Snr (IMA, MSPC, DP8417).
38 *IT*, 15, 26 Aug., 14, 15, 19 Sept., 25–8 Nov. 1922; *II*, 10, 15 Aug., 15 Sept., 17 Oct., 21, 30 Oct., 1, 3, 7, 8, 25, 27 Nov., 6, 7, 23, 28 Dec. 1922; *CT*, 5 Aug., 2, 23 Sept., 4, 11 Nov., 2, 23 Dec. 1922; *CTr*, 5 Nov. 1922; Captured documents, 21, 22, 25 Sept. 1922 (IMA CW/CAPT Lot 20/3); Captured documents, 19 Sept. 1922 (IMA CW/CAPT Lot 20/4); Captured documents, 15 Aug. 1922 (IMA, CW/OPS/03/07); Pension claim of Sarah Woods (IMA, MSPC, 2D162).
39 *II*, 21 Aug., 28 Dec. 1922. See also pension claim of Annie Nealon (IMA, MSPC, DP2624); *CT*, 26 Aug. 1922.

40 Price, *Flame and the candle*, pp 249–50. See also Captured documents, 26 Sept. 1922 (IMA, CW/CAPT Lot 20/3); Captured documents, 18 Sept. 1922 (IMA, CW/CAPT Lot 20/4).
41 Baker, *My stand for freedom*, pp 79–80. See also *WIT*, 14 October 1922; Captured documents, 18 Sept. 1922 (IMA, CW/CAPT Lot 20/4); Captured documents, 24 Aug. to 11 Sept., 2 Oct. 1922 (IMA, CW/CAPT Lot 20/3); *CT*, 2 Dec. 1922; Price, *Flame and the candle*, pp 228, 231.
42 Captured documents, 29 Sept. 1922 (IMA, CW/CAPT Lot 20/1); Captured documents, 24 Aug. to 16 Sept. 1922 (IMA, CW/CAPT Lot 20/3); Captured documents, 18 Sept. 1922 (IMA, CW/CAPT Lot 20/4); *CT*, 12 Aug. 1922.
43 Michael Hopkinson, *Green against green: the Irish civil war* (Dublin, 1988), pp 174–5.
44 Price, *Flame and the candle*, p. 238. See also *CT*, 4 Nov., 23 Dec. 1922; *IT*, 28 Dec. 1922, 5 Feb. 1923.
45 Price, *Flame and the candle*, pp 238–43.
46 General weekly returns (IMA, CW/OPS/03/06); Operation reports, Jan. 1923 (IMA, CW/OPS/03/01).
47 April summary (IMA, CW/OPS/03/08); *FJ*, 15 Feb. 1923; Captured documents, Letter 7 Mar. 1923 (IMA, CW/CAPT Lot 20/2). See also Operation reports, Feb. 1923 (IMA, CW/OPS/03/01); April: summary (IMA, CW/OPS/03/08); *FJ*, 13 Jan., 22 Feb. 1923.
48 Captured documents (IMA, CW/CAPT Lot 19).
49 *FJ*, 24, 26 Feb., 9 Mar. 1923; *II*, 9 Mar. 1923; *IT*, 3, 9 Mar. 1923; Price, *Flame and the candle*, pp 231–2, 250, 254; Operation reports, Mar. 1923 (IMA, CW/OPS/03/01); Radio reports (IMA, CW/OPS/03/08); *CTr*, 14, 21 Apr. 1923; *MN*, 21 Apr. 1923; Pension claim of Delia Corcoran (IMA, MSPC, DP944); Pension claim of Michael Walsh (IMA, MSPC, DP7248).
50 Operation reports, Feb.–Mar. 1923 (IMA, CW/OPS/03/01).
51 Captured documents (IMA, CW/CAPT Lot 20/2). See also Operation reports, Feb.–Mar. 1923 (IMA, CW/OPS/03/01); Captured documents (IMA, CW/CAPT Lot 20/2); *FJ*, 24, 26 Feb. 1923; *IT*, 15 Mar. 1923; *II*, 15 Mar. 1923.
52 Operation reports, Mar. 1923 (IMA, CW/OPS/03/01); Captured documents (IMA, CW/CAPT Lot 20/2); *FJ*, 24, 26 Feb. 1923; *IT*, 15 Mar. 1923; *II*, 15 Mar. 1923.
53 General weekly returns (IMA, CW/OPS/03/06); Captured documents, 10 Mar. 1923 (IE/MA/CW/CAPT Lot 2). See also monthly summaries (IMA, CW/OPS/03/08); Captured documents, 5, 8 Mar. 1923 (IMA, CW/CAPT Lot 19); General weekly returns, 30 Mar. 1923 (IMA, CW/OPS/03/06); *IT*, 10 Feb. 1923.
54 Linda Connolly, 'Towards a further understanding of the violence experienced by women in the Irish Revolution', *Maynooth University Social Sciences Institute*, Working Paper Series, No. 7 (Maynooth, Jan. 2019), http://mural.maynoothuniversity.ie/10416/1/Linda%20Connolly_final.pdf.
55 *II*, 27 Apr. 1923.
56 *FJ*, 20 Apr. 1923. See also Operation reports, Feb.–Mar. 1923 (IMA, CW/OPS/03/01); April summary (IMA, CW/OPS/03/08); General weekly returns (IMA, CW/OPS/03/06); Radio reports (IMA, CW/OPS/03/08); Captured documents (IMA, CW/CAPT Lot 20/2); *FJ*, 18 Jan., 24 Feb., 5 Apr. 1923; *IT*, 27 Jan., 15, 26 Mar. 1923; *II*, 3 Jan., 15 Mar., 27 Apr. 1923; *CT*, 13 Jan. 1923; Pension claim of Patrick Coyle (IMA, MSPC, 3D156).
57 Captured documents, 4 Apr. 1923 (IMA, CW/CAPT Lot 19). See also Price, *Flame and the candle*, pp 247–9; Waldron, 'The Civil War in Ballyhaunis', pp 34–6; General weekly returns, 23 Mar. 1923 (IMA, CW/OPS/03/06); Daily Operations reports, 30 January 1923 (IMA, CW/OPS/03/01); Radio reports of Messages 16 Mar. 1923 (IMA, CW/OPS/03/08); *CT*, 13, 23 Jan., 14 Feb., 21 Apr., 2 June 1923; *IT*, 27 Jan., 16 Feb., 6 Mar., 17, 24, 25 Apr. 1923; *FJ*, 20 Feb. 1923; *II*, 6 Apr. 1923; *WP*, 10 Mar. 1923; *MN*, 10 Mar. 1923.
58 General weekly returns, 27 Apr. 1923 (IMA, CW/OPS/03/06); Captured documents, 11, 21 Mar. 1923 (IMA, CW/CAPT Lot 20/2); Captured documents, 11 Mar. 1923 (IMA,

CW/CAPT Lot 19); *IT*, 14, 16 Feb., 15 Mar., 27 Apr., 7 May 1923; *FJ*, 16, 24 Feb. 1923; *II*, 15 Mar., 27 Apr. 1923.
59 General weekly returns, 23 Mar. 23 (IMA, CW/OPS/03/06); Operation reports, 10, 14 Apr. 1923 (IMA, CW/OPS/03/01); Captured documents, 7 Feb. 1923 (IMA, CW/CAPT Lot 20/2); Radio reports (IMA, CW/OPS/03/08); Daily Operations reports, January 1923 (IMA, CW/OPS/03/01); *IT*, 13 Feb., 17 Mar. 1923; *FJ*, 17 Mar. 1923; *CTr.*, 14, 21 Apr. 1923; *MN*, 21 Apr. 1923.
60 *IT*, 16, 23 Jan., 3, 12 Feb., 5, 13 Mar., 18 May 1923; *CT*, 13, 27 Jan., 7 Apr. 1923.
61 *IT*, 6 Mar., 17 Apr. 1923; *CT*, 13 Jan., 14 Feb., 21 Apr. 1923; *WP*, 10 Mar. 1923; *MN*, 10 Mar. 1923.
62 *IT*, 18 May 1923.
63 *CT*, 13 Jan. 1923; *IT*, 18 May 1923.
64 Operation reports, 5 Apr. 1923 (IMA, CW/OPS/03/01). See also General weekly returns, April (IMA, CW/OPS/03/06); *IT*, 24 Apr. 1923; *FJ*, 20 Apr. 1923.
65 Captured documents, 18 Feb. 1923 (IE/MA/CW/CAPT Lot 2).
66 *CTr*, 14 Apr. 1923, General weekly returns, 27 Apr. 1923 (IMA, CW/OPS/03/06). See also Captured documents, 18 Feb. 1923 (IMA, CW/CAPT Lot 2).
67 May summary (IMA, CW/OPS/03/08); Pension claim of Thomas McNicholas Snr (IMA, MSPC, DP8412); Pension claim of Annie Healy (IMA, MSPC, 51APB72).
68 General weekly returns, 4, 11 May 1923 (IMA, CW/OPS/03/06). See also May summary (IMA, CW/OPS/03/08); General weekly returns, 29 June, 13 July 1923 (IMA, CW/OPS/03/06); *II*, 25 May 1923; *IT*, 25 May 1923; *FJ*, 9 May 1923.
69 Captured documents (IMA, CW/CAPT Lot 19). See also General weekly returns, 8, 15 June 1923 (IMA, CW/OPS/03/06).
70 General weekly returns, 13, 20, 27 July, 7 Sept. 1923 (IMA, CW/OPS/03/06). See also General weekly returns, 13, 27 July, 7 Sept. 1923 (IMA, CW/OPS/03/06); Operation reports, Apr.–Nov. 1923 (IMA, CW/OPS/03/01–02); *IT*, 8, 26 May, 7 June 1923; *FJ*, 21, 22 May, 29, 30 June 1923; *II*, 7, 22, 30 June 1923; Pension claim of Kate Mulvihill (IMA, MSPC, 3D200); Pension claim of Ellen Delaney (IMA, MSPC, 3D143); Pension claim of John Brady (IMA, MSPC, 3D3); Pension claim of Annie Kane (IMA, MSPC, 3D163); Pension claim of Mary McGinty (IMA, MSPC, 3D45); Pension claim of Mary Coyle (IMA, MSPC, 3D13); Pension claim of Bridget Reddy (IMA, MSPC, 3D150); 'Fatalities List' (IMA, MSPC).
71 General weekly returns, 4 May 1923 (IMA, CW/OPS/03/06). See also General weekly returns, 20, 27 July 1923 (IMA, CW/OPS/03/06); *IT*, 18 May 1923.
72 General weekly returns, 27 July, 10 Aug. 1923 (CW/OPS/03/06).
73 https://irelandelection.com/elections.php?detail=yes&tab=constit&elecid=28&electype=1 (accessed 4 July 2022); Price, *Flame and the candle*, pp 260–3; General weekly returns, 10, 17 Aug. 1923 (IMA, CW/OPS/03/06); *CTr*, 16 June 1923; *FJ*, 16, 30 June 1923; *II*, 30 June 1923.
74 General weekly returns, 20, 28 Sept., 19 Oct. 1923 (IMA, CW/OPS/03/06); Monthly summaries (IMA, CW/OPS/03/08–09); *IT*, 8 June 1923; *FJ*, 27 June 1923; Pension claim of Bridget Hogan (IMA, MSPC, 3D29).
75 Operation report, 10 Sept. 1923 (IMA, CW/OPS/03/06).

Select bibliography

PRIMARY SOURCES

A. MANUSCRIPTS

Armagh
Cardinal Tomás Ó Fiaich Memorial Library and Archives
Fr Louis O'Kane papers

Castlebar
Mayo County Library
Items relating to the IRA

Dublin
Irish Military Archives
Papers relating to the War of Independence
Civil War papers
Captured Documents
Radio and Phone reports
Truce liaison material
BMH Witness Statements
Military Service Pensions Collection

National Archives of Ireland
RIC Crime Branch special papers
Dáil Éireann papers

National Library of Ireland
Dr F.S. Bourke papers
Collins papers
Joseph McGarrity papers
MacKenna-Napoli papers
Edward MacLysaght papers
J.J. O'Connell papers
Florence O'Donoghue papers
Seán T. O'Kelly papers
George Noble Plunkett papers
Dr Dorothy Price papers
Several loose statements and collections relating to the IRA

Papers formerly in possession of the late Michael MacEvilly, Dublin
James Chambers, 'Statement'
Thomas Heavey, 'Statement'
Michael Hughes, 'Statement'
Thomas Kettrick, 'Statement'
Edward Moane, 'Statement'
Moane/Malone [tape], Moane, Brigadier E., and Malone, Vice Comdt. B., 'Transcript of tape recordings made in Dublin by the above in January 1967' (transcribed by Michael MacEvilly – Dublin 1983)
John Joe Philben, 'Statement'

Trinity College
J.R.W. Goulden papers
CO904 papers on microfilm

UCD Archives
Richard Mulcahy papers
Ernie O'Malley papers and notebooks

London
Imperial War Museum
Jeudwine papers, Includes 'Record of the Rebellion in Ireland in 1920–21 and the part played by the Army in dealing with it', and 'History of the 5th Division in Ireland, November 1919–March 1922'; Lt.-Gen. A.E. Percival papers, two lectures on 'Guerrilla Warfare – Ireland 1920–21'; Several memoirs of British soldiers who served in Ireland between 1916 and 1921

National Archives, London
Colonial Office papers
Home Office papers
War Office papers

Mayo
Interviews with Volunteers and their relatives
Thomas Conroy, Neale
Luke Gilligan, Taugheen
Thomas Heavey, Dublin
Charles Hughes, Lankill
Tom Maguire, Cross
Patrick Owen Mugan, Cloonskill
Edward O'Malley, Owenwee
J.P. Quinn, Ballyglass
Dan Sammin, Murrisk

Westport
Clew Bay Heritage Centre
War of Independence Centenary – West Mayo (westmayo.ie)
Papers relating to Westport Battalion, West Mayo Brigade
'Activities list Owenwee Company'
Kelly, W.J., 'One of the men of the West'
Kilroy, Michael, 'The awakening'
Kilroy, Michael, 'ASU Operations'
Moran, M., 'With Michael Kilroy during Easter Week 1916 and the years before'
Mugan, Patrick Owen, 'Statement'
O'Donnell, Jim, 'Recollections based on the diary of an Irish Volunteer 1898 to 1924'
'Statement of Michael Kilroy's wife'

B. OFFICIAL RECORDS

Census of Ireland 1901, 1911
Dáil Éireann. Parliamentary debates

C. NEWSPAPERS AND PERIODICALS

An tÓglach
Capuchin Annual
Connaught Telegraph
Connacht Tribune
Freeman's Journal
Irish Bulletin
Irish Independent
Irish Times
Mayoman
Mayo News
Weekly Irish Times
Western People

D. PRINTED PRIMARY MATERIAL

Baker, Joe, *My stand for freedom: autobiography of an Irish republican soldier* (Westport, 1988).
Brennan-Whitmore, William James, *With the Irish in Frongoch* (Dublin, 1917).
Brewer, John D., *The Royal Irish Constabulary: an oral history* (Belfast, 1990).
Carroll, F.M., *The American Commission on Irish Independence 1919: the diary, correspondence and report* (Dublin, 1985).
Griffith, Kenneth and Timothy O'Grady, *Curious journey: an oral history of Ireland's unfinished revolution* (London, Melbourne, etc. 1982).

Mac Giolla Choille, Breandán (ed.), *Intelligence notes 1913–16* (Dublin, 1966).
MacEoin, Uiseann (ed.), *Survivors* (Dublin, 1987).
Macready, Nevil, *Annals of an active life*, 2 vols (London, 1924).
Martin, F.X., *The Irish Volunteers 1913–1915: recollections and documents* (Dublin, 1963).
Neligan, David, *The spy in the Castle* (London, 1968).
O'Malley, Cormac K.H., 'Ernie O'Malley autobiographical letter', *Cathair na Mart. Journal of the Westport Historical Society*, 9:1 (1989), 1–20.
O'Malley, Cormac K.H. and Vincent Keane (eds), *The men will talk to me: Mayo interviews by Ernie O'Malley* (Cork, 2014).
O'Malley, Edward, *Memories of a Mayoman* (Mayo, 1981).
O'Malley, Ernie, *On another man's wound* (London, 1936).
Walker, Brian, *Parliamentary election results in Ireland, 1801–1922* (Dublin, 1978).
With the IRA in the fight for freedom, 1919 to the Truce (Tralee, 1955).

SECONDARY SOURCES

A. PUBLISHED WORK

Augusteijn, Joost, 'The importance of being Irish: ideas and the Volunteers in Mayo and Tipperary' in David Fitzpatrick (ed.), *Revolution? Ireland, 1917–1923* (Dublin, 1990), pp 25–42.
—— *From public defiance to guerilla warfare: the experience of ordinary Volunteers in the Irish War of Independence* (Dublin, 1996; rptd 1998).
Bennett, Richard, *The Black and Tans* (London, 1970).
Bowden, Tom, 'The Irish Underground and the War of Independence 1919–1921', *Journal of Contemporary History*, 8:2 (1973), 3–23.
—— 'The IRA and the changing tactics of terrorism', *Political Quarterly*, 47:4 (1976), 425–37.
Boyce, David George (ed.), *The Revolution in Ireland, 1879–1923* (Basingstoke, 1988).
Burke, John, *Roscommon: the Irish Revolution, 1912–23* (Dublin, 2021).
Casey, James, 'The genesis of the Dáil-Courts', *Irish Jurist*, 9 (1974), 326–38.
Connolly, Linda (ed.), *Women and the Irish Revolution: feminism, activism, violence* (Dublin, 2020).
—— 'Towards a further understanding of the violence experienced by women in the Irish Revolution', *Maynooth University Social Sciences Institute*, Working Paper Series, No. 7 (Maynooth, Jan. 2019).
Costello, Francis, 'The Republican Courts and the decline of British rule in Ireland', *Éire-Ireland*, 25:3 (1990), 36–55.
Davitt, Cahir, 'The civil jurisdiction of the Courts of Justice of the Irish Republic', *Irish Jurist*, 3 (1968), 112–30.
Farry, Michael, *Sligo: the Irish Revolution, 1912–23* (Dublin, 2012).
Fitzpatrick, David, *Politics and Irish life, 1913–1921: provincial experience of war and revolution* (Dublin, 1977).
—— 'The geography of Irish nationalism, 1910–1921', *Past and Present*, 78 (1978), 113–44.

Foster, Robert Fitzroy, *Vivid faces: the revolutionary generation in Ireland, 1890–1923* (London, 2014).
Garvin, Tom, *The evolution of Irish national politics* (Dublin, 1981).
—— 'Priests and patriots: Irish separatism and fear of the Modern', *Irish Historical Studies*, 25 (1986), 67–81.
Greaves, C. Desmond, *The Irish Transport and General Workers' Union: the formative years, 1909–1923* (Dublin, 1982).
Hart, Peter, *The IRA at war, 1916–1923* (Oxford, 2003).
Hay, Marnie, *Na Fianna Éireann and the Irish Revolution, 1909–23: scouting for rebels* (Manchester, 2019).
Heffernan, Brian, *Freedom and the Fifth Commandment* (Manchester, 2014).
Hindley, Reg, *The death of the Irish language, a qualified obituary* (London, 1990).
Holt, Edgar, *Protest in arms: the Irish Troubles, 1916–1923* (London, 1960).
Hopkinson, Michael, *Green against green: the Irish Civil War* (Dublin, 1988).
Hughes, Brian, *Defying the IRA? Intimidation, coercion and communities during the Irish Revolution* (Liverpool, 2016).
Jordan, Donald E., *Land and popular politics in Ireland. County Mayo from the Plantations to the Land War* (Cambridge, 2011).
Keane, Vincent, 'Westport and the Irish Volunteers', *Cathair na Mart*, 22 (2002), 84–8.
—— 'Westport Sluagh Na Fianna Éireann (Irish National Boy Scouts)', *Cathair na Mart*, 25 (2006/7) 37–4.
Keogh, Dermot, *The Vatican, the bishops and Irish politics, 1919–1939* (Cambridge, 1986).
Laffan, Michael, 'The Sinn Féin Party', *Capuchin Annual,* 37 (1970), 227–35.
—— 'The unification of Sinn Féin in 1917', *Irish Historical Studies*, 17:67 (1971), 353–79.
—— *The resurrection of Ireland: the Sinn Féin Party, 1916–1923* (Cambridge, 1999).
Lally, M., *The Tan War in Ballyovey* (n.p., n.d.).
Leonard, Jane, 'Getting them at last: the IRA and ex-servicemen' in D. Fitzpatrick (ed.), *Revolution? Ireland, 1917–1923* (Dublin, 1990), pp 118–29.
Macardle, Dorothy, *The Irish Republic: a documented chronicle* (London, 1937; new edn, London, 1968).
MacMahon, Timothy G., *Grand opportunity: the Gaelic Revival and Irish society, 1893–1910* (Syracuse, 2008).
Maguire, Conor A., 'The Republican courts', *The Capuchin Annual*, 36 (1969), 378–88.
Maguire, George, 'Mayo and Sligo 1920', *The Capuchin Annual,* 37 (1970), 296–9.
Martin, F.X., *Leaders and men of the Easter Rising: Dublin 1916* (London, 1967).
Matthew, Colin & Brian Harrison (eds), *Oxford dictionary of national biography*, 60 vols (Oxford, 2004)
Maume, Patrick, *The long gestation: Irish nationalist life, 1891–1918* (New York, 1999).
McGarty, Patrick, *Leitrim: the Irish Revolution, 1912–23* (Dublin, 2020).
McGuire, James & James Quinn (eds), *Dictionary of Irish biography*, 9 vols (Cambridge, 2009)
Milne, Ida, *Stacking the coffins: influenza, war and revolution in Ireland, 1918–19* (Manchester, 2020).
Mitchell, Arthur, *Revolutionary government in Ireland. Dáil Éireann, 1919–22* (Dublin, 1995).

Nic Dháibhéid, Caoimhe, 'The Irish National Aid association and the radicalization of public opinion in Ireland', *The Historical Journal* 55:3 (2012) 705–29.

Ó Broin, Leon, *Revolutionary underground: the story of the Irish Republican Brotherhood, 1858–1924* (Dublin, 1976).

—— 'Revolutionary nationalism in Ireland: the IRB, 1858–1924' in T.W. Moody (ed.), *Nationality and the pursuit of national independence* (Belfast, 1978), pp 97–119.

O'Donoghue, Florence, 'Guerrilla warfare in Ireland', *An Cosantóir*, 23 (1963) 293–301.

O'Halpin, Eunan & Daithí Ó Corráin, *The dead of the Irish Revolution* (New Haven and London, 2020).

O Mahony, Seán, *Frongoch: university of revolution* (Killiney, Co. Dublin, 1987).

Price, Dominic, *The flame and the candle: war in Mayo, 1919–1924* (Cork, 2012).

Rice, Seán (ed.), *Castlebar Mitchels, 1885–1985* (Castlebar, 1985).

Townshend, Charles, *The British campaign in Ireland, 1919–21: the development of political and military policies* (Oxford, 1975).

—— 'The Irish Republican Army and the development of guerrilla warfare, 1916–21', *English Historical Review*, 94 (1979), 318–45.

—— 'The Irish railway srike of 1920: industrial action and civil resistance in the struggle for independence', *Irish Historical Studies*, 21:84 (1979), 265–82.

—— *Political violence in Ireland: government and resistance since 1848* (Oxford, 1983).

—— *Easter 1916: the Irish Rebellion* (London, 2005).

—— *The Republic: the fight for Irish independence, 1918–1923* (London, 2014)

Waldron, Kieran, 'The Civil War in Ballyhaunis', *Annagh*, 44th edition (2021).

Williams, T. Desmond (ed.), *The Irish struggle, 1916–26* (London, 1966).

—— *Secret societies in Ireland* (Dublin, 1973).

Wusten, Hendrik van der, *Iers verzet de staatkundige eenheid der Britse eilanden, 1800–1921* (Amsterdam, 1977).

Index

1798 Rising, 8

Aberdeen, countess of, 11
Achill Mission, 17, 32
Achill, 2–4, 8, 19–20, 22–3, 27, 31–2, 35, 54, 59, 106, 124–5, 128
Achonry, Co. Sligo, 3
aeridheacht, 98, 100
agnostics, 3
alcohol, 31, 62, 66–8, 83, 89–90, 99, 101, 107, 125, 129
All-for-Ireland League (AFIL), 7, 13–15, 29
Ambrose, Robert, 13, 14
ambushes, 73, 75, 81–82, 85–7, 89–93, 96, 101, 122–4, 128, 132
Ancient Order of Hibernians (AOH), 9, 20–1, 24, 27–8, 37–8, 41–2, 45, 54; *see also* Board of Erin
Anglo-Irish Treaty, 94, 97, 102–4, 106–7, 109–12
anti-Treaty IRA, *see* Irish Republican Army
arbitration courts, 54–5, 62, 67, 69, 70, 83
Ardilaun, Lord, 10
Armistice Day, 59
armoured cars, 80, 108–9, 113, 115, 122, 123–4, 126; *plates 15, 17*
arms funds, 36, 49; concert, *plate 7*
arms, 7–8, 20–1, 36, 38–41, 49–51, 57–8, 66, 72–3, 76, 78, 80–1, 85–8, 91, 96, 102, 107, 113, 121, 125–7, 131–2, 137; raids for, 57–8, 65, 72, 86–7
Armstrong, Thomas, 75
Ashe, Thomas, 47, 51, 58
Asquith, Herbert Henry, 17
atheists, 3
Athlone, Co. Westmeath, 18, 109, 123, 133
Aughagower, 9, 37, 41, 72, 85, 132
Austria, 59
Auxiliaries (Auxiliary Division Royal Irish Constabulary), *see* RIC

Bachelor's Walk killings, 24
Baker, Joe, 125, 127
Balcarra, 36
Balfe, Captain Nicholas, 33
Balla, 1, 8, 18, 21, 29, 37–38, 40, 44–7, 50, 78, 88, 100, 116, 122
Ballaghaderreen, Co. Roscommon, 7, 15, 18, 36, 40–1, 46, 50, 56, 61, 65, 78, 81, 87–8, 90, 92, 119, 124
Ballina Herald, 5
Ballina, 1–5, 10, 11, 15–20, 23, 26–7, 33–7, 39, 43, 45–7, 49–50, 52–3, 56, 58–60, 63–4, 66, 68–9, 75, 78, 80, 83–4, 88–90, 92, 95–6, 101–2, 106–7, 109–10, 115–16, 122–3, 125–6, 129–31
'Ballinalee', armoured car, 122
Ballinrobe, 1–3, 5, 10, 16, 18, 33, 35, 45–6, 59, 63, 67, 69, 78, 85, 90–1, 98, 108–9, 113–17, 120, 125–6, 129–30
Ballycastle, 60, 65, 78, 105
Ballycroy, 72
Ballyderrig, 58
Ballyglass, 23
Ballyhaunis, 4, 15, 21, 25, 37, 38, 65, 76, 78–9, 107, 109, 116, 126, 128
Ballyheane, 48
Ballyvarry, 60
Bangor, 78, 92, 100, 119–20
Beakin, 89
Belclare, 45
Belfast boycott, 21, 98, 101
Belfast, Co. Antrim, 4, 8, 21, 34, 105
Belgian Refugees Fund, 30
Belgium, 34
Belmullet, 2–4, 20, 33, 35, 54, 65, 78, 92, 102, 106, 119–20, 124, 133
Binghamstown, 3
Birmingham, George A., 20
Birrell, Augustine, 19
Black & Tans, *see* RIC
Blacksod Bay, 14, 58
Board of Erin (AOH), 9, 39

165

Board of Guardians, Castlebar, 41
Boer War, 7–9
Bohola, 45, 47–8, 54, 72, 76, 93
Boland, Harry, 118
Bolshevism, 63, 70, 110, 117
bombs, 53, 87–8, 91, 102, 123
Bonniconlon, Co. Sligo, 123, 128, 131
boycotting, 16–17, 19, 21, 67, 70, 73, 98, 101
Boyle, Co. Roscommon, 33, 114
Boyle, Daniel, 13, 19, 61
Breaffy, 48
Britain, 4, 5, 21, 32–3, 56–7, 87, 106, 115, 120
British army, 2, 22–3, 34, 52, 54, 59, 66; 7th Lancers, 40, 96; Connaught Rangers, 24, 34; North Staffordshire Regiment, 40; Staffordshire Regiment, 40
Brockagh, 80
Bunnahowen, 82
Butler, Sergeant, 84, 91
Byrne, Charles, 110

Callaghan, Fr Andrew, 19
Campbell, Thomas, 109–10
Carney, Fr, 67, 86
Carracastle, 23, 38, 60, 82–3
Carrowkennedy, 89, 92, 93
Carson, Edward, 21, 23, 28
Carty, Frank, 126
Cassidy, Patrick, 82, 107, 137
Castlebar, 1–11, 15, 22–4, 27–31, 33–41, 44–7, 49–50, 52–3, 62, 68–9, 78, 80, 82, 84–5, 89, 91, 94–6, 98, 103, 105–6, 108–9, 111, 113, 115–21, 126–7, 130, 133; Aerdrome, *plate 12*; Jail, 108; *plate 10*
Castlehacket, 70
Castlerea, Co. Roscommon, 14, 27, 34, 114, 126
Catholic church, 9, 13–14, 20, 26–7, 33, 35, 38, 40, 42, 46, 48, 56–8, 60–1, 65, 66, 68–70, 80, 84–6, 100–3, 108–10, 116–17, 124–5, 133

Catholic emancipation, 23
Catholics, 2, 4, 21
cattle driving, 2, 7, 20, 32, 63, 104
céilí, 59, 66
Central Council for the Organisation of Recruiting, 34
Central Hotel, Ballina, 64
Chambers, Mrs, 121
Charlestown, 63, 78, 102, 107, 109, 111, 119, 128
Church of Ireland, 3, 4, 35, 110
Civic Guard, 108, 120, 129, 133
Civilian Guards, 118
Clare, County, 16, 19, 47, 60
Claremorris, 2, 3, 11, 14, 17, 20, 28, 33, 35, 45–6, 78, 85, 115–17, 120, 125–6, 129–30
Clarke, Fr, 14
Clifden, Co. Galway, 123
Clogher, 73
Clonalis Castle, Co. Roscommon, 114
Cloonroe, 130
Coleman, Patrick, 49, 52, 66
Colleary, Mr, 28
Collins, Michael, 50, 78, 87, 104, 108–10, 118
Collooney, Co. Sligo, 114
compulsory tillage scheme, 32, 48, 54–5
Comrades of War, 69
Cong, 10, 41, 86, 126
Congested Districts Board (CDB), 14, 16, 19–20, 35, 63, 73
Conlan, Thomas John, 71
Connacht, 2, 3, 5, 24, 28, 43, 74, 119
Connemara, 7, 46, 98, 131
Connolly, Fr, 38
Connolly, James, 49
Conroy, Fr J.P., 65
conscription, 26–7, 33, 35–6, 43, 50, 56–59, 61, 63–4
Cooney, Edward, 116–117
co-operative movement, 63
Corbally, Co. Sligo, 78
Corbett, Éamon, 99
Corcoran, Seán, 40, 41, 45–6, 50, 52, 78
Cork, County, 1, 7, 15, 21, 24, 36, 60, 87

Index

Cornacool, 108
Corpus Christi, 113
Corrib, Lough, 70
Costello, P.J., 10
Coyle, Henry, 133
Cressenlough band, 53
Crimlin, 48
Croagh Patrick, 47, 57, 89
Cross, 43, 45, 75, 78, 126
Crossard, 92, 107
Crossboyne, 131
Crossley tenders, 78
Crossmolina, 15, 19, 34, 36, 45, 64, 78, 92, 104–5, 117
Crowley, John, 59, 61, 63, 97, 103
Crown forces, 81, 102
Cryan, Battie, 48
Cuban Revolution, 135
Cumann na mBan, 38, 44–5, 55, 57–8, 82, 128
Cumann na nGaedheal, 133–5
Cunningham, Fr, 85
Cushlough, 51; Fife and Drum Band, *plate 5*

D'Alton, Canon, 125
Dáil courts, 62, 69–71, 73–4, 83, 85, 99–101, 105, 107, 113
Dáil Éireann, 62–3, 67, 69, 70–2, 74, 83, 85, 94–5, 97–101, 103–4, 106, 109, 134–5
Dáil loan, 67–8
Davis Bros., 104
Davitt, Michael, 1, 7, 71
de Valera, Éamon, 47, 52, 56, 59–61, 97, 100, 106, 111, 131–2
Defence of the Realm Act, 26, 36
Delaney, Michael, 25
Derrig, Thomas, 9, 38, 49, 78, 80, 86, 97–8, 101, 126, 133, 135
Derry, County, 81
Derrygorman, 45
Dever, Mr, 10
Dillon, John, 1, 7, 9, 12–13, 15–18, 22, 28–9, 32–3, 41, 47, 53, 56, 59–61, 86; *plate 1*

Doherty, Margaret, 128
Donegal, County, 4
Donnelly, Stephen, 43, 64, 80, 85
Dooagh, 22
Doogary, 81
Dooliage, 92
Doris, Patrick, 6, 57
Doris, William, 6, 14–16, 18–21, 27, 33, 46, 61, 137
Dorr, Frank, 8
drilling, 22–4, 37, 48, 50–2, 55–8, 64, 66, 72–4, 96, 98, 100, 125, 133
Dromin, 45
Dromore West, Co. Sligo, 109, 131
Drummin, 51, 61, 72, 89
Dublin city, 4, 8–11, 21, 24, 33, 36–7, 39–41, 43, 45–9, 54, 59–60, 63–4, 66, 68, 70–1, 78–9, 90, 93, 97–8, 103–4, 107, 112–14, 130, 135, 137
Duffy, Jim, 100
Duffy, Paddy, *plate 13*
Dwyer, Joe, 12

Easter Rising (1916), 7, 9, 26, 36, 38–44, 47, 49–50, 59, 93
Egan, Bernard, 13–14, 110
elections: East Clare by-election, 47; general, 6, 7, 12–16, 48, 59–63, 86, 109, 110–11, 132–5; county council, 74; local, 65, 69, 74, 94–5; North Roscommon by-election, 47; RDC, 74; South Longford by-election, 47; UDC, 11, 68
emigration, 4, 30, 33, 57, 100–1, 133
Enniscrone, Co. Sligo, 76, 85, 92, 120, 128, 131
Erris, 106, 120
evictions, 12, 16, 19, 34, 100, 104
executions, 7, 44, 47, 76, 119, 127
Expelled Workers' Fund, 105

Fahy, Frank, 23
Fallmore, 2
Famine, 2, 95, 100, 120
Farmers' Union, 103
Ferran, Francis, 103

Fianna Éireann, 9, 21–2, 37–41, 45, 52, 55, 58, 64, 134, 137; *plate 6*
Fianna Fáil, 134–5
Figgis, Darrell, 22, 29, 36–37, 39–41, 47–8, 59, 60
First World War, 1, 6, 9, 21, 24, 26–35, 38, 42–3, 49, 54, 58–9, 62–3
Fitzgibbon, John, 14, 16, 18, 21, 34, 60
Flaherty, Jimmy, *plate 14*
flying columns, *see* Irish Republican Army, Active Service Units
Fogarty, Bishop Michael, 103
Fogarty, Mrs, 110
Foley, Major, 86
Ford cars, 78, 124
Forde, Seán, 46
Fountain Hill farm, 69–70
Four Courts, 107, 112
Foxford, 2, 5, 8, 16, 31, 71, 78, 113, 117, 126, 128–9
France, 28, 51, 56
freethinkers, 3
Frongoch, 41
fyfe and drum band, 47

Gaelic Athletic Association (GAA), 5, 7–8, 24, 37, 43–4, 55, 106, 118
Gaelic football, 48, 59, 118
Gaelic League, 5, 22, 41, 43–4, 55, 58, 65, 106
Gallagher, Patrick, 46
Galway, County, 2–6, 14, 16, 19, 21, 33, 46, 49, 69, 83–4, 91–3, 96–9, 101, 107, 123, 130
Geesalagh, 133
German Plot, 58
Germany, 21, 26, 28–9, 32, 34–5, 37, 40, 51–2, 56, 58–9
Gibbons, Seán, 29, 84, 95, 97, 137
Gildea, Charles, 78
Gilmartin, Archbishop Thomas, 65, 103, 117
Ginnell, Laurence, 54
girl scouts, 36
Glasgow, 119

Glendinning, George (statue of), Westport, 106
Glenhest, 100, 129
Glenisland, 9, 46
Glenree Valley, Co. Sligo, 131
graziers, 2, 7, 13, 16–17, 19–20, 32, 55, 63, 69, 104
Great Southern and Western Railway, 114
Gregg, Hugh, 102
grenades, 88, 99, 113, 115, 120, 123
Griffith, Arthur, 48, 70, 118

Hannay, J.O., *see* Birmingham, George, 20
Harney, A., 89
Hawley, Thomas, 92
Headford, Co. Galway, 127
Healy, Joseph, 131
Healy, Michael, 69, 70, 100
Heavey, Thomas, 8, 108, 116, 137
Hegarty, Patrick, 45, 64, 68, 71, 79
Henry, Michael, 45, 130, 137
Hibernian Rifles, 37
Hoban, John, 46, 78, 80
Hobson, Bulmer, 24
Hogan, Michael, 126
Hollymount, 19, 76
Home Affairs, minister for, 70, 99, 130
Home Rule Act (1912), 17, 21–3, 26–7, 44, 86
home rule, 1, 6, 13–14, 16–29, 32, 42, 44, 46–7, 56, 64, 86
House of Commons, 7, 17, 21, 27, 41
House of Lords, 13, 16, 27
Howth gun-running, 24
Hughes, Charles, 9, 101
Hughes, Michael, 89, 137
Hughes, Owen, 9
Humbert monument, Castlebar, 53
hunger strike, 47, 51–2, 108
Hurst, George, 7, 41
Hyland, John, 69–70

Imperial Hotel, Castlebar, 106
informers, 83
internment, 41, 44, 76, 97, 124

Index 169

intimidation, 14, 16–17, 19, 61, 63, 68, 73–5, 82, 84, 102, 110
Irish American Alliance (IAA, AOH), 9, 22, 29, 37, 39
Irish Civil War, 1, 106–7, 113–34
Irish Convention, 1917, 17, 44–5, 56
Irish Free State, 117, 124–5, 129, 131, 134–5
Irish language, 5, 18, 98, 100, 137
Irish National Aid Association, 44
Irish National Teachers' Organisation, 97
Irish Parliamentary Party (IPP), 5–7, 12–18, 21–9, 32–3, 36, 38, 42–3, 45–4, 53–6, 59–61, 65, 134
Irish Republican Army (IRA), 1, 8, 43, 62, 64, 66–90, 92–102, 104–35; 2nd Western Division, 98, 119; 4th Western Division, 98, 121–2, 124, 126, 127; Active Service Units (flying columns), 79–81, 83, 85–94, 96, 100, 106, 120, 124–6, 128, 133, *plate 11*; anti-Treaty, 1–2, 104, 107–33; election of officers, 24; general convention, 50; General Head Quarters (GHQ), 36, 38, 49, 58, 62, 65–7, 71–2, 75, 78, 80–2, 85–7, 93, 97–9, 106, 108, 129, 132
Irish Republican Brotherhood (IRB), 1, 6, 8–9, 21, 22, 24, 29, 38–40, 45, 50, 55, 60, 62, 103–4
Irish Volunteers, 1, 18, 21–9, 35–66, 68, 71–2, 74
Irish Volunteers' Dependents' Fund, 44
Irishtown, 14
Islandeady, 23, 91
Irish Transport and General Workers' Union (ITGWU), 11, 30, 54, 62–3, 104

Jones, Rick, *plate 13*
Jordan, Colonel, 54–5
Joyce, Patrick, 89

Keel, 31
Keleghan, John Joe, 72
Kelly, Joseph, 65
Kelly, Patrick, 87, 89
Kenny, Patrick, 46
Kettrick, Thomas, 9, 38, 49, 66, 78, 81, 88–90, 96, 137
Keville, Patrick, 50
kidnapping, 70, 96
Kilkelly, 56, 60, 126
Killala, 2–3, 33, 97, 125
Killaloe, Co. Clare, 103
Killevaly, 45
Kilmaclassen, 48
Kilmaine, 108
Kilmeena, 8, 9, 37, 39, 91, 121
Kilroy, John, 121
Kilroy, Michael, 8–9, 22, 37, 39, 41, 45–6, 50, 53, 58, 66, 80, 90, 98, 106–8, 110, 113, 115, 119, 121–4, 133–4, 137; *plate 14*
Kilroy, Mrs, 38, 121
Kilroy, T.J., 30
Kiltimagh, 37, 40, 45–6, 50, 54, 72, 78, 99, 101, 114, 122, 132
Kinaffe, 48
Knock, 85, 99

labour, 11, 21, 26, 30, 32, 54, 56, 59, 62–3, 68–9, 79, 95, 101, 104, 133, 135
Lackey, Thomas, 122
Lahardane, 45, 126
Lambert, Butch, *plate 13*
land: acts, 4, 7, 12, 16, 19, 135; agitation, 1, 2, 13, 16, 20, 25, 51, 55, 62, 66, 75, 83, 129, 134; landlords, 2, 15, 16, 18–20, 29, 54, 63, 69, 100–1, 105, 115, 135; sale of, 19, 54, 63
Land League, 1, 14–15, 134
Larkin, James, 11–12, 30
Lavelle, Michael, 103
Lawlor, General, 126
Leenane, Co. Galway, 40, 46, 85
Leitrim, County, 1
license, for dogs, 129; for liquor, 99, 120
Limerick, County, 4, 21, 39, 109
Liscull, 81

Lisgorman, 45
Lloyd George, David, 13, 97, 100, 103
London, 97, 137
Longford, County, 84
Louisburgh, 30, 40, 46, 64–5, 70, 75, 78, 89, 124, 132
Lynch, Diarmuid, 37, 108

Mac Eoin, Seán, 116
MacBride, Anthony, 8, 46
MacBride, John, 7–9, 21, 22, 29, 37, 39, 41, 47, 69, 104, 106, 130
MacBride, Joseph, 8, 24, 37, 40, 46–8, 50, 58, 60–2, 66, 68, 78, 86, 97, 103, 111, 129, 133–4, 137; *plate 2*
MacDonagh, John, 8
MacDonagh, Thomas, 8
machine-guns, 91–2, 96, 99, 102, 116, 122–3, 126
MacHugh, Fr Patrick, 85
Madden, Dr John, 126, 134
Magdalene asylums, 95
Maguire, Conor, 44, 67–70
Maguire, John, 127, 130
Maguire, Thomas (Tom), 43, 45, 70, 78, 86, 90–1, 98, 100, 103–4, 113, 119, 124, 127, 133–4, 137; *plate 3*
Mallin, George, 10
Malone, Broddie, *plate 13*
Markievicz, Countess Constance, 38, 111
Marley, Patrick, 100
Maxwell, Sir John, 41
Mayo County Council, 7, 10, 14, 17, 49, 64, 66, 74, 94–5, 97, 103–4, 106, 109, 130
McCabe, Mr, 110
McDonnell, James, 65
McDonnell, Mrs, 19
McDonnell, Patrick, 41
McDonnell, Peter J., 39, 96, 115, 121
McDonnell, Peter, 72
McGrath, Joseph, 133
McGreal's pub, 91
McGuinness, Joseph, 47
McHugh, Michael, 39, 46, 50, 76, 78, 137
McNicholas, Thomas, 131

Meehan, Fr J.W., 38, 44, 84–5
Mellows, Liam, 39
Men's Sodality of the Sacred Heart, 117
Methodists, 4
Midland railway line, 114
Military Service (Ireland) bill, 56
Millford house, 124
Milling, John Charles, 65
Milling, Mrs, 69
Mills bombs, 8, 87, 89
mines, 88, 113, 115, 123, 126–7
Mitchells GAA club, 118
Moane, Edward (Ned), 8, 38, 45, 51–3, 58, 134, 137; *plate 14*
Moclair, Mr, 28
Mogaugh, 48
Moore Hall, 129, 130
Moore, Colonel Maurice, 23–4, 48, 129
Moore, George, 129–30
Moran, Fr Andrew, 44
Moran, Lieutenant, 122
Moran, William, 114, 137
Motor Drivers' Union, 102
Moy river, 88
Moylett, Patrick, 25, 38, 47
Mulranny, 126
Murphy, John, 58, 69–70
Murrisk, 45

National army, 106, 108, 111–16, 119–33, *plates 15, 16*
National Registration Act, 32
National Volunteers, 22, 29, 35–8, 40, 45, 48, 66
nationalists, 1, 5–7, 9, 13, 15, 17, 20, 24, 33, 42, 46, 56, 113
Naughton, bishop of Killala, 39, 56, 125
Neary, Brigadier, 123
Nephin Mountain, 92, 129
New Irish Mining Company, 10
Newport, 8, 9, 20, 22, 27, 29, 33, 36–8, 41–2, 45–7, 57, 66, 78, 80, 84, 90–1, 98, 100, 105, 119–22, 124–8
North Mayo Farmers' Association, 103
North Roscommon by-election, 47
Northern Ireland, 86, 109, 113

Index

Ó Murthuile, Seán, 104
O'Brien, Michael, 91
O'Brien, William, 1, 6–7, 13–15, 18, 29
O'Connell, Tom, 135
O'Connor, Art, 70, 137
O'Donnell, John, 7, 13–14
O'Donnell, Patrick, 29
O'Donovan Rossa, Jeremiah, 37
O'Higgins, Kevin, 130
O'Kelly, Conor, 13–15
O'Leary, Colm, 41, 44
O'Leary, Michael, 36
O'Malley, Ernie, 89, 137
O'Rahilly, Michael Joseph, The, 39
O'Rourke, Daniel, 104
O'Shiel, Kevin, 70
O'Sullivan, Gearóid, 78
Oldcastle, 100
Oranmore and Browne, Lord, 28, 34
Owenwee, 81
Ox Mountains, 119, 123, 126, 128, 131–2

Paris Peace Conference, 47, 59, 71, 97
Parke, 33
Partry Mountains, 91, 100, 119
Partry, 85, 88–91, 119
Pearse, Patrick H., 24
petty and quarter sessions, 30, 50, 52–4, 71, 73, 99, 118, 129
Pioneer Total Abstinence Association, 113
poor law union, proposed amalgamation, 95, 130
Pratt, Mrs, 105
Presbyterians, 4
Price, Eamon, 78
Protestants, 3–4, 6, 13, 20, 60, 90, 101, 105, 135
Provisional government, 104, 106–9, 112–13

'Queen of the West', armoured car, 124, *plate 17*

Ralph, Annie, 49
rape, 128
Ratepayers' Association, 69
rates, 31, 35, 69, 94–5, 118, 130
recruiting, 9, 24, 27–9, 33–6, 38, 43, 46, 52, 54, 57–9, 108, 110, 114, 117
Red Cross, 121
Redmond, John, 6–7, 14, 18, 22, 24, 26–9, 37–8, 53
republican police, 99, 101–2, 105, 107
Restoration of Order in Ireland Act, 76
Ring, Joseph (Joe), 46, 48, 51, 97, 108, 110, 115, 123, 135; *plates 15, 16*
Rooney hall, Castlebar, 36, 38
Roscommon, County, 1–4, 7, 14, 16, 18, 20, 33, 44, 46–8, 51, 54–5, 67, 69–70, 75, 78, 83, 86, 93, 95, 98, 104, 108, 110, 114–15, 137
Rotunda, Dublin, 21
Rowland, John, 57
Royal Irish Constabulary (RIC), 4, 7, 9, 11, 16, 20, 29, 34, 37, 40, 42–3, 45–6, 50–3, 58, 60, 63–4, 67, 71–5, 78, 81–9, 92, 95–102, 107, 113, 118, 127; Auxiliary Division, 76, 80, 84, 96, 101; *plate 9*; Black and Tans, 75–6, 85, 88, 118; inspector-general, 16, 19–21, 23, 26, 29, 43–4, 48, 52, 77; Westport officers, *plate 8*
Ruane, Seán, 79
Ruane, Thomas, 45, 50, 52, 78, 99, 108, 114, 137
Rural District Council, 47, 95, 114, 130
Russian Revolution, 135
Ruttledge, Patrick Joseph, 97, 106, 133, 134

Scottish Potato Merchants' Association, 54
Sears, William, 59, 60, 86, 97, 100, 103–4, 125, 129–30, 133–4
sexual violence, 68
Sheeane Hill, 36, 48
shotguns, 49–50, 57, 66, 81, 88, 99
Shraheen, 45
Shramore, 126–7, 133
Shrule, 46, 72, 124
Sinn Féin billiards club, 49

Sinn Féin (SF), 1, 5–6, 8, 10, 21, 24, 29, 38, 42–3, 45–8, 50–1, 53–6, 58–65, 67–70, 73–4, 76–7, 81–4, 86, 95–6, 98–103, 107, 112, 133–4, 137
Slattery, Michael, 107
Sligo Brigade, 88
Sligo, County, 2–5, 16, 18, 23, 33, 44, 46, 48, 51, 54, 67, 69, 76, 78, 84, 86, 93, 95, 103, 109, 114, 119, 122, 130
Sligo jail, 52
Sligo, Lord, 16, 24, 34, 36, 39, 106; estate, 48
Sligo town, 33, 52
sniping, 92, 122–3, 127–9, 132
Society of St Vincent de Paul, 105
Solohedbeg ambush, 65
South Africa, 7
Srah, 45, 82
St Patrick's Day, 20, 39, 53
Steadman, David A., 41, 77–8, 86
Straide, 60, 105
suffragettes, 10–11, 26
suicide, 68
Sweeney, Thomas J., 30, 131
Swinford, 2, 3, 33, 35–6, 46–8, 60, 71, 78, 95–6, 100, 102, 105–7, 109, 114, 118, 122, 126, 128
Symonds, Commandant, 108

Tarmey, Thomas, 22
tax offices, 72
Temporary Discharges Act (also 'Cat-and-Mouse' Act), 55
The Neale, 45, 67
Timony, John, 45, 137
Tipperary, County, 65, 81, 93
Titanic, 17
Tolan, Michael, 101
Toromeen estate, 54
Town Tenants Act, 12
Town Tenants' League, 15
Townshend, Charles, 62, 75, 86
tricolour, 42, 47–8, 56, 64, 96
Tuam, archbishop of, 14, 84
Tuam, Co. Galway, 3, 33, 63, 70, 103, 109, 117, 126–7

Tubercurry, Co. Sligo, 27, 36
Tudor, General Henry Hugh, 86
Tullyhill, 88
Turkey, 59

Urban District Councils, 2, 68, 69; Castlebar, 30–1, 34, 38, 41, 111, 117–18; Westport, 10, 65, 106, 130
United Irish League (UIL), 1, 2, 6–7, 9, 14–16, 18–19, 32, 45, 54–5
Ulster Volunteer Force (UVF), 20, 23
Ulster, 20–1, 86, 109
Union Jack, 44, 60, 80, 84
unionists, 7, 13, 15, 21, 27, 34, 86, 134
United Irish League (UIL), 1, 134

Victoria Cross, 36

Walsh, John, 48
Walsh, Bridget, *plate 4*
Walsh, Michael, 90
Walsh, Richard, 8, 21, 24, 37–8, 40, 45–6, 49–50, 57–8, 62, 68, 76, 78, 104, 134, 137
War of Independence, 38, 62, 66, 75, 103, 106, 123, 125, 133
Wellington, duke of (Arthur Wellesley), 23
Westport, 1–11, 15–16, 18–20, 22, 24, 27–30, 33, 34–41, 44–50, 52–3, 55, 58, 63, 65–6, 69, 73, 76, 78–80, 82, 89–91, 96, 100–2, 106, 108–10, 114–16, 119–20, 126, 130, 132, 134–5, 137
Wexford, County, 81
White Cross Fund, 105
White, Captain, 83, 92
Wicklow, County, 28
Wilhelm II, Kaiser, 29
William, King, 23
Willington, J.W., 10
Wimborne, Lady, 39
Wimborne, Lord, 31, 39
Women's National Health Organization, 10
Woodenbridge speech, 28–9, 37
workhouses, 3, 35, 95, 102, 115, 130